IDENTITY AND CULTURE: NARRATIVES OF DIFFERENCE AND BELONGING

ISSUES in CULTURAL and MEDIA STUDIES

Series Editor: Stuart Allan

Published titles

IDENTITY AND CULTURE

Chris Weedon

OPEN UNIVERSITY PRESS

Open University Press
McGraw-Hill Education
McGraw-Hill House
Shoppenhangers Road
Maidenhead
Berkshire
England
SL6 2QL

email: enquiries@openup.co.uk
world wide web: www.openup.co.uk

and Two Penn Plaza, New York, NY 10121-2289, USA

First published 2004

A catalogue record of this book is available from the British Library

ISBN 0 335 20086 9 (pb)   0 335 20087 7 (hb)

Library of Congress Cataloging-in-Publication Data
CIP data applied for

Typeset by RefineCatch Limited, Bungay, Suffolk
Printed and bound by CPI Group (UK) Ltd, Croydon, CR0 4YY

13990217

CONTENTS

SERIES EDITOR'S FOREWORD

'Belonging,' Stuart Hall once observed, 'is a tricky concept, requiring both identification and recognition.' In considering what it means to be 'British', for example, he highlighted the ways in which familiar ideas about national belonging can be embedded in relations of power and discrimination. 'If people from ethnic minorities are to become not only citizens with equal rights but also an integral part of the national culture,' he wrote, 'then the meanings of the term "British" will have to become more inclusive of their experiences, values and aspirations.' In other words, he pointed out, for any society to claim to be both multi-ethnic and, at the same time, mono-cultural would be a contradiction in terms. Each of us, as individuals, needs to see something of ourselves given expression in our everyday cultural forms and practices. And yet, as some know more than others, inclusion is all too frequently defined by exclusion. 'Only deep and rigorous measures to end discrimination,' Hall reminded us, 'can help us navigate these treacherous waters.'

For Chris Weedon, as she acknowledges on these pages, Stuart Hall has been a lifelong inspiration. In important ways, *Identity and Culture* has been shaped by her engagement with his writings, but also by her grassroots involvement in a multi-ethnic cultural initiative – Butetown History & Arts Centre – in Cardiff Bay. As will soon be apparent to the reader, this book looks at how different forms of cultural narrative and cultural practice work to constitute subjectivity and identity for individuals and groups in multi-ethnic, 'postcolonial' societies. Weedon begins the discussion by engaging with several theoretical challenges, before moving on to look at examples of historical, political, fictional and visual narratives of identity and belonging. Her examples are drawn from British, Australian and US contexts, each of them engendering critical insights into the social power relations that structure the subject positions and forms of identity in play. Through a number of related case studies, she analyses how cultural texts and practices offer new forms of identity and agency, and in so doing serve as ways of negotiating, even subverting dominant forms of identity.

The *Issues in Cultural and Media Studies* series aims to facilitate a diverse range of critical investigations into pressing questions considered to be central to current thinking and research. In light of the remarkable speed at which the conceptual agendas of cultural and media studies are changing, the series is committed to contributing to what is an ongoing process of re-evaluation and critique. Each of the books is intended to provide a lively, innovative and comprehensive introduction to a specific topical issue from a fresh perspective. The reader is offered a thorough grounding in the most salient debates indicative of the book's subject, as well as important insights into how new modes of enquiry may be established for future explorations. Taken as a whole, then, the series is designed to cover the core components of cultural and media studies courses in an imaginatively distinctive and engaging manner.

Stuart Allan

PREFACE

As I write this preface at the end of a dull, late November week in 2003, I have not been looking out for items on race, ethnicity or difference. Despite this, a number of things have come to my attention over the past few days. I have heard from several different sources details of the increasing levels of tension between young Cardiff Somalis, who are the children of refugees, and white and other non-Somali people in Cardiff. These included vicious attacks on young Somalis by white youths with baseball bats. I also listened to an announcement by the Home Secretary of plans to bring in legislation that would allow the removal of the children of asylum seekers, from their parents. This would punish people who had lost their appeals but refused to leave the country. Their children would be placed in care, so that the parents could be denied all state benefits. Meanwhile, BBC *News 24* announced that the French government is to ban the wearing of headscarves in all public buildings in the interests of maintaining a secular state. France has a Muslim population of some five million, about 7 per cent of the total population. At the same time, in the current monthly paper produced by Cardiff County Council, there is an article announcing a new help line for victims of racial abuse or attack and a note that such attacks have increased dramatically over recent months.

If these types of social developments were not enough in themselves, two aspects of my own life have made difference an issue of great concern to me. One is sharing my life with someone who is an inspirational African-American writer and activist. The other is my involvement, since 1990, in a multi-ethnic history and arts project, Butetown History & Arts Centre (www.bhac.org), located in the old 'Tiger Bay' docklands community that has recently become part of the new 'Cardiff Bay'. While neither of these parts of my life feature in this book (except for the illustrations which come from Butetown History and Arts Centre's archive), they have both shaped my understandings of difference, identity and the need to belong. I am indebted above all to Glenn and also in various ways to many people in Butetown. I would like to thank Butetown History and Arts Centre archive for permission to reproduce the photographs in Chapters 2 and 5. I am also grateful to those who have discussed issues with me and commented on the material used in various chapters of this book, including the series editor Stuart Allan. My particular thanks go to Jackie Huggins and Bronwen Levy in Brisbane. Finally I would like to thank Stuart Hall for remaining an inspiration over decades.

My hope is that *Identity and Culture* might provoke interest in questions of difference, particularly as raised by those who are not part of that privileged space of belonging that is whiteness. Tackling discrimination in all its forms requires changes in all areas of life: social, economic, political and cultural. It also requires an understanding of why people have such a strong investment in marking and policing difference and why identities assume so much importance in particular contexts. While cultural texts and practices cannot be or do everything, they are important. They can and should contribute to the development of a society in which difference is not only tolerated, or grudgingly accepted, but welcomed and celebrated as enriching.

Earlier versions of material used in this book appeared in the following publications. Material from Chapter 3 in 'Historia, voz y representacionen el feminismo postcolonial: Las mujeres indigenas en Australia,' *Asparkia Investicacio feminista* (2002) (13), 115–28. Material from Chapter 4 in 'Discourses of Race and Ethnicity in Contemporary Britain,' in D. Walton and D. Shultz (eds) *Culture and Power: Unofficial Knowledges*, pp. 47–62. Bern: Peter Lang (2002). Material from Chapter 6 in 'Redefining Otherness, Negotiating Difference: Contemporary British Asian Women's Writing', in B. Neumeier (ed.) *Contemporary British Women's Writing*, pp. 223–36. Amsterdam: Rodopi (2000). Material from Chapter 7 in '*Goodness, Gracious Me*: Comedy as a Tool for Contesting Racism and Ethnocentrism', in M.J.C. Aguilar (ed.) *Cultural and Power V: Challenging Discourses*, pp. 261–9. Valencia: University of Valencia (2000). Material from Chapter 8 in 'Miss World in Nigeria: Eurocentrism and the Problem of Islamophobia,' *Revista Canaria de Estudios Ingleses*. University of La Laguna, Canary Islands, April 2004.

An enlarged and expanded version of some of the material drawn on in Chapter 4 will appear in Victoria Arana and Lauri Ramey (eds) (2004) *Black British Writing*. New York: Palgrave Macmillan.

INTRODUCTION

Just now everybody wants to talk about identity. As a key word in contemporary politics it has taken on so many different connotations that sometimes it is obvious that people are not even talking about the same thing. One thing at least is clear – identity only becomes an issue when it is in crisis, when something assumed to be fixed, coherent and stable is displaced by the experience of doubt and uncertainty. From this angle, the eagerness to talk about identity is symptomatic of the postmodern predicament of contemporary politics.

(Mercer 1990: 43)

Identity is about belonging, about what you have in common with some people and what differentiates you from others. At its most basic it gives you a sense of personal location, the stable core to your individuality. But it is also about your relationships, your complex involvement with others and in the modern world these have become ever more complex and confusing. Each of us live with a variety of potentially contradictory identities, which battle within us for allegiance: as men or women, black or white, straight or gay, able-bodied or disabled, 'British' or 'European' . . . The list is potentially infinite, and so therefore are our possible belongings. Which of them we focus on, bring to the fore, 'identify' with, depends on a host of factors. At the centre, however, are the values we share or wish to share with others.

(Weeks 1990: 88)

Identity is a key concept in the contemporary world. Since the Second World War, the legacies of colonialism, migration, globalization, as well as the growth of new social movements and forms of identity politics have put the question of identity at the centre of debates in the humanities and social sciences. National liberation struggles and ethnic conflicts throughout the world, the fall of Communist regimes in Eastern Europe and the rise of the extreme right in Europe as a whole have placed identity on the mainstream political agenda. In Western societies, the successful mobilization by the right of exclusive, racist discourses of national identity has, in part, fed upon media representations of a perceived threat from increasing numbers of economic migrants from developing countries and asylum seekers escaping repressive regimes.

In order to understand the power of identity, and particularly the role it plays in repressive individual and social practices, we need to theorize it within broader conceptualizations of subjectivity that can account for the unconscious, non-rational and emotional dimensions of identity. Often tied to racism, ethnocentrism, sexism and homophobia, exclusive forms of identity can lead to discriminatory behaviour towards others and violence of all kinds. These aspects of subjectivity and identity have come to the fore in recent years in a range of bitter ethnic conflicts, most visibly in Europe, Asia and Africa. They are also implicated in the rising levels of Islamophobia and Muslim fundamentalism that have become increasingly visible since the events of 11 September 2001, when the twin towers of the World Trade Center in New York and a section of the Pentagon in Washington were destroyed by passenger planes, hijacked by disaffected Muslims linked to Al Qaeda.

Perceived threats from the West's 'others' have profoundly affected mainstream politics in Western countries, setting the agenda not only for the right, but also for centre and centre-left parties. The events of 11 September have been used to justify emergency laws that allow a range of repressive measures towards those defined as suspect aliens, including, in some states, imprisonment without trial. Migration from the developing world has been met by xenophobic policies and campaigns, which do not only target poor or unskilled migrants. For example, the recruitment by industry of highly qualified South Asian IT specialists in Germany was countered by campaigns in Bavaria under the slogan '*Kinder statt Inder*' (Children not Indians), in which German women were called upon to have more children, echoing an aspect of Germany's Nazi past. In another hemisphere, the refusal of the Australian government in 2001 to accept refugees, stranded on-board ship off the coast of Australia, helped secure the re-election of what was, until then, a highly unpopular government. In Britain the moral panics around asylum seekers continue to feed xenophobia and have resulted in a range of repressive government policies that seek to contain asylum seekers and assuage popular fears. In January 2003 the leader of the Conservative opposition in the British parliament went so far as to urge that all asylum seekers be held and screened by the security forces to ascertain whether or not they were connected with terrorism. All these political issues feed on and keep alive discourses of identity and belonging, of who we are and what 'they' are, and who has the right to live where we do.

Identity and culture are key issues in the 'post-colonial', 'post-modern' West. This is a world in which the legacies of colonialism, including migration and the creation of diasporas, along with processes of globalization have put taken-for-granted ideas of identity and belonging into question. Organized around a series of case studies, this book focuses on how cultural texts, ranging from history and fiction to film and television, address and seek to shape identities in societies where ethnicity, gender and class are still paramount, and where racism is still alive and well. It asks how forms of racism continue to structure both the ways in which people are defined and how they see themselves.

Since the early modern period in Western Europe, different peoples and cultures have come into contact – actually or virtually – and mixed with each other to ever increasing degrees. This meeting of cultures in its various manifestations via colonialism, the slave trade, white settlement outside Europe, war, migration to the West and globalization, has involved relations of power, foremost among them attempts to dominate or assimilate others under the various banners of civilization, Christianization, modernization, progress and development. These processes have involved a profound 'othering' of colonized peoples as different and less advanced than people of European descent. Often, for example in the cases of slavery, genocide and even contemporary forms of racism, it has involved a denial of a common humanity. This strategy of othering has persisted into the present. For example, in early 2003, the language of the US administration in its 'War on Terror' and war against Iraq continued to divide the world into the civilized and uncivilized, the good and the evil. Lost from view in much of this Western political rhetoric are double standards in foreign policy, and the material causes of social unrest, especially in developing countries. This in turn leads to a failure to understand the reasons for the popular appeal, particularly but not exclusively outside the West, of groups such as Al Qaeda.[1] This appeal is in part organized and catered for through a number of internet sites that link the global and the local in an imagined community and create a space from which to speak in a world in which Western powers are dominant (see Khatib 2003).

One of the legacies of colonial history is the multi-ethnic, multi-cultural and racially mixed nature of contemporary Western societies. This book looks at questions of culture and identity in the contemporary 'postcolonial' West, drawing on examples and case studies from the UK, the United States, Australia and Africa. The book has three major concerns. The first is how we might usefully theorize the relationship between subjectivity, identity and agency and understand their constitution in and through cultural texts and practices. This is the focus of Chapter 1. The second concern is the importance of history to identity. This is taken up in different ways in Chapters 2, 3 and 4, and includes issues such as the significance of having a voice that is recognized and heard, and its role in the formation of positive forms of identity. It further includes the social, ideological and political role of narratives of the past that depict a collective experience for marginalized groups and the relations of dominant groups to these narratives and to the histories they inscribe. An example of this – the subject of Chapter 3 – is the Australian government project of 'reconciliation' with the Aboriginal people of Australia, which was to culminate in the 100th anniversary of the establishment of Australia as a sovereign state in 2001. Part of this process involved the government-sponsored 'Bringing Them Home' project, which raised, once again, the painful issues of Aboriginal history since white settlement and white Australia's relationship to its past. This oral history project sought to collect the life stories of the 'Stolen Generation': those mixed-race children forcibly removed from their Aboriginal families to be brought up on missions, in orphanages and in white adoptive families, and the various white Australians involved in the process. This is a history that was made widely visible outside Australia by Sally Morgan's *My Place* (1988) and in 2002 by the film *Rabbit Proof Fence*.[2] Linked to questions of history and voice is the importance of roots and the appeal of narratives of origin and belonging. This is the focus of Chapter 5. While this is especially true for those minorities marginalized by mainstream discourses of national identity, it is also a major component of extreme white supremacist thinking, as examples in Chapter 5 suggest.

The third focus of the book is how people negotiate identity and difference in postcolonial, multi-cultural societies and the importance of hybrid cultures and identities. This is the focus of Chapters 6 and 7. Negotiating difference includes issues of conflicting cultures and values and their effects on identity, an area that has come to the fore in Western Europe with the establishment and growth of substantial minority Muslim communities and the strengthening of Islamophobia. Postcolonial Western societies are faced with competing ideas of how we should live, especially as regards, gender norms, religious practices, food and dress. State institutions such as schools, the health service and social services are increasingly being asked to address diversity in the interests of accommodating difference. This is the focus of Chapter 8. The final issue that the book addresses is how one might make hegemonic forms of subjectivity and identity strange, problematizing and relativizing them in the interests of a more tolerant and diverse society.

Yet, we also need to ask why these discourses have such a powerful hold over us. To begin to answer this question I want to turn to theories of subjectivity and identity, which are the focus of Chapter 1.

SUBJECTIVITY AND IDENTITY

Identity is not as transparent or unproblematic as we think. Perhaps instead of thinking of identity as an already accomplished fact, which the new cultural practices then represent, we should think. Instead, of identity as a 'production', which is never complete, always in process, and always constituted within, not outside, representation. This view problematises the very authority and authenticity to which the term, 'cultural identity' lays claim.

(Hall 1990: 222)

The knowing self is partial in all its guises, never finished, whole, simply there and original; it is always constructed and stitched together imperfectly, and *therefore* able to join with another, to see together without claiming to be another.

(Haraway 1991b: 193)

'Hey, you there!'

In his classic and influential essay, 'On Ideology and Ideological State Apparatuses. Notes Towards an Investigation,' French Marxist philosopher, Louis Althusser theorizes the process of identification through which individuals become 'knowing subjects' (Althusser 1971). A 'knowing subject' is an individual conceived of as a sovereign, rational and unified consciousness, in control of language and meaning. It is the 'I' that thinks and speaks and is the apparent author of meaning. This is the theory of the subject that is usually assumed in commonsense discourses. Althusser describes an everyday situation in which an individual is walking down the street and hears a police officer or other voice call out 'Hey, you there!' Almost always, Althusser suggests, the hailed individual will turn around. In the process s/he becomes a subject. Althusser comments on the reasons for this, suggesting that it occurs:

> Because he [or she] has recognised the hail was really addressed to him [or her], and that 'it was really him [or her] who was hailed' (not someone else). Experience shows that the practical telecommunication of hailings is such that they hardly ever miss their [woman or] man: verbal call or whistle, the one hailed always recognises that it is really him [or her] who is being hailed. And yet it is a strange phenomenon, and one which cannot be explained solely by 'guilt feelings', despite the large numbers who 'have something on their consciences.'
>
> (Althusser 1971: 163)

Faced by this 'strange phenomenon', Althusser theorizes the process of hailing, that is, the process of the constitution of the individual as subject within language and ideology, as fundamental to human societies. In Althusser's theorization, the process of recognition by the individual of herself or himself as the one addressed by the call to recognition *interpellates* the individual as a subject within ideology. The individual is hailed, and responds with an identification through which s/he is a subject in a double sense. S/he becomes both the agent of the ideology in question and subjected to it. This process of identification, Althusser argues, inserts individuals into ideologies and ideological practices that, when they work well, are lived as if they were obvious and natural. In Althusser's theorization, a range of what he terms 'Ideological State Apparatuses' such as religion, education, the family, the law, politics, culture and the media produce the ideologies within which we assume identities and become subjects.

Identities may be socially, culturally and institutionally assigned, as in the case, for instance, of gender or citizenship, where state institutions, civil society and social and cultural practices produce the discourses within which gendered subjectivity and citizens are constituted. Often they solicit active identification on the part of the subject so defined. For example, forms of dress and many children's games are marketed as gender specific and encourage normative gender identification and behaviour. In the case of citizenship, an elaborate bureaucracy monitors and allocates the markers of citizenship, for example, birth certificates, passports and electoral registers. National anthems, sung at official state occasions and at cultural and sports events, seek to recruit subjects, drawing on emotional as well as rational forms of identification in order to interpellate individuals as citizens of a particular nation. In the cases of both gender and national identity, a wide range of social practices come into play in recruiting subjects to identify with the identities on offer. The meaning of a particular social practice, for example, the singing of a national anthem, is, however, never fixed. It will change according to the context in which it is used.

Forms of identity are often internalized by the individual who takes them on. This process can be theorized in terms of what Judith Butler has called 'performativity'. This refers to the repeated assumption of identities in the course of daily life. Butler, who concentrates on the example of gender, argues that 'there is no gender identity behind the expressions of gender . . . Identity is performatively constituted by the very "expressions" that are said to be its results' (Butler 1990: 24–5). Thus, for example, feminine identity, manifest in dress, ways of walking and behaving, does not give rise to this femininity but is the product of it. It is acquired by performing discourses of femininity that constitute the individual as a feminine subject. Whereas common sense suggests that femininity and masculinity are natural, in this mode of theorization they are culturally acquired through repetition. In Butler's language, this 'performativity must be understood not as a singular or deliberate "act", but, rather, as the reiterative and citational practice by which discourse produces the effects that it names' (1993: 2). As individuals inserted within specific discourses, we repeatedly perform modes of subjectivity and identity until these are experienced as if they were second nature. Where they are successfully internalized, they become part of lived subjectivity. Where this does not occur, they may become the basis for dis-identification or counter-identifications which involve a rejection of hegemonic identity norms.

Other identities rely explicitly on active processes of identification, for example membership of a club or religion, and may involve a conscious counter-identification against institutionally and socially assigned identities, and the meanings and values that they are seen to represent. An example of this would be gay and lesbian forms of identity that mobilize common signs and symbols to signify difference from a heterosexual norm. Identity is made visible and intelligible to others through cultural signs, symbols and practices. This can be seen most obviously in the case of gender identity, where cultural codes of the body, dress and behaviour signify gender. Discourses of gender help shape the materiality of both female and male bodies, through, for example, differential gender roles, physical education and work. Yet these same codes can also be used to subvert hegemonic meanings, as in the case of Queer appropriations of the signifiers of heterosexuality. The visual dimensions of identities are often pronounced, as, for example, in the case of sub-cultural groups such as the wide range of Western youth cultures from teddy boys through punks to Goths, seen in the West since the 1950s. Religious identities, too, are often marked by dress and hairstyle as in the case of Christian or Buddhist nuns, monks and priests, Muslims, Sikhs and Rastafarians.

In Althusserian theory, as in the Lacanian psychoanalytic theory of the subject on which it draws, identification is central to the mechanisms through which individuals become knowing subjects. Yet the wide range of identities available in a society and the modes of subjectivity that go with them are not open to all people at all times. They are often restricted to specific groups, usually on the basis of discourses of class, gender and race, that are exclusive to and policed by the groups in question. Non-recognition and non-identification leaves the individual in an abject state of non-subjectivity and lack of agency. At best the individual concerned must fall back on subject positions other than the ones to which s/he is denied access. Toni Morrison, in her novel *The Bluest Eye*, for example, vividly describes a scene in which the poor, Black child,

Pecola, goes to buy sweets from the local store and comes up against a racism that denies her access even to the position of a shared humanity:

> She pulls off her shoe and takes out three pennies. The gray head of Mr Yacobowski looms up over the counter. He urges his eyes out of his thoughts to encounter her. Blue eyes. Blear-dropped. Slowly, like Indian summer moving imperceptibly towards fall, he looks towards her. Somewhere between retina and object, between vision and view, his eyes draw back, hesitate and hover. At some fixed point in time and space he senses that he need not waste the effort of a glance. He does not see her, because for him there is nothing to see. How can a fifty-two-year-old white immigrant store keeper with the taste of potatoes and beer in his mouth, his mind honed on the doe-eyed Virgin Mary, his sensibilities blunted by a permanent awareness of loss, *see* a little black girl? Nothing in his life even suggested that the feat was possible, not to say desirable or necessary.
>
> (Morrison 1981: 47)

Mutual recognition between self and other has been a feature of theories of subjectivity. In 1807, Hegel argued in the *Phenomenology of Mind* that the Other is essential to the realization of self-consciousness (Hegel 1971: 153–78). This idea fed directly into twentieth-century phenomenological and existentialist approaches to the individual, identity and subjectivity, which also inform commonsense assumptions about the self.

In commonsense discourse, people tend to assume that they are 'knowing subjects', that is sovereign individuals, whose lives are governed by free will, reason, knowledge, experience and, to a lesser degree, emotion. They are subjects who, in Althusser's terms, work by themselves. As sovereign, knowing subjects, they use language to express meaning. They acquire the knowledge that they convey in language from their socialization, education and experience of life. The assumptions that they hold about themselves as fully conscious, knowing, intentional subjects derive from Enlightenment ideas of rationality, combined with aspects of a humanism that privilege the individual, consciousness, language and lived experience over theories which ground the essence of the human in biology and natural science or in social structures such as class. In humanist thought the subject and subjectivity are assumed to be unified and rational and the subject is governed by reason and free will, which give it agency.

Humanism is a powerful discourse which, when linked to discourses of human rights and equality, can serve as a positive basis for a tolerant and caring society. It is a discourse based on an assumed sameness in which all human beings share a common humanity, with specific needs and rights. The United Nations, for example, aspires to the humanist goal of universal human rights for all. States that seek to resist this discourse tend to deny the universality of the rights in question and argue that they are culturally specific. Yet, when it comes to understanding how subjectivity and identity work in societies fractured by power relations of class, gender, sexual, racial and ethnic privilege and disadvantage, the theoretical basis on which humanism grounds its aspirations requires problematization. There is more to the constitution of subjectivities and identities than humanism is readily able to theorize. In drawing on other theories we necessarily both think and act as knowing subjects, and, at the same time, need to stand back from this position in order to question our assumptions and to analyse how subjectivities and identities are socially constituted in ways that serve particular interests, even while they may appear or be lived as obvious and natural.

Subjectivity and the subject

Subjectivity and the subject are crucial terms in social and cultural theory. Cultural studies, film and media studies and literary studies all draw on a range of competing theories of subjectivity and identity, variously derived from humanism, Marxism, psychoanalysis, poststructuralism and feminism. Various political, philosophical and cultural movements have challenged Enlightenment and humanist ideas of subjectivity. If the seventeenth century in the West is often seen as the age of reason and the scientific revolution, in the late eighteenth and early nineteenth centuries, romanticism, reinstated the centrality of emotion and sensibility. In a radically different vein, Marxism, which developed from the 1840s onwards, constituted one of the most important challenges to the sovereign rational subject and towards the end of the nineteenth century Freud developed his influential critique of the rational subject. His psychoanalytic theories of the unconscious have remained profoundly influential up to the present day. How, then, might these and more recent poststructuralist theories of the subject, language, meaning and power help us understand subjectivity and identity?

Different theoretical approaches to subjectivity and identity will produce different types of analysis and forms of knowledge. This raises the question of how to choose between theoretical approaches. Traditionally, proponents of particular theories have appealed to science and truth to justify the validity of the theory in question. For example, Marxists have often claimed the scientific status of historical materialism and Freud attempted to clothe psychoanalysis in the language of science. More recently, postmodern theory, particularly the work of Jean-François Lyotard, has questioned the truth status of universalizing theories that claim to explain societies and the process of history. Lyotard (1984) calls such theories 'metanarratives' and suggests that they are never universal but merely one among many competing narratives. In the light of such critiques, theory effectively becomes a tool kit that offers different ways of analysing and theorizing social and cultural phenomena and practices. According to this logic, the theory that one chooses will be that which has the most explanatory power in relation to the questions that one wishes to understand. Important, too, in choosing theories are the social and political implications of the type of knowledge produced. For example, I would argue that it is necessary to have a theory of the unconscious in order to understand the irrational dimensions of racism, sexism and homophobia. The most developed theory of the unconscious is Freudian, yet this might not be the most productive approach to understanding irrational hatred of others, given its reliance on the fear of castration and on the Oedipal complex as they relate to the acquisition of subjectivity. While psychoanalysis's positing of a split subject based on lack and of the unconscious raises questions that are arguably central to understanding subjectivity and identity, Freudian psychoanalysis itself remains a theory that explains these things in terms of universal drives and illicit repressed sexual desires. Maybe we need a more historically and culturally specific theory of the unconscious that does not ground human behaviour solely in Freudian drives.

The questions with which this book is primarily concerned are how different forms of cultural narrative and cultural practice: historical, political, fictional and visual work to constitute subjectivity and identity for the individuals who engage with them. It is further concerned with how cultural practices can offer new forms of identity and agency and serve as ways of subverting and negotiating dominant forms of identity. In analysing how cultural narratives work, the book is primarily concerned with the social power relations that structure the subject positions and forms of identity in play. While these include class, gender and sexuality, the book's major focus is on the mobilization of forms of ethnic identity in societies still governed by racism. I want to return now to some of the theoretical approaches to subjectivity and identity that may prove useful in this project.

Class, ideology, identity

Class remains a key ingredient of subjectivity and identity. If people often do not positively acknowledge the social class to which social theories assign them, they certainly know the classes with which they do not identify. Whereas in the twentieth century the Labour Movement in the UK and other industrial societies appealed to 'class' as if it were something obvious, identifiable and the source of positive forms of identity, in contemporary society such appeals have become less convincing. In cultural analysis in recent years, class has become the poor relation of gender, sexuality, race and ethnicity. This is not unrelated to broader social changes that range from the demise and discrediting of socialism in Eastern Europe to the decline of explicitly class-based politics. In Britain, for example, recent decades have seen a fading of traditional forms of class identity and the rise in a range of discourses and social practices of the idea of a 'classless' society. This has become central to conservative political rhetoric, popular culture, the leisure industries and the expansion of consumerism. Few people in Britain today identify with traditional versions of class politics, though these still have a home in more left-wing trade unions and in far-left political organizations.

Despite the demise of class as a clearly articulated form of identity, it still has important theoretical purchase as a way of conceptualizing social relations that can lead to an understanding of inequalities within society. One of the questions that we need to ask of particular forms of identity is how they relate to the reproduction of economic and social inequalities. Class signifies differences that imply inequalities that can be variously understood as necessary and inevitable or social and undesirable; either way class remains a highly politicized concept. Moreover, class as a form of identity is still significant in many social contexts; it shapes, for example, the meanings given to particular ways of speaking and dressing, to exclusive forms of education, cultural pursuit, and the membership of particular organizations and clubs. It also affects the ways in which individuals interact with one another.

Ideas about class are an important aspect of common sense as well as social and political theory. Commonsense assumptions tend to identify class with particular ways of living to which individuals are born or naturally suited. For example, popular notions of organic working-class life, in which ordinary people are the salt of the earth, remain popular in British television soap operas and cinema and are arguably as strong as commonsense assumptions about the natural 'class' of the aristocracy. Commonsense notions of class tend to focus on its cultural dimensions, for example, whether people speak with class-specific regional accents or use received pronunciation, or what they do in their leisure time, rather than emphasizing the ways in which class is firmly grounded in economic and educational relations of difference and inequality. It is Marxist theories of class that have defined class in more radical ways and produced critiques of the relation between social class, identity and power.

In the Marxist tradition, the individual is the product of class relations, and subjectivity and identity are governed by ideology. For Marxism, subjectivity is always class subjectivity. According to the classical Marxist tradition, economic relations shape both society and the individuals within it. Class is first and foremost an economic category that characterizes the relation of specific groups within society to the mode of production.[1] Yet class position is also a crucial determinant in the formation of subjectivity and identity. According to Marx, in modern capitalist states the relations between capital and labour appear in the form of contracts between apparently free individual subjects – workers and employers. These relations of production are secured by ideology, which is embedded in social and cultural practices. In Marxist theory, ideology shapes subjectivity. As Marx and Engels put it in their early formulation in the *German Ideology*: 'Life is not determined by consciousness, but consciousness by life' (1970: 47). The forms which ideology takes vary in different Marxist texts, ranging from Engels' notion of ideology as false consciousness to the Althusserian notion of ideology as the subject's lived relation to his or her real conditions of existence (Althusser 1971: 152–4). It is this latter formulation that has been most influential in media, cultural and literary studies and which, as suggested above, offers one useful model for theorizing identity.

Louis Althusser's theory of ideology and subjectivity is concerned both with the mechanism of interpellation and with the role of identity and subjectivity in the reproduction of capitalist relations of production. According to Althusser, ideological state apparatuses play a central role in the reproduction of individuals as class subjects. Each apparatus contributes to the reproduction of capitalist relations in its own specific way, creating subjects through the process of interpellation: 'The political apparatus by subjecting individuals to the political state ideology, the "indirect" (parliamentary) or "direct" (plebiscitary or fascist) "democratic". ideology. The communications apparatus by cramming every "citizen" with daily doses of nationalism, chauvinism, liberalism, moralism etc.' (Althusser 1971: 146). Individual subjects internalize particular meanings and values and take up the identity offered to them by the institution in question, for example, that of worker, mother or citizen of a particular state.

Language and the split subject

Crucial to theorizing subjectivity and identity is the question of language. In the Althusserian model of the interpellation of individuals as subjects within particular ideologies, it is the linguistic category of the speaking subject 'I', who identifies with and speaks and acts according to the ideology in question.[2] For Althusser, who draws on the psychoanalytic theory of Jacques Lacan, this subject is split. The subject who says 'I think' is not the same as the subject whose existence is assumed in the act of thought. Thus, in this model, the subject can no longer be seen as unified and the source of knowledge and truth, since the very structure of language points to the implausibility of such models of subjectivity. Identity categories can be understood as attempts to mask this gap between the subject who speaks and the subject who is spoken. It is a gap that individuals, constantly attempt to cover over and for Lacan, it marks the subject's inability to control meaning and the symbolic order.

In his critique of the unified, intentional, knowing subject, Lacan takes as his starting point Descartes' *cogito, ergo sum* – I think therefore I am. He rewrites Descartes' proposition as 'where I think "I think, therefore I am" that is where I am not' (Lacan 1977: 195). Privileging one particular emphasis in Freud's work, which can be found in texts such as *The Interpretation of Dreams* (1976) and *The Psycho-pathology of Everyday Life* (1975), Lacan develops Freud's theory of the acquisition of gendered subjectivity into a general theory of society and culture. Lacan argues that the symbolic order of language, law and meaning is founded on the unconscious, which is itself structured like a language. Subjectivity is an effect of language, governed by lack. The intentional subject (which is equivalent to the ego) is a subject based on identifications created via a structure of misrecognition, laid down in the mirror stage of psychosexual development.

It is useful to understand the mechanisms in play in the mirror phase, since this has become an influential part of recent theories of identity. Its importance lies in the way it theorizes the subject as split and governed by a lack that is produced by the non-unified, non-sovereign status of the subject as an effect of language. It points to lack of control over meaning in the symbolic order and the non-sovereign status of the subject.[3] In Lacanian theory, the infant repeatedly identifies with a mirror image and, in the process, misrecognizes itself as whole, unified and autonomous. Lacan suggests that prior to the mirror phase, infants do not have any sense of distinct identity. The pre-Oedipal stage of development is governed by the experience of the body in fragments, lacking a definite sense of unified, embodied self, separate from the world around it. This state is compounded by the lack of control over the satisfaction of needs and desire that will become the motivating force behind language. Governed by a fragmented sense of self and unable to distinguish itself as a separate entity, the infant overcomes its fragmentation by identifying with the visual image of an 'other', an external mirror image.

According to Lacan, this process of misrecognition becomes the basis for all future identifications by the subject of itself as autonomous and sovereign, once it has entered the symbolic order of language. Apparently unified, subjectivity is thus divided and based on misrecognition. It is the subject's lack of fullness, lack of self-presence and inability to control meaning that motivates language. The process of assuming subjectivity within language invests the individual with a temporary sense of control and of sovereignty which evokes identity according to what Derrida has called a 'metaphysics of presence' in which s/he becomes the source of the meaning s/he speaks and language appears to be the expression of meaning fixed by the speaking subject (see Derrida 1976: 49).

Yet, in Lacanian, Derridean and other poststructuralist theories, the speaker is never the author of the language within which s/he takes up a position. Language pre-exists and produces subjectivity, identity and meaning. For example, language in the form of competing discourses offers the individual meanings and forms of subjectivity that they can assume and live as if they were true. In the process they become subjects. Yet access to the forms of subjectivity and identity constituted for the individual within different discourses is structured through power relations of inclusion and exclusion, often based on visual signifiers of difference that acquire particular meanings in racist, heterosexist and patriarchal societies.

The importance of the visual

'But you do not have the look.'

This was the comment, probably non-committal in its intention but potentially disheartening in its effect, which I repeatedly received in response to what may loosely be called an 'identity claim' that I made, and through which I first started to develop an interest in the alienating relation between how I perceive myself and my visible image: I did not always look what I was, or more precisely, what I tried to claim I was. Sometimes the identity for which I did not have the look was not the one that I wanted to claim anyway, in which case it did not greatly concern me.

I remember the pride and satisfaction that I felt when, at the age of eleven, I transferred from Southeast Asia to a school in Japan and some of the new classmates immediately picked up on my appearance, which they saw as 'darker', 'non-Japanese' and 'native'. Since I did not necessarily want to be a Japanese after having spent most of my childhood in Southeast Asia, I was glad to know that I apparently did not look like one, at least to some of my friends, no matter what it said on my passport. My appearance, in a sense, seemed to truthfully convey what I thought was important about myself at that time. At other times, however, it was precisely what I considered to constitute a large part of who I was that seemed to fail to show.

(Shimizu 2003: 1)

It is not only the speaking subject that is disunified in poststructuralist approaches to subjectivity and identity. There is also often a radical difference between how individuals see themselves and how others define them. At issue here are often discourses of the body and what it means. The body is central to identity – both chosen identities and those imposed by institutions. Competing regimes of meaning seek to define bodies according to gender, sexuality, skin colour, phenotype, norms of beauty and ugliness, age and physical ability. In the above quotation the child in question has spent eleven years as a Japanese girl in Southeast Asia where attitudes to Japan are often negative. She has learned that to be Japanese is problematic outside Japan in areas previously colonized by the Japanese army and state. Inside Japan her body fails to match up to hegemonic norms of Japaneseness and she is relieved to find herself 'othered'. Later in life, when she come to realize that she is sexually attracted to other women, yet appears to most people to be classically feminine and heterosexual, she feels that a large part of who she is fails to show.

The meanings discursively attributed to bodies are never static but rather a constant site of struggle in which meanings can change. For example, one of the more successful dimensions of Western feminist political struggle over the last thirty-five years has been the recognition and legitimation of a range of different ways of being a woman, and indeed a man. This is, in part, an offshoot of the widespread acceptance that femininity is neither natural nor one thing, and that many media images of femininity are neither possible nor desirable. Yet the diversification of acceptable modes of femininity combined with the seductive, postmodern fascination with difference as style and lifestyle, has often served to detract attention from the ongoing inequalities in women's position in society. Similarly the postmodern commodification of racial and ethnic otherness often hides the persistence of racism as a negative and discriminatory force in Western societies.

In racist and sexist societies, most women, and women and men of Colour cannot help but know that they are embodied subjects. Hegemonic discourses of gender and race constantly reassert the centrality of the body but in different ways. Thus, if white women in Britain, whatever their class and background, can participate to some extent – real or imagined – in the postmodern culture of difference and choice, this is much less the case where women who are not white are concerned. Everyday racism insists on attributing fixed sets of meanings to non-white bodies. They are defined as 'other' to a white norm on the basis of how they look. As Richard Dyer has argued in his book *White* (Dyer 1997), predominantly white Western societies privilege white bodies as an unmarked norm against which difference is measured and defined. Whiteness is seldom recognized as an explicit identity by those who live it, except in relation to those it excludes. It is assumed to be natural and the norm. This practice of assuming the universality of whiteness as a marker of the quintessentially human has deep roots in the development of Western culture since the Renaissance. One of its outcomes has been white supremacy: the belief in the natural superiority of white people.

Power limits the possibilities of identity. The meaning of the visual is not at the disposal of individuals but is overdetermined by the history of representation. The rise of modern conceptions of race and racism, which still inform aspects of twenty-first-century life, coincided with the beginnings of modernity and colonial expansion. In Volume One of his study of sexuality, Foucault (1981) attempted to map what he called the 'incitement to discourse' in relation to sexuality, that is the ways in which the modern discursive field of sexuality was created by the constitution of sexuality within discourses as wide-ranging as medicine, psychiatry and demography. In a similar vein, African-American philosopher and cultural critic, Cornel West, has attempted to out-line the 'incitement to discourse' in relation to race. He argues that three factors, in particular, came together in the early modern period to make white supremacy an inevitable outcome of the incitement to discourse that produced modern ideas of race. They were, he argues, inherent in: 'the very structure of modern discourse at its inception [and] produced forms of rationality, scientificity, and objectivity, as well as aesthetic and cultural ideals which require the constitution of white supremacy' (West 1982: 47). West acknowledges that many other factors also gave rise to or helped sustain discourses of race, for example, the demands of the mode of production (capitalist and colonialist expansion), the political interests of colonial powers and of the slave owning classes, and the psychological needs of the dominant white racial group. However, he is interested in what he sees as a neglected area: the endemic racist structure of modern discourses which he sees as the product of a creative fusion at the beginnings of modernity of three things: scientific investigation, Cartesian epistemology and classical ideals of beauty. He argues that they work to circumscribe the ways in which it was possible to conceive of and live discourses of race:

> To put it crudely, my argument is that the authority of science, undergirded by a modern philosophical discourse guided by Greek ocular metaphors and Cartesian notions, promotes and encourages the activities of observing, comparing, measuring, and ordering the physical characteristics of human bodies.
>
> (West 1982: 48)

This project of the natural sciences with its objective of classifying the natural world, was extended to human beings and gave rise to a 'racial science' that incorporated within it classical aesthetic and cultural norms that implied white supremacy:

> The creative fusion of scientific investigation, Cartesian epistemology, and classical ideals produced forms of rationality, scientificity, and objectivity which, though efficacious in the quest for truth and knowledge, prohibited the intelligibility and legitimacy of the idea of black equality in beauty, culture and intellectual capacity. In fact to 'think' such an idea was to be deemed irrational, barbaric or mad.
>
> (West 1982: 48)

The important point here is that the discursive field of racial theory did not allow for forms of subjectivity and identity based on the equality of the races that it constituted. These could only emerge from the contradictions between racialized thinking and other discourses that emphasized a common humanity such as those of human rights and religion. Yet, in the hands of white people, these, too, were often rendered compatible with hierarchical racialized thinking, giving rise to attempts to ground racial science in the Bible, and to segregated religious institutions.[4] The supposedly objective, descriptive classifications produced within eighteenth-, nineteenth- and twentieth-century discourses of race consistently included judgements about intelligence, level of cultural development, beauty, sexuality and morality (Jordan and Weedon 1995: 261–314). These judgements became firmly linked to racial categorization. Nineteenth-century racial theories ranging from Gobineau in Europe to Morton and Nott in the United States, shared a hierarchization of the races in which the white, Caucasian body was placed at the top of the scale (for more on racial science see Stanton 1960, Harris 1968, Gould 1981 and Young 1994). It was said by whites to signify the most beautiful and desirable body and the most advanced and intelligent mind.

While racial science has long since been discredited, many of its assumptions and the stereotypes to which it gave rise, have entered mainstream culture and become part of a collective 'common sense'. The meanings and status often attributed to non-white and non-Western bodies and the modes of subjectivity and identity that they constitute can be traced both in discourses of racialized difference and in the visual iconography of the West. If we look, for example, at the legacies of classical racism and Orientalism in a postmodern Western world we find ongoing stereotypes of difference, particularly in popular culture. Pop music videos, in particular, recycle images of Black people as hypersexual, physically strong, athletic and rhythmic. The popular press repeatedly depicts Muslims and Islamic societies as extreme, fundamentalist, often violent and more primitive than their Christian and secular counterparts (see Said 1981 and Runnymede Trust 1997).

Racialized identities are more often imposed through the assertion of hierarchized oppositions than freely embraced. The liberal humanist identity of being a unique individual insists on the unimportance of constructions of race or gender to who one is. In practice liberal humanist subjectivity often corresponds to white subjectivity. Whiteness is rarely acknowledged as a racialized subject position, yet this freedom from the burden of race is a luxury most often denied to people who are not classified as white. While mainstream discourses fail to acknowledge whiteness as a privileged identity and subject position, the white supremacist far right affirms and celebrates a racialized white identity which relies on the explicit denigration of those who are not white (see Daniels 1997 and Chapter 5 of this book).

Racialized forms of subjectivity and identity, constructed within Western societies, produce resistances. This is an issue taken up in different ways in the following chapters. Often, oppressed groups seek to reclaim some form of positive identity out of racialized discourse, creating what Foucault has called 'reverse discourses' (Foucault 1981: 101, see below). For example, in her novel about slavery, *Beloved*, Toni Morrison depicts an ex-slave woman preaching a new religion of self-love that focuses on the Black body that was so abused and denigrated by slavery:

> 'Here,' she said, 'in this here place, we flesh; flesh that weeps, laughs; flesh that dances on bare feet in grass. Love it. Love it hard. Yonder they do not love your flesh. They despise it. They don't love your eyes; they'd just as soon pick em out. No more do they love the skin on your back. Yonder they flay it. And O my people they do not love your hands. Those they only use, tie, bind, chop off and leave empty. Love your hands! Love them. Raise them up and kiss them. Touch others with them, pat them together, stroke them on your face 'cause they don't love that either. You got to love it.'
>
> (Morrison 1988: 88)

In a similar vein, the Black Power Movement in the West in the late 1960s and 1970s attempted to counteract racist definitions of Black people with its affirmative, campaigning slogan 'Black is beautiful' and its move away from Eurocentric norms of beauty.

Subjectivity, discourse and power

How we see bodies is an effect of the discursive field within which we are located. For the Japanese children invoked in the quotation from Akiko Shimizu above, particular hegemonic norms, produced within the discursive field that constitutes Japaneseness, insist that they deny this identity to the new child recently returned from Southeast Asia. Particular regimes of power inform the discursive fields that define and shape both the materiality and meaning of bodies. Discursive fields are themselves made up of competing discourses that produce different subject positions and forms of identity. In this poststructuralist theoretical approach to subjectivity and identity, language *constitutes* rather than reflects or expresses the meaning of experience and identity. This approach opens up subjectivities and identities to processes of cultural struggle and resistance. Subjectivity (consisting of an individual's conscious and unconscious sense of self, emotions and desires) is also constituted in language, and rational consciousness is only one dimension of subjectivity. It is in the process of using language – whether as thought or speech – that we take up positions as speaking and thinking subjects and the identities that go with them.

This book is concerned with how cultural texts and practices ranging from literature and history to film and television, constitute modes of subjectivity and identity in multi-ethnic, postcolonial societies. While these societies may officially subscribe to discourses of tolerance and, in some cases, even the celebration of cultural diversity, they remain fractured by racism and ethnocentrism. Discourses of identity and difference take many competing and often contradictory forms. Following Foucault, the various chapters of this book see discourses of identity as part of specific discursive fields that are structured in relation to a range of cultural and other institutions. They constitute our subjectivity for us through material practices that shape bodies as much as minds and involve relations of power. Some discourses, and the subject positions and modes of subjectivity and identity that they constitute, have more power than others. For example, as suggested above, with the racist othering of non-white bodies in Western societies, only the white body enjoys an apparently neutral position as universal. Black and Asian bodies, are burdened with a long history of negative, orientalist or primitivist representations and an individual finds herself or himself defined not just as a man or woman but as a specific racially coded man or woman. Primitivist discourses define the other in binary opposition to rational Western 'man', celebrating those feature that the other is said to have to a much larger degree than his/her Western counterpart, for example spirituality, emotionality, closeness to nature, sensuality and sexuality. In primitivist narratives these features are often said to belong to an earlier stage of 'Western man's' development (for primitivism see Hiller 1991, for orientalism see Said 1978). In Foucault's work discourses produce subjects within relations of power that potentially or actually involve resistance. For example, Foucault give the instance of the homosexual in the nineteenth century who, he argues, is discursively produced as a subject and an identity within discourses as diverse as psychiatry, jurisprudence and literature, whereas previously homosexuality had only been a mode of sexual behaviour:

> There is no question that the appearance in nineteenth-century psychiatry, jurisprudence and literature of a whole series of discourses on the species and subspecies of homosexuality, inversion, pederasty, and 'psychic hermaphrodism' made possible a strong advance of social controls into this area of 'perversity'; but also made possible the formation of a 'reverse' discourse: homosexuality began to speak on its own behalf, to demand that its legitimacy or 'naturality' be acknowledged, often in the same vocabulary, using the same categories by which it was medically disqualified.

(Foucault 1981: 101)

His example well illustrates how power is both repressive and enabling. For Foucault, power is a relationship that implies resistance. It is not something held by a particular group, but rather, it is a relationship that inheres in all discourses (economic, media, familial and so on), that serves particular interests. It is dispersed across a range of social institutions and practices and functions through the discursive constitution of embodied subjects within discourses. The subject positions and modes of embodied subjectivity constituted for the individual within particular discourses allow for different degrees and types of identity and agency both compliant and resistant. As will be seen from many examples in this book, the discursive fields, which produce meanings and subjectivities, are not homogenous. They include discourses and discursive practices which may be contradictory and conflicting and which create the space for new forms of knowledge and practice. While there is no place beyond discourses and the power relations that govern them, resistance and change are possible from within.

Subjectivity and identity: the local and the global

How then can we usefully conceptualize the relation between subjectivity and identity? Identity is perhaps best understood as a limited and temporary fixing for the individual of a particular mode of subjectivity as apparently what one *is*. One of the key ideological roles of identity is to curtail the plural possibilities of subjectivity inherent in the wider discursive field and to give individuals a singular sense of who they are and where they belong. This process involves recruiting subjects to the specific meanings and values constituted within a particular discourse and encouraging identification. A wide range of social practices, for example, education, the media, sport and state rituals, offer subject positions that encourage identification. While it is possible to be a subject without identification, identity presupposes some degree of self-recognition on the part of the subject, often defined in relation to what one believes one is not. For example, from our earliest years we learn who we are and what this should mean. We learn that we are female or male, even though we may not identify with or conform to 'socially appropriate' forms of female or male behaviour.

Like the structure of meaning in language, identity is relational. It is defined in a relation of difference to what it is not. Thus, for example, most cultures create polarized binary oppositions between what they define as masculine and feminine. All identities have their 'others' from which they mark their difference. This assertion of difference is often at the expense of similarities, for example, in the British context, Scottishness and Welshness are often defined in opposition to Englishness and the differences in play are not always apparent to those not directly involved. Similarly, an outsider to the dispute between India and Pakistan over Kashmir might wonder at the level of passion that fuels the conflict, given the many similarities and fundamental shared problems faced by the inhabitants of the two countries. In this case, as in many others, the legacies of colonialism have created questions of ownership and control of territory that lie at the heart of the dispute and are fuelled by political interests that mobilize religious differences (see Chapter 8).

National identity, too, is defined in an exclusive relationship of difference from others that is most often tied to place or lack of it, as for example, in the demands of the Kurds in Iraq, Iran and Turkey for their own state. It is also linked to language, history and culture. Often these different factors are seen as inextricably linked, as for example in the case of the indigenous peoples of Australia, New Zealand and North America. Discourses of national identity most often appeal to ideas of a shared culture, history and place. A common language is often assumed to signify a common culture and identity, though the need actively to construct this has long been recognized by cultural critics and politicians. In Britain, Matthew Arnold, writing in the 1860s, looked to literature, and poetry in particular, for the means to instil a common culture and shared national values that would cut across class divisions in the face of increasing social unrest and the rise of trade unionism and other forms of working-class radicalism (see Arnold 1869). Some 131 years later, the Parekh Report on the *Future of Multi-ethnic Britain* (Parekh 2000), which is discussed in detail in Chapter 2, would urge the importance of rethinking British history, Britishness and the national heritage to the process of creating a tolerant and vibrant multi-cultural society.

As noted above, states mobilize flags, anthems, monuments and rituals to promote narratives of identity and belonging. Other agencies and institutions, from tourist boards to industry and commerce, market national costumes, crafts and customs, cuisines and landscapes in their constructions of what makes a nation different and, in this case, worth visiting. Often these images have little to do with life as it is lived. Identity in all its forms, even national identity, is never singular but is plural, fractured and reconfigured by gender, ethnic and class relations. Constructions of identity are always historically specific, for example, the much maligned attempt by New Labour in Britain to rebrand the country as 'Cool Britannia'. As will be seen from examples in Chapters 2 to 5, more often, attempts to construct identity appeal to history for their legitimation, often creating both hegemonic discourses of history and invented traditions (see Hobsbawm and Ranger 1992).

In recent years there has been much debate about the implications of globalization for identity. The term globalization is widely applied to many different aspects of contemporary life, ranging from the spread of multi-national corporations to the international appropriation of popular cultural forms and practices and the world-wide web. Writers on globalization point to the ways in which the structures and integrity of nation states are being challenged by economic and cultural developments, as well as postcolonial diasporas and the migration of peoples, particularly from the 'South' to the 'North'. The effects of globalization on identity have been varied and are always contextual and shaped by the particular social relations of the society and social group in question. The worldwide spread of commodities such as Coca-Cola and McDonald's burgers has led to theories of the 'McDonaldization' of the world (see Ritzer 2000). Here community and place are apparently rendered less important in the formation of identity, as people strive for Western and mostly US influenced life-styles. The meaning and significance of such symbols of Western capitalism and Western values in non-Western countries will vary according to location and specific context. Some critics have pointed to the ways in which the spread of American capitalism, media and the values they incorporate has spurred the development of oppositional and resistant forms of national and religious identity. The post 11 September increase in Islamophobia and US policies in the Middle East have further strengthened this process.

In the second half of the twentieth century, inward migration changed the face of most West European societies. If throughout the colonial period, white Europeans settled outside of Europe, encountering others on their own terrain, the twentieth century saw large-scale non-European settlement in former colonial powers. One of the concerns of this book is how migration affects identity, both that of states and of individuals and groups within these states.

In the chapters that follow, I argue that identity is central to the desire to be a 'knowing subject', in control of meaning. I look at the ways in which, in defining their own sense of identity, individuals tend also to fix the identity of others working within long-established binary modes of thinking. I ask how we might begin the process of dislodging these binaries. Is such a process not crucial to the development of plural societies that are accepting of difference, and that even celebrate it? What forms do and might cultural political struggle over identity take? Can we move beyond identities? How important is having a voice, representation and respect? Do people need to belong to a recognized group or community? How, in the cultural arena, might we challenge hegemonic constructions (white, male and middle-class) of histories and traditions? It is to these questions that I now turn in Chapters 2, 3 and 4.

Further reading

Althusser, L. (1971) On Ideology and Ideological State Apparatuses. Notes Towards an Investigation, in *Lenin and Philosophy and Other Essays*, pp. 121–73. London: New Left Books.

Donald, J. and Rattansi, A. (eds) (1992) *'Race', Culture and Difference*. London: Sage in association with the Open University.

Dyer, R. (1997) *White*. London: Routledge.

Rutherford, J. (ed.) (1990) *Identity: Community, Culture, Difference*. London: Lawrence & Wishart.

Woodward, K. (ed.) (1997) *Identity & Difference*. London: Sage in association with the Open University.

2 | HISTORY, NATION AND IDENTITY

I wouldn't say I'm British, I'd say I'm Welsh. I always say Welsh.

Yeah. My children would say they feel Welsh because they were born in Wales.

No matter what colour you are, if you are not white, you're not British.

(Parekh 2000: 8)

Ethnocentrism the explicit and arrogantly held action-guiding belief that one's culture and cultural ways are superior to others; or the disrespectful, lazy, arrogant indifference to other cultures that devalues them through not seeing appreciatively *any* culture or cultural ways except one's own when one could do otherwise; or the disrespectful, lazy, arrogant indifference that devalues other cultures through stereotyping of them or through non-reflective, self-satisfied acceptance of such stereotypes.

(Lugones 1990: 46)

Colonial history is the terrain where the project of 'Western' culture's self-definition became a project heavily dependent upon its 'difference' from its 'Others' both internal and external. The contemporary self-definition of many Third-World cultures and communities are also in profound ways political responses to this history.

(Narayan 1997: 80)

In contemporary Britain, more especially since the Labour Government came to power in 1997, funding bodies in the arts and museum sectors have been required to pay more attention to questions of representativeness and to what has come to be termed 'cultural diversity'. The 'National Heritage' is no longer transparent or obvious. In the words of a path breaking conference 'Whose Heritage?' held in Manchester in 1999, cultural diversity is changing Britain's 'Living Heritage'.[1] Like other countries before it, Britain is now officially a multi-cultural society in which the conditions need to be created to enable full participation by minorities in all aspects of national life. Government, state institutions, education and quasi-autonomous authorities like arts funding bodies, as well as royalty, repeatedly restate this point. The Prince of Wales, for example, talks of his future role, once he ascends the throne, as defender of faith, not *the* Faith. ('Defender of the Faith' was a title bestowed on King Henry VIII by the Pope prior to Henry's split with Rome, which lead to an independent Anglican Church of England.) Attempts are made, both at the level of official discourse and in the rituals of official state occasions, to reinforce the view of Britain as culturally diverse. For example, the opening ceremony of the devolved Welsh Assembly in 1999 was marked by a multi-faith religious service and ethnic minority figures were conspicuously present, leading the way in the opening procession alongside White Welsh dignitaries, famous personalities and politicians. Similarly the Queen's golden jubilee celebrations in the Mall and in front of Buckingham Palace in London in June 2002 were carefully planned to be inclusive. The televised celebrations began with parades of beautiful, colourful costumes from recent Notting Hill Caribbean carnivals. These were followed by several thousand gospel singers representing another Black cultural form. This attempt at inclusiveness marks a major shift from the immediate post-war decades, when exclusively white norms of Britishness were hegemonic and assimilation dominated thinking about migrants to Britain (see Solomos 2003). In discourses of assimilation minorities are required to adapt culturally to the dominant culture, that is to say to become like 'us'. The shift away from this means that in order to count as British, ethnic minorities are no longer required to become culturally the same as the white majority.

'Britishness' can be usefully theorized in Foucauldian terms as the product of a specific discursive field in which a number of key institutions play crucial roles. These include, for example, education, the museum and heritage sector, the monarchy, the press and the media. Britain is one of many societies in which questions of cultural and ethnic diversity, multi-culturalism, nation and identity have come to the fore in recent decades. While changes in different societies have their own local dimensions and momentum, the global moves towards decolonization, post-coloniality, post-modernism and globalization, have helped shape these developments in many countries. From critiques of Western colonialism to the struggles of indigenous peoples in white settler societies, moves have been made to redefine hegemonic discourses of culture, nation and identity. Central in this process has been the challenging of dominant narratives of history, racial and ethnic stereotyping and white supremacy. These challenges have produced both counter-hegemonic discourses and new forms of identity. These are all important factors in the current debates about Britishness and the forms of identity and belonging that different conceptions of Britishness allow, preclude or enable.

In Western societies both individual and collective forms of identity are closely tied to ideas of national, local and family history and tradition. These, together with the personal and collective memories that sustain them, create a sense of where one comes from and where one belongs. For most people, this sense of history and tradition is learned informally in the family, through media representations and in school. National anthems, flags, costumes and holidays, state rituals, national sports teams, pageantry, museums, heritage centres, buildings and monuments all help to create and sustain narratives about who we are and where we have come from. A sense of history and tradition is created and sustained not only through history books, but also in historical novels, drama, films and documentaries. Battles over the meaning and control of history and historical symbols can, on occasion, be used to justify wars, as in the case of Serbian narratives about Kosova, or Northern Ireland, where competing Unionist and Republican accounts of history and their symbolic manifestations reinforce religious differences and social and economic discrimination. Where dominant narratives of history play important ideological roles, they often feed prejudice, exclusion and discrimination, and may lead to social unrest and violence that do not reach the level of outright war.

In societies where there is more than one ethnic group and/or tradition in play, dominant versions of history and culture and the forms of identity that they encourage often function to exclude, silence, stereotype or render invisible those who do not fit within hegemonic narratives. Western narratives of colonization, for example, that of the white man's burden in colonial British India or of white America's 'heroic' conquering the indigenous peoples in the move westwards, long held sway, both in history writing and in popular cultural representations such as fiction and cinema. These representations portrayed colonized peoples as inferior, reaffirming those racist stereotypes found in classical nineteenth-century racist science. In recent decades, alternative, previously marginalized versions of history, often emphasizing agency and resistance, have established counter-narratives that demand to be taken seriously among Western as well as indigenous historians, novelists and filmmakers.

History, both in its academic and popular forms, plays a key role in the construction of what Benedict Anderson (1991) has termed the 'imagined community' that constitutes a nation. In an attempt to define the concept of nation, Anderson proposes seeing it as:

> an imagined political community – and imagined as both inherently limited and sovereign.
>
> It is *imagined* because the members of even the smallest nation will never know most of their fellow-members, meet them or even hear of them, yet in the mind of each lives the image of their communion. . . . In fact, all communities larger than primordial villages of face-to-face contact (and perhaps even these) are imagined. Communities are to be distinguished, not by their falsity or genuineness, but by the style in which they are imagined.
>
> (Anderson 1991: 6)

Anderson argues further that:

> nationality, or, as one might prefer to put it in view of that word's multiple significations, nation-ness, as well as nationalism, are cultural artefacts of a particular kind. To understand them properly we need to consider carefully how they have come into historical being, in what ways their meanings have changed over time, and why, today, they command such profound emotional legitimacy.
>
> (Anderson 1991: 4)

The question of emotional legitimacy is important since it points to the ways in which national and ethnic identities go beyond the rational and acquire much of their force – both positive and negative – from an articulation with emotional and sub-conscious dimensions of the individual. Poststructuralist theory has long taught us that a productive way of understanding culture and society is to see meanings, values, individual subjectivities and identities as produced within language and other signifying practices and as sites of contest between competing interests. The current debates in the UK over the meaning of Britishness well illustrates this point. They have come to the fore with moves towards a greater British involvement in the European Union and as a response to demands to recognize the changing ethnic composition of Britain as a multi-cultural society in which both immigrant and indigenous ethnic groups are articulating their difference from a specific set of English norms and narratives of history. Devolution in Wales and Scotland, for example, are, in part, the political manifestation of a long cultural struggle to assert the specificity of Welsh and Scottish histories and culture. Wales was linked to the English crown from the thirteenth century onwards and was fully incorporated into the English crown in the 1536 Act of Union. In contrast, Scotland retained its own legal and educational systems after the Act of Union in 1707. This has arguably led to a stronger form of cultural nationalism in Scotland, which, for example, acquired a national museum of Scottish history in Edinburgh in 1998. For a long time nationalism in Wales was firmly tied to the Welsh language, though in the wake of devolution the institutional bases for national identity have been strengthened and diversified. The media, in particular, have helped to reinforced a sense of national identity through their coverage of the 'national news of Wales' and of the Welsh Assembly government. As Prys Morgan (1992) has shown in some detail, it was in the eighteenth century, with the demise of the last remnants of a traditional, popular oral culture, that educated Welsh men and women, many of them based in London, sought to 're-invent' forms of traditional Welsh culture ranging from Welsh language poetry, to the Eisteddfod and a national costume and flag. Following nineteenth-century laws and practices outlawing the use of the Welsh language in education and administration, the twentieth century saw struggles to reassert the legitimacy of the Welsh language, which involved acts of civil disobedience and the fire bombing of English-owned properties. In both Wales and Scotland, the success of nationalist parties was, in part, rooted in a positive revaluing of notions of Welshness and Scottishness in opposition to a long history of derogatory representations of the

Welsh and Scots emanating from England. It involved a rejection of Englishness and all things identified as English.

In the wake of Marxist, feminist and postmodern theories and critiques of historiography, the idea that the best history writing produces transparent narratives, describing past occurrences in an objective or scientific fashion has long since lost credence (for a critical introduction to historiography see Berger 2003 and for post-modern history writing see Jenkins 1997). Analyses of the ideological underpinning and rhetorical strategies of history writing have shown how both history and tradition are articulated and mobilized to promote particular values. As will be seen from discussion of press reception of the Parekh Report on *The Future of Multi-Ethnic Britain* (Parekh 2000) later in this chapter, those values most often cited by British politicians and commentators of all political complexions are tolerance and commitment to democracy and the rule of law. These values are grounded in specific narratives of British history articulated not only in education, books, television documentaries, museums and monuments, but also in the rituals of daily life. Britain's role in the Second World War is an important part of those hegemonic narratives of Britishness and in recent years in the UK, for example, increasing emphasis has been placed by the state and the media on the importance of marking Armistice Day. This is manifest in state support for the introduction of two minutes' silence, originally sponsored by the veterans' charity, the British Legion, at 11 o'clock on both 11 November and Armistice Sunday. The government's justification for this move is in part the desire to inform and educate the younger generations about war, its effects and the specific sacrifices made by men and women in the two world wars in the twentieth century (and subsequent conflicts since 1945) as the number of those with personal memories and direct involvement dwindles.

Yet history and tradition have another role to play: the interpellation of subjects and the inducing of a sense of identity and belonging. Individual constructions of identity are affirmed by seeing something of oneself and one's forebears in representations of the history of the nation. Inclusion is important since having a history and set of traditions with which one can identify and within which one can position oneself other than as victim, gives the interpellated individual a position of dignity from which to speak. While aspects of white British national identity still rely on narratives of empire that celebrate Britain's imperial past, 'Empire' is increasingly being subject to selective amnesia and disavowal. When it does appear, empire is largely narrated from the viewpoint of the colonizers, though in recent years, in a more critical and differentiated fashion than previously, as, for example in major cinema films of the 1980s dealing with India under the British Raj (see Hall 1999: 16). The conservative press's response to the Parekh Report on *The Future of Multi-Ethnic Britain* offers a good example of these old style, if now somewhat defensive, views of empire:

British history is the story of freedom and respect for the law, and Britain's relationship with the world beyond our shores is the story of benefaction, not exploitation, of justice, not oppression, and the desire to enlighten, to improve, to teach and to help.

(Paul Johnson, *Daily Mail* Essay, 11 October 2000)

For the descendants of the peoples of Britain's former colonies, now living in Britain, whose ancestors were often transported half way round the world as slaves or indentured labour, alternative narratives of empire, which privilege resistance, are important in establishing a history and tradition that allows for positive identification and not merely for narratives of victimhood. In this context the celebration of empire and the disavowal of its horrors hinder the development of an inclusive discourse of Britishness that acknowledges the multifaceted, complex and profound interconnections between the history of Britain and those of her colonies.

History serves as a repository of symbols for the cultural politics of the present. For example, in attempts to justify recent conflicts involving Britain in the Middle East and Afghanistan, the government turned to forms of rhetoric that are derived from Britain's role in the Second World War and reference Churchill's speeches. In the process Saddam Hussein, the Taliban and Al-Qaeda have on occasion implicitly been aligned with Hitler and Nazism in ways that deny the specificity of the issues in play. Particularly striking examples of the oppositional cultural politics of history can be found in recent imaginative accounts by writers of African descent of the slave trade both in Britain and the United States, and in the reclaiming of history by the indigenous people of Australia, where the struggle for justice is conducted in part through an appeal to a silenced history. These issues will be taken up in later chapters. I want to turn now to look in some detail at the case of contemporary Britain, where culture, heritage and tradition have, in recent years, become significant sites of debate in relation to devolution and the ethnic diversity of the UK.

The second half of the twentieth century saw major changes in British culture and society. Following the introduction of secondary education for all in the immediate post-war years and the subsequent massive expansion in further and higher education, general levels of education rose among large sectors of the British population. At the same time there was an expansion in leisure time for many people who also saw their disposable income increase. The development of new technologies made a range of previously elite cultural forms widely accessible, as did the development of state sponsorship of the arts and the expansion of museums and the culture industries. Popular culture, too, saw massive expansion and with these changes, cultural class distinctions became less rigid and often less obvious. Furthermore, migration to Britain from countries of the former British Empire and other parts of the world radically increased the diversity of British cities, which previously had been largely white (with the exception of London and ports such as Liverpool, Bristol and Cardiff). These changes to the face of Britain have raised important questions about the role of history in the construction of Britishness and, in particular, questions of whose history is recorded, displayed, and taught to multi-ethnic Britain.

Plate 1. The Changing Face of Britain. Local artist, Jack Sullivan, with children from St Mary's Primary School, Cardiff.
(Butetown History & Arts Centre archive.)

The question of history

The relationship between history and national identity has become a live topic in recent historiography and museology (see Boswell and Evans 1999). History plays a central role in defining both individual and group identity. Dominant narratives of history construct both national identities and broader categories such as 'The West'. Moreover, dominant narratives of history tend to naturalize the social relations of the present, showing how they have evolved naturally out of the past. In mainstream history writing, in television films and in museums and galleries, the materials presented as History often represent a narrow and exclusive view of who makes history and whose lives and experiences are important. For a long time working-class history barely existed, though developments in social and labour history since the 1960s have done much to remedy this state of affairs. Until the 1970s women, as a social group, had little or no visible history. Here feminist historians are filling this absence. The exclusiveness of traditional narratives of British history thus became a key theme in history writing in the second half of the twentieth century. Efforts were made on several fronts to extend the national story to make room not only for the history of the working classes and of women, but also for critiques of prevailing accounts of the nation's imperial past and its relation both to its ex-colonies and to the immigrant communities who migrated to Britain from the Empire and Commonwealth.

History matters. It is important both to our sense of who we are and to our understanding of the present. The voices that count in the telling of history shape the narratives and the perspectives from which both past and present are understood. Misrepresentation and non-representation are both damaging. It is, in part, the recognition of this that has changed museum and arts policy and led to the beginnings of a rewriting of British history and the representation of the history of minorities and women within public institutions. Thus, for example, in 1995 the Liverpool Museum opened a new gallery on the slave trade, which had been, until then, the unspoken past on which the wealth of ports such as Liverpool and Bristol was built. Black history month, which began in the US in 1926 as Negro History week and became Black History month in the late 1960s is celebrated in the US in February and more recently in Britain in October. It is becoming increasingly institutionalized in Britain as television companies as well as museums begin to include it in aspects of their programming (see, for example, Channel 4's Black History Month website[2]).

The need to address the relation of history, both to national identity and the current state of multi-ethnic Britain, was one important aspect of the Parekh Report on *The Future of Multi-Ethnic Britain*, published in October 2000. The Commission on the Future of Multi-Ethnic Britain had been set up three years earlier by the Runnymede Trust, with financial support from the Joseph Roundtree Charitable Trust and the Nuffield and Paul Hamlyn Foundations. Its remit was 'to analyse the current state of multi-ethnic Britain, and to propose ways of countering racial discrimination and disadvantage and making Britain a confident and vibrant multi-cultural society at ease with its rich diversity' (Parekh 2000: viii). Although not a government report as such, the project had the backing of the Labour administration and the report was officially launched by the then Home Secretary, Jack Straw.

The Future of Multi-Ethnic Britain (which does not cover Northern Ireland) argues that England, Scotland and Wales have reached a turning point in their history, can either become 'narrow and inward looking, with rifts between themselves and among their regions and communities' or they can develop as 'a community of citizens and communities' in which difference and diversity are welcomed and celebrated (Parekh 2000: xiii). The second of these options would, the report argues, require radical changes in British society, which would include:

- developing a balance between cohesion, equality and difference;
- addressing and eliminating all forms of racism;
- rethinking the national story and national identity;
- reducing material inequalities;

- understanding that all identities are in a process of transition; and
- building a pluralistic human rights culture.

(Parekh 2000: xiii)

The report is divided into sections that cover culture, social institutions and strategies for change. Among the main themes of the section of the report that deals with cultural questions are discussions of 'how to reimagine English, Scottish and Welsh history so that it includes everyone; how to understand identities in transition; how to balance cohesion, difference and justice, how to deal with racism' (Parekh 2000: 6). The arguments currently in play in the battle over Britishness, history and tradition were clearly articulated in the press reception of the report, which is discussed in detail below. Of all the suggestions that it made for change, it was the call to rethink the national story and national identity that aroused the most hostile reception in the conservative press.

The Parekh Report works with a sophisticated understanding of the nature and social role of history and its importance in the formation of national identity. It argues that:

A sense of national identity is based on generalisations and involves a selective and simplified account of a complex history. Much that is important is ignored, disavowed or simply forgotten. Many complicated strands are reduced to a simple task of essential and enduring national unity, with everything in past history leading inexorably up to a triumphal conclusion.

(Parekh 2000: 16)

The processes of selection and simplification involved in the construction of dominant narratives of national history are, it is argued, crucial to its ideological role in the creation of a shared national identity:

Of course its effectiveness in binding society together is no less real because much of it is invented or distorted. Its purpose is not to give an accurate historical account but to enable individuals to position their personal life-stories within the larger, more significant national story. Identification not knowledge is its raison d'être. It allows individuals to identify with something outside, and greater than, personal experience. It binds individuals into a broader interdependence with others in the nation-building project.

(Parekh: 2000: 16–17)

Yet the process of selection involved in the construction of hegemonic narratives of history may mean that certain groups or individuals find themselves excluded and without a place from which to belong.

That conservative Britain is not yet ready to accept the need for changes to the national story to include minority populations is clear from the press reception of the Parekh Report. In the tabloids and conservative broadsheets, the complexities of the arguments about Britishness detailed in the report were reduced to bald caricatures, focused on questions of history and national identity. Complex arguments were represented in the form of headlines such as 'Straw wants to rewrite our history', 'British is a racist word says report' (Johnston, *Daily Telegraph*, 10 October 2000); 'Curse of the Britain Bashers' (Kavanagh, *Sun*, 11 October 2000), 'Endorsed by Ministers, the report which calls for our entire national identity to be consigned to the politically correct dustbin of history' (Doughty, *Daily Mail*, 11 October 2000). Writing in the left liberal broadsheet, the *Guardian*, on 11 October 2000, columnist Gary Younge perceptively commented: 'If you really want to take the racial temperature in Britain, you would be better off examining the reactions to the report on multi-ethnic Britain rather than the report itself (Younge 2000: 7). The press discussion of the report continued for several days and an analysis of it throws a clear light on the types of argument invoked to resist moves towards more diverse and inclusive accounts of history, traditions and identity.

The changing face of Britain

> Cultural meanings appeal to people's imaginations but are difficult to pin down. They are embedded not in formal rules and laws but in all the informal aspects of cultural life that are taken for granted: customs, habits, daily rituals, unwritten social codes, the way masculinity and femininity are expressed, speech idiom and body language, feelings for the landscape, and collective memories of national glories – especially those associated with war. . . . Image metaphor and shared symbols play a crucial role in constructing and maintaining the idea of England as an imagined community. They not only express solidarity but also construct a solidarity that was not there before.
>
> (Parekh 2000: 20)

The Parekh Report identified a number of key factors instrumental over the last thirty years in changing the face of Britain. These include migration, devolution, globalization, the end of Empire, Britain's long-term decline as a world power, the development of a widespread moral and cultural pluralism and an increasing degree of integration with Europe. Almost all these factors can be seen as directly contributing to a more diverse and less homogeneous Britain in which the informal aspects of cultural life are less widely shared. While the conservative press in the UK continues to deplore most of these developments, it does not usually deny that they are happening or have occurred. Yet the Parekh Report's critiques of Britishness, of dominant narratives of British history and of racism, provoked a very different response: one of total denial.

The Commission on the Future of Multi-Ethnic Britain argued that, given the changes to Britain that had occurred in the second half of the twentieth century, there is a pressing need to redefine current norms of Britishness (Parekh 2000: 55). It identified problems with traditional, cosy, all white and predominantly southern, rural images of England. It took issue with hegemonic narratives of the history of the nation, accusing them of exclusiveness and challenged the implicit white racial superiority of traditional norms of Britishness. All these problems, it suggested, have their roots in the British Empire, the legacies of which live on. The end of empire, the report argued,

> Is often described as the shedding of a burden whose time has past. However, expunging the traces of an imperial mentality from the national culture, particularly those that involved seeing the white British as a superior race, is a much more difficult task. This mentality penetrated everyday life, popular culture and consciousness. It remains active in projected fantasies and fears about difference and in racialised stereotypes of otherness. The unstated assumption remains that Britishness and whiteness go together, like roast beef and Yorkshire pudding. There has been no collective working through of this imperial experience.
>
> (Parekh 2000: 25)

The absence of this collective working through of the imperial experience and its legacies, the report suggested, allows racist attitudes to persist unchallenged:

> The absence from the national curriculum of a rewritten history of Britain as an imperial force, involving dominance in Ireland as well as in Africa, the Caribbean and Asia, is proving from this perspective to be an unmitigated disaster.
>
> (Parekh 2000: 24–5)

The Parekh Report in the press

For the majority of the British population access to, and knowledge of, the report on the *Future of Multi-ethnic Britain* was mediated through press coverage and much of this sought to offer readers a discursive position that encouraged outright rejection of its findings. The conservative press reacted with marked hostility to the report's critical stance on Britishness and British history and did its utmost to discredit both the report and the commission that produced it. The *Daily Telegraph*, perhaps the most conservative British broadsheet, conducted a debate on the report over several days. Its responses warrant detailed consideration, since the newspaper uses the full range of discursive strategies that are also found in much of the tabloid press. Discussion of the report in the *Daily Telegraph* began on 8 October, three days prior to its official publication, when the *Daily Telegraph*'s social affairs correspondent, Betham wrote an article on how the report was a celebration of the state of Britain's race relations. The headline 'Critics of a "racist" Britain are misguided, says report' suggests a document very different both in tone and content from that actually published. Quoting from the chair of the committee, Professor Bhikhu Parekh, Betham suggested that 'race relations in Britain are the best in Europe and the notion that the country has severe racial problems is a "skewed and partisan" lie'. He further claimed that the Parekh Report had declared that 'the suggestion that Britain was a country in which racism was wider spread – which emerged in the wake of the Macpherson Report into the death of Stephen Lawrence – was wrong'.[3] This discursive strategy of praising race relations in Britain and asserting that they are better in the UK than in both the rest of Europe and the USA, encourages readers to assume a complacent self-satisfaction and sense of superiority to other countries. It can be identified as an important feature of right-wing responses to the report. The *Telegraph*'s seizing the opportunity to disparage the Macpherson Report is also characteristic of conservative views on racism in Britain.

By 10 October the *Daily Telegraph* had radically changed its focus to attack the report's treatment of British history and Britishness. Under the headlines 'Straw wants to rewrite our history' and 'British is a racist word says report' (Johnston 2000), the paper briefly summarized some of the report's recommendations and the government's response to them. Its headlines suggest a sense of common ownership of history, shared by the newspaper and its readership, and of property under attack. The paper quotes two right-wing members of parliament, Lord Tebbit and Gerald Howarth to reinforce its position. While Tebbit is introduced to attack multi-ethnic and multi-cultural states for having the 'greatest conflicts', Howarth introduces a new note, dismissing the report as 'an extraordinary affront' to the 94 per cent of the population which does not belong to an ethnic minority. This signals a second conservative response to multi-ethnic Britain: to downplay the numerical significance of non-white ethnic minorities and thus their rights to determine the shape of contemporary culture and social policy. It marks a radical shift from the earlier right-wing strategy, usually associated with Enoch Powell MP, which suggested that white Britain would be overwhelmed by non-white immigrants.

A third widespread strategy employed to discredit the report in the conservative press, both broadsheet and tabloid, is the use of negative language with left-wing connotations. In its various comments, the *Daily Telegraph* repeatedly resorts to disparaging descriptions such as 'caldron of political correctness' (Philip Johnston, 10 October 2000), 'sub-Marxist gibberish' (editorial, 10 October 2000), 'drivel' 'balderdash', 'thoroughly nasty', 'offensive to blacks and whites alike' (Tom Utley in the Wednesday Column, 11 October 2000). The commission is described as a 'crack-brained think tank' (Boris Johnson, Thursday Column, 12 October 2000), and it is suggested that the authors are self-serving individuals 'supported by the taxpayer', an accusation guaranteed to alarm its conservative readership. The charge of political correctness was one made repeatedly in conservative discussions of the report. For example, Tom Utley, writing in the *Daily Telegraph*'s Wednesday Column on 11 October 2000, painted a disturbing picture of political correctness, informing its readership that the Commission wanted:

Everyone to be thinking about race all the time [instead of 'letting things develop naturally']. They would have schools, the police and all public authorities treating everyone differently, according to their ethnic origins.

They would force television companies to appoint staff according to the colour of their skin, rather than their ability to read the news or to present a game show. They would have my sons describe a friend as 'Afro-British', rather than 'the fat one with specs'. Most wickedly of all, they would like to rewrite British history, and to 'jettison' whole chapters of it because so much of it is about white people.

(Utley, *Daily Telegraph*, 11 October 2000)

This column explicitly addresses white people as a homogenous group whose interests are threatened by the report. On 12 October 2000, the *Daily Telegraph* turned to the question of Britishness, claiming that even the government was distancing itself from the suggestion that the term 'British' had racist undertones. Next to a large photograph of the Home Secretary giving a speech, the paper printed carefully chosen extracts from the report (*Daily Telegraph*, 12 October 2000: 10). The choice is telling. It covered 'What is Britain?', 'Inescapable change', the future of 'Britishness', 'Racial Coding' and selected recommendations that allowed the *Daily Telegraph* to privilege the theme of political correctness. On the page opposite was a large spread, dominated by a photograph of Black, Olympic gold medallist Denise Lewis wrapped in the union flag, entitled 'I feel so proud when I see our Union flag'. The use of 'our' here, drawn from a completely different context, suggests that there is no difference between white and Black Britons. The photograph itself has no direct connection to the written text. The article consists of six accounts by 'leading figures' of what it means to be British. Views range from Liberal Democrat Party Chairman, Scottish Charles Kennedy's stress on diversity, multiple identities and the shared British values of 'tolerance and decency, a spirit of innovation and a willingness to get the job done together', to Angela Browning, shadow leader of the House of Commons, claiming that 'You can feel Britishness in your bones. That sense of history, fairness, justice and landscape that makes you proud just to be part of it' (Laville, *Daily Telegraph*, 12 October 2000). There are two non-white Britons among the six contributors. Lord Alli, Managing Director of the television company, Carlton Productions, stresses diversity and shared values:

We are a diverse nation and we are richer for that. Our heritage is drawn from many traditions but at its heart is a Britishness with values which I share of tolerance, individualism and inclusiveness. To say that is not to deny my roots. But I was born here and I am part of this country. Being British should not be a political statement. It should, for all of us, just be what we are.

(Laville, *Daily Telegraph*, 12 October 2000)

Lord Paul stresses multi-culturalism and anti-racism, claiming to feel both a proud Indian and a proud Briton.

The selection of contributors also reflects recent moves in Britain towards political devolutions. Professor Brian Walker, director of the Institute of Irish Studies, Queens University, Belfast writes of British identity in Northern Ireland, arguing that the peace process allows for less polarized, more diverse identities. Christie Davies, described as a professor of sociology born in Surrey and brought up in Wales, claims original Britishness for the Welsh, but stresses that this heritage now belongs to all. Picking up a common thread in right-wing thinking about multi-ethnic Britain, he attempts to dissolve difference and assimilate all to a shared tradition:

> Caradog and Boudicca were our ancestors alone. Yet they belong equally to the English or to the Hindus, Sikhs, Parsees and Barbadians who are part of our nation. For we are all equally British. To become British is to acquire *all* our history and culture as one's own possession. What we must do is to consolidate our Britishness by abolishing terms such as English, Cymru, Pict and Geordie. We must become one nation.
>
> (Laville, *Daily Telegraph*, 12 October 2000)

While the tradition that Davies constructs here privileges ancient Celtic Britain, a similar assumption can also be found in more usual Anglo-centric accounts of British history, in other words that it should be the basis for a single common culture, wherever people come from and whatever their own histories. The *Daily Telegraph* editorial on page 31 returns to the material effects of political correctness, arguing that the substantive proposals, from which the government had not distanced itself, would bring about 'an explosion in the power of the state to regulate vast swaths of national life, in the name of "diversity"'. Thus, if broadcasters wanted franchises renewed, they would have to demonstrate sufficient cultural sensitivity in recruitment and programming. This would give the 'likes of the commission' 'a meal ticket for life'. It calls on Conservatives to 'make good their past silence on Macpherson'. They must expose the government's collusion in this attempt to destroy a thousand years of British history (Laville, *Daily Telegraph*, 12 October 2000).

The conservative recognition that history matters and that specific narratives of history serve to justify or challenge the legitimacy of the status quo, fuelled the vehemence of responses to the report. Boris Johnson in his 'Thursday Column' (*Daily Telegraph*, 12 October 2000) warned that the report was part of 'a war over culture' in which the government was on the side of the enemy:

> The reason we oppose Ouseley [Sir Herman Ouseley, former chair of the Commission for Racial Equality], and the rest of the Runnymede rhubarb, is that we can sense that these people want to demolish things that are valuable in our culture . . . Yes, the Runnymede lot would be just a bunch of cranks and losers, if their ethos – their agenda – was not found all over the Government. For at least

10 years it has been the plan of far-sighted Left-wingers to break up the United Kingdom, or Ukrania, as they call it, into its constituent parts, and thence to dissipate the embarrassing allegiance to Britain. Their motives are not always the same. Some of them, such as Tony and Sir Herman, don't like British history and tradition; some of them want to create a new European identity; some of them are inspired by Celtic fringe-ism.

All that we have to recognise is that these people are powerful and influential, and the burblings of Yasmin [Alibhai-Brown] and Herman will in five years be found in our children's curriculum. . . .

This is a *war over culture*, which our side could lose. Why should children be taught that the British Empire was an unadulterated evil, when it plainly wasn't? You won't encourage Britain's minorities – the vast majority of whom think of themselves as British – to achieve more or feel more at home, by deprecating the achievements of dead white men. And it is not just British triumphs that this Government would like to erase, but the British character.

(My emphasis, Johnson, *Daily Telegraph*, 12 October 2000)

The theme of cultural threat was taken up again on 13 October 2000 by William Hague, the then leader of the Conservative Party, who described the report as a threat to Britain which 'manifests itself in the tyranny of political correctness and the assault on British culture and history. We should call it the anti-British disease.' Hague claimed that the commission was 'stuffed with Left-wing cronies' and warned that there was a danger in the Government taking it seriously:

For if the commission's principal recommendations were implemented, then our police would be paralysed, school exams would be fiddled, classroom discipline would collapse and our political institutions would be stuffed with people on the basis of their colour rather than on whether they could do the job . . .

Hague took particular exception to the historical linking of Britishness with white racism:

I believe that the commission – and, by extension, New Labour – could not be more wrong in describing 'Britishness' as 'racially coded'. Britain is not a racial group. It is a nation forged from different peoples, from the Scots, the Welsh, the English and the Northern Irish, and from millions of people who have come to our shores from around the world to share in our national life.

Indeed, a proper understanding of our history, instead of the ignorant clap-trap displayed by the report, shows that the British nation is a nation of immigrants: Celts, Picts, Saxons, Angles, Normans, Jews, Hugenots, Indians, Pakistanis, Afro-Caribbeans, Bengalis, Chinese, and countless others. These are the British people, all of them.

The apparent inclusiveness of Britishness is stressed:

Together we have created one of the most exciting, diverse, prosperous, democratic and tolerant nations on earth, with a history of standing up to tyranny and genocide of which we can be proud.

(Hague, *Daily Telegraph*, 13 October 2000)

The editorial that accompanied this piece made clear just how much right-wing commentators continue to resent the findings of the MacPherson Report on the Stephen Lawrence case. In the view of the *Telegraph*'s editorial writer:

No more disgracefully unfair document has ever been produced by a judge in modern British history. At every turn, it decided to assume, without anything that a proper court would consider as evidence, that the police were guilty of 'institutional racism'. Its bigoted conclusions were accepted with only a whimper of protest by the institutions it criticised. The bullying of the 'anti-racists' had won.

In a similar tone the editorial dismissed the Parekh Report:

It is an outrageous lie that the history, identity and character of the British people is racist. Whatever else may be said about our imperial past, it helped to breed in the British an openness to other nations that was not part of the collective experience, of say, Germany or Japan. Britishness is explicitly a political not a racial concept. The word regained usage to describe the union of kingdoms and later of parliaments, and maintains that meaning today. It never had anything to do with whiteness, although – as is still the case even today – the overwhelming majority of Britons were white.

(Editorial Comment, *Daily Telegraph*, 13 October 2000)

The question of racism and what should be done to remedy it is consistently picked up and dismissed in conservative responses to the Parekh Report:

'Anti-racism', in short, requires a big lie, just as much as, we all know from 20th-century history, does racism. To say that British whites are collectively racist is essentially similar to saying that Jews are undermining the country. It stigmatises untruthfully, and for a political purpose . . .

The Runnymede report proposes, at our count, 50 new programmes, target bodies and reviews to impose the racial attitude that it favours. It wants to regulate schools, businesses, police, the law, the health service, newspapers and government so the 'diversity' (by which is meant racial quotas and anti-British ideology) is enforced. This agenda is at last exposed. At the next election it must be defeated.

(Editorial Comment, *Daily Telegraph*, 13 October 2000)

The discursive strategies in play in the coverage of the Parekh Report work to create a collective white British subject position with which the readership can identify. This subject is proud to be British, proud of a singular and obvious true British history, dismissive of the realities of racism and self-satisfied in his or her knowledge that Britain is a better place to live, whatever the colour of your skin, than the rest of Europe or the USA. The strategies of interpellation in play, rely on direct address to readers who are encouraged to identify with 'our' shared understanding of Britishness and British history.

Tabloid coverage of the Parekh Report, while less extensive, mobilized many of the same themes and strategies found in the conservative broadsheet press. The mass-selling tabloid the *Sun*, owned by Rupert Murdoch, carried a large two-page headline on the day that the report was published (11 October 2000). It read 'Curse of the Britain Bashers' with a sub-headline 'Ministers welcome report which says "British" is racist and all our history must be rewritten'. Describing the report as 'rambling' with 'a muddled conclusion', the article summarized some of the recommendations and quoted the report on 'the rule Britannia mindset'. Like the *Daily Telegraph*, the *Sun* mobilized a Black Briton in its attack, printing a large photograph of Black decathlete Daley Thompson carrying the Union Jack over a headline 'It's ridiculous'. Employed as a 'SunSport columnist', Thompson is described as the son of a Nigerian father and Scottish mother with three British-born children, and he 'tells us why he is proud to be British'. Daley rejects as 'ridiculous' the idea that it is possible to rewrite history and claims that Britain 'is still the best country in the world', valued by immigrants for 'freedom and tolerance, the right to a free health service and respect for the law' (Thompson, *Sun*, 11 October 2000). Mobilizing typical tabloid, anti-intellectual populism, he appeals to the government to listen to the voices of ordinary people, 'the "multi-cultural Britons" in the streets – and that is all of us', rather than 'the race industry – largely people who are paid to tell us what we need without asking us'. The discursive strategies in play here involve appealing to 'we, the people' in a way that explicitly includes non-white Britons, while rejecting the role of experts on race in Britain.

While acknowledging racism, Daly stresses the progress that has been made over the past decades, and rejects the suggestion that 'minorities associate Britishness with colonisation and empire'. He admits that some of his Black friends suffer discrimination, telling him that 'they get stopped by the police for just walking about'. He comments that he agrees with the commission that 'the anger this causes should be looked at' – misreading the report's recommendation that it is the *causes* of this anger that require attention. Like many *Daily Telegraph* commentators, Thompson chooses to stress progress in race relations, though his example of progress is at best modest: 'But not so long ago, most people assumed that a black man in possession of a nice car must have stolen it and I believe it is an achievement that most people in Britain don't think that way any more' (Thompson, *Sun*, 11 October 2000).

Echoing Thompson's piece, the *Sun*'s editorial set itself up as the voice of ordinary people against the 'the chattering classes, the metropolitan elite', who are accused of despising 'our heritage'. It links the project of rewriting history to Stalin and the Soviet politburo. It rejects the idea of Britain as a 'community of communities', rather than a single nation which is central to the Parekh Report, rather than a single nation, equating it with racism and appealing to the common sense of the common people:

OF COURSE we cherish the diversity that makes the British way of life so rich.

OF COURSE we recognise that our island is home to many cultures, all of which have equal rights and needs – and responsibilities.

But the idea that we are not a nation but should be viewed as 'a community of communities' is abhorrent.

THAT way is racist. THAT way encourages the ghetto mentality.

This country has a proud record of fairness and tolerance.

It is home to people from around the world who have fled persecution or seek to better themselves.

The easy-going way ordinary folk handle their everyday lives is what makes Britain Great and makes Britons so proud.

The Home Secretary is a good and sensible man.

He should stick this report in the bin.

(*Sun*, 11 October 2000)

The interpellation of readers as part of a popular collective 'we' is also central to the *Daily Mail*'s coverage of the report. Also a conservative tabloid, it signalled its response to the report on its front page with a headline: 'The flashy vacuity of the Dome, the trashy icons of Cool Britannia . . . and now the idea that to be British is racist. This is a government that knows nothing of our history and cares about it even less' (*Daily Mail*, 11 October 2000). In a two-page spread with the large headline 'Racism slur on the word "British"' the *Daily Mail* ran an article under the emotive heading: 'And Empire is linked to the Holocaust' (Doughty, *Daily Mail*, 11 October 2000). Like other conservative newspapers, the *Daily Mail* used a photograph of a successful Black British athlete to suggest that the report has no substance. The front-page headline was inset with a large image of Olympic gold medallist Denise Lewis wrapped in the Union Jack. In the accompanying text, the *Daily Mail* selectively quoted some of the report's statements about Britishness and history, together with the views of the then Tory party Chairman, Michael Ancram. In another move common to the conservative press, it brought in a non-white Briton, in this case Raj Chandran, the longest serving member of the Commission for Racial Equality, to dismiss the report. Chandran does not deny racism, but prefers not to focus on it in the interest of being accepted. Under a large print headline, 'An insult to all our countrymen', he claims that Britain is 'an increasingly tolerant multicultural society' and that he is proud of his British passport. Chandran disingenuously uses a partial and false logic, which excludes consideration of the economic factors influencing immigration, to ask: 'If the UK is not hospitable and accepting, why would millions of people – black, brown and yellow – have struggled so hard, first to come here, and then to become British citizens over the past half century?' (Chandran, *Daily Mail*, 11 October 2000). He suggests that accusations of institutional racism are counter productive to the interests of people like himself who wish to be accepted: 'Constant nagging about what a prejudiced and racist lot the British are can only breed unease and resentment in the host community, and that resentment will inevitably be focused on the recently arrived minorities.' In line with the rest of the *Daily Mail*'s coverage, his comments on empire highlight only those things that he sees as positive, ignoring Britain's centuries-long involvement in the slave trade and relieving Britain of any responsibility for the events in post-imperial Sri Lanka, India or Africa:

> The British kept the peace in my old country, Ceylon, where I grew up as part of the minority Tamil population. Since independence, ethnic cleansing and civil war has decimated that beautiful country.
>
> Something similar happened with India, which tore itself apart during partition. Moslems and Hindus murdered each other by the million as the British withdrew.
>
> Or look at Africa, where British colonialism, for all its faults, brought stability and a degree of prosperity. It is certainly debatable whether, say Sierra Leone, Gambia or Mugabe's Zimbabwe are better off now than they were under British rule.
>
> (Chandran, *Daily Mail*, 11 October 2000)

His account of history is both partial and interested:

> If the history that I learned at school is any guide, it was the reviled British Empire which led the fight against slavery in the 19th century – to the fury of Arab traders and many African leaders who were colluding in it for profit.
>
> (Chandran, *Daily Mail*, 11 October 2000)

On pages 12 and 13 of the same edition, the *Daily Mail* published a double spread under the headline 'An Insult to History and Our Intelligence'. This consisted of an editorial comment and a '*Daily Mail* essay' by Paul Johnson entitled 'In Praise of Being British'. The headline sets the tone of the two pieces, suggesting that history is a fixed given and inviting us, as readers, to align ourselves against those who wish to suggest otherwise.

Drawing on popular narratives of Britishness, the comment column opens with a quotation from Churchill's 'Battle of Britain' speech and goes on to portray an inclusive struggle by Britain, her colonies and Commonwealth against Nazi tyranny. The effect is to suggest a culturally and ethnically diverse group pulling together. This inclusive portrayal of the Second World War is a relatively new phenomenon in the UK. Even as recently as the fiftieth anniversary of the end of the Second World War in 1995, Black and Asian veterans had to campaign for recognition of their part in the fight. The inclusive portrayal sets the tone for the broader rhetorical argument which structures both the comment column and the essay, namely that Britain has always

Plate 2. Welsh Somali veteran, Said Shuqule, with outreach worker Akli Ahmed in front of the 'Windrush' photographic exhibition held at Butetown History & Arts Centre, Cardiff, April–June 2001. This exhibition helped to make visible the history of Caribbean service men and women's involvement in the Second World War and of that generation's experience of migration to Britain.
Photo Glenn Jordan. (Butetown History & Arts Centre archive.)

been multi-cultural and that by implication the Parekh Report is manufacturing a problem that does not exist. It continues:

> And now we are told that the Empire was a human disaster, a brutal engine of oppression and slavery, guilty of 'holocausts' against the helpless – a term clearly intended to equate the imperial experience with the mass slaughter committed by the Nazis.
>
> And Britain? This country, we are assured, has no national identity worthy of the name. Indeed the term 'Britishness' is tainted by racism. What is needed, therefore, is 'a rethinking of the national story and the national identity' to reflect the views of Asian, Afro-Caribbean and Irish people.
>
> (*Daily Mail*, 11 October 2000)

This characterization of the report serves to set readers, against the Parekh Commission which is likened to Stalin and Hitler:

Such were the means by which Stalin and Hitler twisted the past to suit their own political purposes. Now there is pressure for Britain to go through the same corrupting process – inspired this time not by a savage dictator, but by those self-satisfied champions of liberal orthodoxy, the Runnymede Trust.

(*Daily Mail*, 11 October 2000)

Yet, we are told, it is not only the Commission that is behaving like dictators, but also the New Labour government that is backing the report's recommendations.

The comment column's narrative of British history and empire is an inclusive one, which seeks to assimilate the history of both the different parts of the UK and Ireland and the former colonies and Commonwealth into one story:

The authors of this pathetic report barely acknowledge that the Empire was largely built by the Scots. They don't seem to know that the Welsh founded the Tudor dynasty, which brought about the most profound changes in our national experience. Or that Ireland and England have been inextricably intertwined since the Elizabethan plantation.

Of course these smaller nations have their own proud histories, too. But they are still an essential part of Britishness – as indeed are the waves of people who have settled here, from the Saxons and the Vikings to the Afro-Caribbean and Asian peoples of our own day.

(*Daily Mail*, 11 October 2000)

The terms of the inclusion are, however, extremely problematic, as the reference to the interweaving of British and Irish history, in particular, suggests. Absent is any mention of the colonial power relations involved. Indeed colonization is unproblematic for the *Daily Mail*. It suggests that the empire was for the most part positive:

Never mind that the slave trade existed for millennia before British imperialism was heard of. Never mind that the Royal Navy stamped it out on the high seas in one of the most remarkable operations conducted by any nation at any time. Never mind that the Empire was by and large a force for good. . . . How Churchill would have despised them.

(*Daily Mail*, 11 October 2000)

Adjacent to this editorial is a '*Daily Mail* Essay' by Paul Johnson: 'In Praise of Being British' (Johnson, *Daily Mail*, 11 October 2000). This includes a large photograph of 'the best of British', a line up of five kings and queens, one general and William Wilberforce, an MP active in the campaign for the abolition of slavery. The inclusion of Wilberforce among Charles I, Elizabeth I, Wellington, James I, Cromwell, Henry VIII and Queen Victoria reflects the way in which recent critiques of empire and the slave trade have become powerful enough for even the conservative press to feel that it must engage with them. In the opening paragraph of the essay, readers are informed that: 'The Runnymede Trust report, calling for a total rewrite of our history and the banning of such terms as "English" and "Britain" as racist, looks like the first move in a New Labour brainwashing exercise designed to destroy our sense of nationhood' (Johnson, *Daily Mail*, 11 October 2000). The use of 'our' immediately sets the readers against the Trust and the government. Describing the Parekh Commission as 'loaded with reliable Left-wingers', and the report as a 'brutal exercise in Labour racial theology' which has 'a distinct smack of totalitarianism about it too', Johnson likens it to attempts by Lenin, Hitler, Mao Tse-tung, Mobutu, Saddam Hussein, Colonel Gadafy and Milosovic to rewrite history for their own purposes.

In marked contrast to this, Johnson suggests, that true History is an objective given. He asserts that 'Britain has a long tradition of unbiased, objective and truthful historical writing, avoiding propaganda and hagiography, and not fearing to criticise the ruling elite when necessary.' He grounds this assertion in the ethnocentric claim that 'Britain was the first truly free country in world history and because our history has always been free, we can trust it.' Throughout his essay, Johnson emphasizes both what he sees as positive aspects of British history and the diverse populations that have always-already made up Britain:

> British history is the story of freedom and respect for the law and Britain's relationship with the world beyond our shores is the story of benefaction, not exploitation, of justice, not oppression, and the desire to enlighten, to improve, to reach and to help.
>
> It is not a story of which any one of us need be ashamed. Nor is it a story which needs to be rewritten. On the contrary: it can be rewritten only by inserting bias and dogma, propaganda and downright lies.
>
> (Johnson, *Daily Mail*, 11 October 2000)

Here, as in other Conservative responses to the Parekh Report, an attempt is made to suggest that the problems that the report is addressing do not really exist. Since Britain has the 'best' race relations in the world and has always been made up of people from diverse backgrounds, the report is painting a false picture of the UK and undermining the truth of history and empire in the interests of biased political correctness. British history, the *Daily Mail* argues, already includes everyone who lives in Britain.

Conclusion

In a section entitled 'The Future of Britishness', the Parekh Report argues that:

> Full acceptance is a deeper notion than inclusion. Since inclusion is offered on terms already set by the wider society, it involves assimilation, sharing current norms of what it means to be a British or a good citizen, and demands a heavy cultural entrance fee. Full acceptance, however, involves renegotiating the terms

and redefining the current norms of Britishness so as to create secure spaces within them for each person's individual qualities.

(Parekh 2000: 55)

It is precisely this process of renegotiation and redefining that conservative Britain finds so alarming, whether in education, the arts or the museum and heritage sectors.

History and tradition play a central role in shaping hegemonic constructions of national identity. This was recognized both by the Parekh Commission on the Future of Multi-ethnic Britain and by those who attacked the report that it produced. Shifts in conservative discourse, apparent in some of the press reception discussed above, suggest that there have been the beginnings of profound changes in attitudes to Britishness and Britain's non-white populations. The move from discourses of assimilation to the embracing of diversity, much of it brought about by the active engagement of non-white Britons, have begun to have profound effects on cultural policy and some aspects of British life. It has led to calls for a rethinking of history and the National Heritage both in the arts and museum sectors as well as in education. This is seen by its proponents as crucial to a fully multi-cultural society. As Stuart Hall has argued:

> A shared national identity thus depends on the cultural meanings, which bind each member individually into the larger national story. Even so-called 'civic' states, like Britain, are deeply embedded in specific 'ethnic' or cultural meanings, which give the abstract idea of the nation its live 'content'. The National Heritage is a powerful source of such meanings. It follows that those who cannot see themselves reflected in its mirror cannot properly 'belong'.

(Hall 1999: 14)

Moves to rewrite British history in more inclusive ways are precisely aimed at creating a space in which non-white Britons can belong. The next two chapters turn to detailed examples of attempts to rewrite national histories in more inclusive ways. Chapter 3 looks at moves in Australia to recover the unrecorded history of what has become known as Australia's 'Stolen Generation'. Chapter 4 turns to fictive attempts by Black British writers to depict the diasporic Black experience both since 1945 and during slavery.

Further reading

Anderson, B. (1991) *Imagined Communities: Reflections on the Origins and Spread of Nationalism*. London: Verso.

Boswell, D. and Evans, J. (eds) (1999) *Representing the Nation: A Reader*. New York and London: Routledge in association with the Open University.

Hall, S. (1999) 'Un-settling "The Heritage": Re-Imagining the Post-Nation' in *Whose Heritage? Keynote Addresses*, pp. 13–22. The Arts Council of England.

Parekh, B. (2000) *Report of the Commission on the Future of Multi-Ethnic Britain*. London: Profile Books.

Pilkington, A. (2003) *Racial Disadvantage and Ethnic Diversity in Britain*. Basingstoke: Palgrave Macmillan.

HISTORY, VOICE AND REPRESENTATION: ABORIGINAL WOMEN'S LIFE WRITING

3

I understand why there is a lot of hatred in the Aboriginal community where children have been forcibly removed from their families by white governments. How could anyone think that apologies or money could make up for the lost years and the terrible traumas and emotional damage caused to my family?

(Kartinyeri 2000: 12)

In the act of pinpointing and dissecting racial, sexual or class 'differences' of women-of-color, white women not only objectify these differences, but also change those differences with their own white, racialized, scrutinizing and alienating gaze. Some white people who take up multicultural and cultural plurality issues mean well but often they push to the fringes once more the very cultures and ethnic groups about whom they want to disseminate knowledge. For example, the white writing about Native peoples or cultures displaces the Native writer and often appropriates the culture instead of proliferating information about it. The difference between appropriation and proliferation is that the first steals and harms; the second helps heal breaches of knowledge.

(Anzaldúa 1990b: xxi)

It is difficult to imagine a more polarized example of the cultural politics of identity, race and representation than that of the indigenous peoples of Australia. Denied citizenship until 1962 and excluded from the census until 1967, indigenous Australians have been subject to two centuries of repressive white policies ranging from genocide to forced assimilation. With no civil rights or access to positive forms of white-defined Australian identity, Aboriginal people were subjected to racialized categorizations within a discursive field dominated by racist anthropology and the legacies of generations of colonial administrators. Until recently, the dominant images of

Aboriginal people outside of their own communities were of 'primitive', 'tribal' people – the 'dying race' of the anthropologist, *National Geographic* and documentary films; the dark-skinned primitives of cultural evolutionist texts. More recently they have become the romanticized, authentic nature people and gifted traditional artists of Australian travel brochures and the tourist industry. Here the images are of tribal people with their boomerangs, stone axes and spears, their ancestral sites and secret rituals, their traditional songs, dances and Dreamtime stories, their bark paintings and body decorations – living in harmony with nature.

Both the boldly negative racism of much popular representation of indigenous people by white Australia and the primitivist celebration of tribal culture, now highly visible in the marketing of Australia to tourists from abroad, help determine the discursive field within which Aboriginal people are seeking to develop positive modes of subjectivity and identity. They are expressions of a deep-rooted Eurocentric, colonial gaze, which has shaped representations of indigenous people since the arrival of the First Fleet in 1788. It is only in recent years that the history of Australia, since the beginnings of white settlement, has begun to be told from Aboriginal perspectives in ways that allow for positive forms of identification. Traditional culture and ways of living were massively disrupted or destroyed by white settlement and the appropriation of the land. It was as recently as 1992, with the path-breaking Mabo case, that the Australian High Court overturned the doctrine of *terra nullius*, which had governed attitudes to land rights since the founding of the Australian federal state in 1901.[1] Aboriginal issues remained under the control of the individual state legislatures even after the creation of a federal state and the Commonwealth Government of Australia only assumed joint responsibility for Aboriginal affairs with the individual states in 1967.

Until the 1930s, anthropologists and administrators assumed that the indigenous people would die out. Those people who survived white settlement were rounded up and relocated on reserves, which they were not free to leave. Mixed-race children were removed from Aboriginal mothers and communities to be brought up on missions and in other government institutions or, in some cases, fostered by white families as part of a policy of assimilation. Most of this 'Stolen Generation' would become a pool of forced cheap labour for white Australia. Denied access to their culture and classified 'Black' in a racist society, many would turn to alcohol and die early deaths. As individual indigenous people, brought up on reserves and missions gradually obtained their freedom to travel and settle where they wanted, they tended to migrate to towns and cities. Yet it was not until the Federal Government took on joint legislative responsibility for Aboriginal affairs in 1967 that control of movement was abolished.[2] With lives governed by dispossession, racism and unemployment and alcohol, many Aboriginal people found themselves the most socially excluded sector of Australian society with children who continued to underachieve. For them, questions of identity and self-esteem are key issues, alongside the material relations that perpetuate their social exclusion.

Aboriginal people are markedly absent from the discursive field that constitutes mainstream Australian history. Though markers of Aboriginal languages surface in some place names, many are British in origin, and the other material signifiers of history, for example, monuments, museums, textbooks and school history syllabuses, largely ignore Aboriginal history or relegate it to anthropological studies of 'primitive' cultures. Although the history of Aboriginal people has been closely interwoven with that of the white settlers since 1788, this has yet to receive full and widespread recognition. For example, in 2001, the 100th anniversary of the founding of the (white) Australian nation in 1901, the Australian Broadcasting Corporation produced a series of five fifty-seven minute programmes called *100 Years: The Australian Story*.[3] The episodes cover Australia's constitutional links with Britain, employment, the white Australia policy, the Aboriginal question and Australia's current position in the world particularly in relation to the United States. What is most remarkable about this series is that viewers can watch all the episodes, with the exception of number four, without hearing any mention of Australia's indigenous population. While the fourth programme (20 per cent of the whole) is dedicated to the Aboriginal question since 1901, the others render Aboriginal people totally invisible, despite the fact that many of the issues dealt with did involve or have implications for Aboriginal people. It is as if indigenous people are simply a special issue, unimportant to the rest of Australian history.

In 1992, faced by increasing demands for land rights, Australian Prime Minister Paul Keating called for a process of 'reconciliation' with the indigenous population. This process was due to reach its culmination in the centenary celebrations of the founding of the Australian state in 2001. It involved conscious, public recognition of past and present wrongs: dispossession, genocide, murder and removal of mixed-race Aboriginal children from their families and communities. As part of this process, a Royal Commission was set up to look into the plight of the Stolen Generation. Known as the 'Bringing Them Home' inquiry, it presented its report in April 1997 and among its recommendations was provision for the collection of the history of the Stolen Generation. In December 1997, as the National Library of Australia's leaflet on the 'Bringing Them Home' project explains:

> In response to the first recommendation of *Bringing Them Home*, the report of the National Inquiry into the Separation of Aboriginal and Torres Strait Islander Children from Their Families, the Commonwealth Government announced that $1.6 million would be allocated to the National Library of Australia. This was for an oral history project that would collect and preserve a substantial range of stories from Indigenous people and others involved in the process of child removals.
>
> The aim of the project is to create a rounded history by recording a selection of the experiences and perspectives of various people who were involved.
>
> Those who will be given the opportunity to make their stories public will include:

•separated children
•family members affected by separations
•foster parents
•administrators
•missionaries
•hospital workers
•police

The National Library of Australia leaflet goes on to comment that:

> The recording of these oral histories is crucial to documenting a significant period
> of Australia's history and making it available as a public record. The process of
> recording, and the oral histories themselves, can play an important part in healing
> and reconciliation, and in helping Australians to understand their history.

In addition to proposing the 'Bringing Them Home' oral history project, the report of
the Royal Commission called upon white Australia to apologize to the Aboriginal
population and to compensate the victims of this policy. While the state legislatures
agreed to apologize, federal Prime Minister John Howard refused and compensation
has not been forthcoming. For indigenous people, who continue to be the poorest,
unhealthiest, least educated, most imprisoned and least employed sector of Australian
society, with a life expectancy of fifty-seven years for men and sixty-two years for
women, this was at best a symbolic gesture.

History, voice and identity

At stake in the 'Bringing Them Home' project are questions of whose history is
collected and told, who does the telling and where this history is preserved and for
whom. Underlying these questions is the issue of what sort of imagined community of
'Australianness' Aboriginal people can participate in without a knowledge and recognition of this history within the wider society. If history is fundamental to many forms
of identity and belonging, it involves processes of interpellation that also give the
subject thus created a voice. The 'Bringing Them Home' project can be seen as the
beginnings of an institutionalization of an important aspect of Aboriginal cultural
politics, which includes oral history, written life stories and the fictional evocation of
Aboriginal history since white settlement. This chapter turns to another aspect of
Aboriginal attempts to reclaim the past as a source for positive forms of identity. It
looks in some detail at examples of written life stories by indigenous women, two of
who were Stolen Generation children, in the context of contemporary debates within
feminism about history, identity, voice and representation.

Writing of Aboriginal women, indigenous feminist writer, Aileen Moreton-
Robinson has described how:

White Australia has come to 'know' the 'Indigenous woman' from the gaze of many, including the diaries of explorers, the photographs of philanthropists, the testimony of white state officials, the sexual bravado of white men and the ethnographies of anthropologists. In this textual landscape Indigenous women are objects who lack agency. The landscape is disrupted by the emergence of the life writings of Indigenous women whose subjectivities and experiences of colonial processes are evident in their texts.

(Moreton-Robinson 2000: 1)

In this reflection on Aboriginal women's life writing, Moreton-Robinson points to some of the most important issues at stake in the process of life writing that is located in the pre-existing discursive fields of white Australian history and white constructions of indigenous women. These are subjectivity, agency and voice and they are preconditions for positive forms of identity. If one is interested in histories of Australia that do not marginalize or exclude Aboriginal voices and perspectives and that document the relations between Black and white Australians, one has to look, for the most part, to indigenous sources. Given this situation, Aboriginal feminist and historian, Jackie Huggins has asked: 'Is it possible for white Australians to write "Aboriginal" history? Aboriginal history differs from white history in its concerns and perspectives and probably its methods' (Huggins 1998: 2). Answering her own question, she suggests that while the approaches to history may be different, whites already play a fundamental and often *unacknowledged* role:

Whites too are crucially part of the process. Whites are exercising power and making decisions which affect Aboriginal lives. White norms and values are enshrined in our institutions and white knowledge and ways of valuing are taught and recorded in our schools. We are all products of history and, as a consequence, occupy particular positions of privilege or disadvantage.

(Huggins 1998: 2–3)

While Aboriginal history cannot be thought without the role of white Australians, the articulation of Aboriginal voices and perspectives are necessary starting points for a history that is able both to represent indigenous experience and give Aboriginal people a sense of positive identity, ownership and agency. Over the last twenty years increasing numbers of life histories and fictional representations of the history and present of Aboriginal Australia have been published. In what follows, the chapter looks at the question of history, identity and voice, in examples of published life stories by women from different parts of Australia.[4]

Voicing Aboriginal women's experience

In 1994, Queensland-born Rita Huggins and her daughter Jackie published Rita's life history: *Auntie Rita*. The text tells of Rita's forced removal with her family in the

1920s from her people's country to what would become the Cherbourg Aboriginal Reserve, where her family were imprisoned under the Aboriginal Protection Act. It recounts her time in forced domestic service, her obtaining freedom from the Act, her marriage, widowhood and subsequent life in Brisbane, where she became active in Aboriginal affairs. *Auntie Rita* deals with many themes common to life writing by Aboriginal women. These include, first and foremost, questions of identity and culture raised by the forced expulsion of Aboriginal families from their traditional lands and the removal of mixed-race children from their families. Both issues are shown to pose key questions of identity and belonging. Forced Christianization, the banning of the use of Aboriginal languages and traditional tribal customs and practices over the decades gave rise to the question for Aboriginal people today of what it means to be Aboriginal outside of traditional tribal communities. Yet as Jackie Huggins points out, even this question is overdetermined by the assumptions and prejudices of white society which determine how Aboriginal people are viewed and defined. Commenting in *Auntie Rita* on a visit with her mother to New Zealand, she writes:

> Our experience in New Zealand showed the preconceived ideas people have about Aboriginals. Because we did not fit the stereotype of the 'savage,' we were not considered 'real' Aboriginals. You meet this often. Like the time it was said to me that I didn't sound like an Aboriginal because I didn't have an accent. Styles of dress, speech, abode, where we shop or what car we drive do not lessen our relation to Aboriginal culture and identity. Nor do they heal the emotional scars from our experiences living in Western society.
>
> The ultimate insult is 'You're not a real Aboriginal'.
>
> (Huggins and Huggins 1994: 128)

This problem of white definitions of Aboriginality is not only confined to everyday life, it is institutional. For example, it permeates academic scholarship, even by white women who see themselves as feminists. Writing of recent work by white women anthropologists in her book *Talkin' up to the White Woman: Indigenous Women and Feminism*, Aileen Moreton-Robinson points to the ways in which white people construct models of Aboriginality which are then used to disallow the authenticity of actual Aboriginal people's claims to Aboriginal identity.

> The use of culture as *a priori* essential meanings to construct the traditional Indigenous woman in anthropological literature raises questions about the representation of such a woman. If she exists, she does only what anthropology decides for her and she has completely escaped colonisation. Her lack of subjectivity means she is an object, whom anthropologists have constructed in their imagination and on paper. The traditional woman is the woman against whom all Indigenous women are measured, yet in her pristine state she does not exist. What do exist are different Indigenous women who have different cultures that do not mirror anthropological representations.
>
> (Moreton-Robinson 2000: 88)

This process of the dominant group constructing the 'other' as a homogeneous group lacking diversity can be found throughout Western societies. It points to a major cultural political task both within multi-ethnic societies and beyond, that involves promoting recognition of the diversity of marginalized groups. Invariably this relies on the positive intervention by people from the groups in question who challenge hegemonic constructions of their otherness. In indigenous women's life writing, family and community form a crucial counterweight to white stereotypes of and assumptions about Aboriginal people, whether primitivist or simply negatively racist. This factor made the plight of the Stolen Generation all the more profound. Jackie Huggins writes of herself:

> I am a PRIVILEGED Aboriginal woman. I am privileged because:
>
> – I have grown up with my family
> – I have never been taken away
> – I have been socialised into believing that the dignity of the human spirit is tied up in my Aboriginality
> – I have a mother like Rita.
>
> (Huggins 1998: 94)

Life writing by Aboriginal women strongly articulates the need for a sense of belonging rooted in forms of Aboriginal culture that distance indigenous people from the Western, racist, white mainstream and can feed positive conceptions of identity. Aboriginal writers often suggest that family and community offer a strong source of alternative values, crucially denied to the Stolen Generation. These values include the importance of the extended family, of history, traditions, the land and above all spirituality. These alternative versions of the roots of identity resignify aspects of traditional culture, also emphasized in Western primitivist versions of the Australian 'Black other'. This reappropriation and resignification marks an anti-Western, anti-colonialist stance. Aileen Moreton-Robinson, for example, emphasizes in her chapter on 'Self-Presentation within Indigenous Women's Life Writings' how the ways in which writers present Aboriginal spirituality is very different from the Christianity of white Australia:

> Unlike White constructions of Christian spirituality. Indigenous spirituality encompasses the intersubstantiation of ancestral beings, humans and physiography. The spiritual world is immediately experienced because it is synonomous with the physiography of the land. In the life writings, the reality of spirituality is a physical fact because it is experienced as part of one's life.
>
> (Moreton-Robinson 2000: 19)

This points to a felt need in the construction of positive narratives of identity and belonging not to be like the oppressor, even if one is an apparently westernized Aboriginal woman. It involves a fundamental rejection of many of the norms and values of white Australia. As life-writing texts suggest, this is a form of spirituality that the Stolen Generation have to learn late in life and that becomes, in their narratives, an important basis for the development of a positive sense of identity and belonging.

For indigenous women in urban environments, and above all for the Stolen Generation, history, too, is shown to be crucial to identity. For the Stolen Generation, learning about Aboriginal history becomes a journey of self-discovery. Yet, even for those not taken away, it is an important factor in the acquisition of positive forms of identity. Jackie Huggins writes 'my love of history stems from my displacement as an Aboriginal person. Like most students I was fed on a diet of lies and invisibility from a very young age' (1998: 120). The absence of this Aboriginal history from most mainstream education contributes to the continual marginalization of Aboriginal people in mainstream Australian society.

I want to turn now to look in some detail at two life stories by Aboriginal women from different parts of Australia that tell of the experiences of women of the Stolen Generation: *Kick the Tin* by Doris Kartinyeri (2000) and *It is no Secret: the Story of a Stolen Child* by Donna Meehan (2000). Kartinyeri was taken from her family as an infant and brought up in a rural children's home run by a religious order outside Adelaide, South Australia. Meehan was removed from her family as a small child and adopted by a loving white family in industrial Newcastle, New South Wales.

Kick the Tin [5]

> I have an illness. It has taken me a long time to come to terms with it. My healing began when I decided to write my autobiography and I continued to write throughout my illnesses.
>
> (Kartinyeri 2000: 1)

For Doris Kartinyeri, life writing is explicitly seen as a form of healing, a way of coming to terms with a past that has blighted her life. *Kick the Tin* was published by the feminist publishing house, Spinifex, with subsidies from both central and state government sources. The narrative recounts how Doris Kartinyeri was removed from her family against their wishes, after her mother's death in childbirth. She was brought up at the United Aboriginal Mission in South Australia until she was sent into service at the age of 14. The absence of any experience of family is shown to have profound effects on her life, including her sense of who she is. Kartinyeri tells how, having no early contact with her family, she learns to see the other Aboriginal children in the home as her 'brothers' and 'sisters' and has no sense of natural family ties even though, as she grows up, her father and siblings are able to visit her at Colebrook Home:

> During my father's visits to Colebrook, there was no mention of my mother or her death, nor did I ask. I had lost my culture and language. The word 'mother' did not have any meaning for me. I just did not know the word. I vividly remember using my pillow to cuddle at night for comfort and security. Even though my

brothers and sisters accompanied my father on his visits, I felt no bond with them. Doreen said, 'I am your sister' and I replied. 'No you're not my sister! These are my brothers and sisters here.'

(Kartinyeri 2000: 47)

Her upbringing in the home makes the process of bonding with her family as an adult difficult. It requires that she learn a language and culture and get to know a large extended family.

Kick the Tin focuses a detailed, critical, adult eye on the practices of the mission. Life at the home is described as strict and sometimes brutal. It includes both the widespread use of physical punishment and sexual abuse, which produce a sense of resistant solidarity among the children. Kartinyeri writes:

There were some children who were favoured and others who, for unknown reasons, were treated badly. But we supported one another. We always knew who wet the bed from the boys' dormitory. They were outside in the cold, peeling potatoes in the early hours of the morning, preparing vegetables for the evening meal. The other bed-wetters could be punished by standing for all meals and eating dry weetbix. Then they were punished by having cold showers.

(Kartinyeri 2000: 43)

Colebrook Home is described in the text as 'a haven for sexual deviants' and Kartinyeri recounts how, as a young child, she was made to fondle the upper part of a 'religious' woman's legs during film shows. She tells of how she later heard of many Colebrook boys being sexually abused. Such abuse is not restricted to her experience in the home. Sent into domestic service at the age of 14, she describes how she was subjected to men exposing themselves and to the constant threat of sexual assault. Reflecting on this common experience, shared by many of the Stolen Generation, she tells of how an often brutal mission upbringing, isolated from family, culture and community, led many of the children to develop alcoholism and mental illness in later life. After describing the punishments inflicted on children in the home, Kartinyeri comments: 'To me this was physical and mental abuse. . . . This is one of the reasons I believe a majority of our sisters and brothers went either to gaol or mental institutions. Others suffered with alcoholism. All in the name of religion' (Kartinyeri 2000: 43). Some Colebrook children, Doris Kartinyeri recounts, did go back to their families on leaving the home, some, indeed, succeeded despite the barriers set up by racist white society, and became professionals and trades people, but many turned to alcohol or became mentally ill, as she herself did. Reading *Kick the Tin*, it is noticeable how many of the children, especially boys, depicted in the photographs in the book have died prematurely and looking back on her life and that of other children of the Stolen Generation, Kartinyeri powerfully comments:

It angers me now to think that the system of the so called Aboriginal Protection Board and so called Christians had the power to remove Aboriginal children from their families and place them into Christian institutions. These institutions rammed Christian beliefs into children, brainwashing them into a system that stripped them of their people, their culture, their beliefs, their rules, their traditions. We had our own rules, our own ways of living, We had our own creation stories, our spirituality. What right did they have to crush our spirituality, our language, our kin? What right did they have to crush our spirit and replace it with their myths and stories and rules which they did not live up to. And which they used to violate our lives?

(Kartinyeri 2000: 110)

It is no Secret: the Story of a Stolen Child

For a long time, one of the responses of white Australians to the plight of the Stolen Generation was statements of ignorance of what had been done to Aboriginal families over generations. This issue is explicitly addressed by Donna Meehan in her life story, where she writes: 'If white society legitimately doesn't know about the consequences of government policies, then someone has to inform them' (Meehan 2000: 257). Meehan's life story was published by Random House. It tells of how the author was sent away from the Aboriginal camp in the outback where she was born. Put on a train at the age of 5, she travels hundreds of miles to be fostered and adopted by a childless, white, European, immigrant couple in Newcastle, New South Wales. Donna is never told the reason for her removal from her family but grows up Black in a white environment. While she has very loving adoptive parents, they cannot protect her from white racism or the feelings of abandonment produced by her forced removal from her family. It is only as an adult, when she finds her Aboriginal mother, that she learns that they were all victims of the assimilationist policies of the white Australian state. When they finally meet, her birth mother, Beatrice, tells her: 'The government took all you kids away. I lost all seven kids that day. It was terrible. They put the eldest five on the train and kept the three-month-old twins at the hospital' (Meehan 2000: 129). When Donna asks 'Why did you give me away?' Her mother hangs her head and says quietly, 'I dunno, they just took youse all away. I dunno why' (Meehan 2000: 137). As she researches her life story, Donna learns about the profound effects that the loss of her mother's children had on her mother: often she was suicidal and she only survived through extended family support. Her relatives would tell her: 'They'll all come 'ome when they're ol' 'nough. You wait an see. You gotta be 'ere waitin for them. You know that ol' Murri spirit will come looking for its own' (Meehan 2000: 147). Beatrice, like many Aboriginal women in this position, turned to alcohol.

Meehan tells how, in Newcastle, she was brought up by devoted parents and suffered none of the abuse or poverty of children brought up on missions or in children's homes. Yet, as in many life stories of the Stolen Generation, questions of racism and identity caused her serious problems:

I was nine years old when I first saw an Aboriginal person in the city, on the television. . . . Mum and dad were so excited and said, 'Look, there is one of your people. See how beautiful he is and look how the white people love him. This is your country, you be proud of it. We are the new Australians. Don't you be ashamed, you be proud you're Aboriginal.

(Meehan 2000: 58–9)

While her white immigrant parents understand the importance of self-esteem to identity, they are unable to protect her from racism. Despite the best endeavours of her parents, Donna learns the negative, racist meanings given to Aboriginality by white Australia. After the television incident, she does not see another Aboriginal person until she is 14, when an Aboriginal girl joins her high school. They do not, however, become friends: 'Although by my features people knew I was Aboriginal, within, I was in denial. I felt confronted. I had learned it was shameful to be Aboriginal, so instead of being happy to see her I was embarrassed' (Meehan 2000: 59). Donna's wish to belong becomes a wish to be white: 'All I wanted was simply to be like all the other kids – white – but I couldn't pass the colour test (Meehan 2000: 53). Nor does her schooling offer any way forward, since it does not include 'Aboriginal perspectives or Aboriginal guest speakers, nor were Aboriginal people encouraged to become teachers' (Meehan 2000: 61). Working in her parents' petrol station, she deflects white racism by telling customers that she is Maori or Fijian. Once married and away from parental support, however, she finds herself constantly trying to prove that she is not the white stereotype that white people have of Aboriginals:

I kept house trying to please others, trying to prove to white society that I wasn't dirty. For close to a year I was taking three showers a day, all to prove I was clean. I still felt inferior about being different, and I had an ocean of anger within me about many things in my life, past and present. I grew more lonely and miserable to the point where I wanted to commit suicide.

(Meehan 2000: 84)

Later in life she comes to interpret her constant feelings of inadequacy as a growing identity crisis, fuelled by anger at being sent away by her mother and 'years of grieving that was never acknowledged, identified or resolved' (Meehan 2000: 86).

It is no Secret offers a detailed account of the painful process of coming to terms with a denial of Aboriginality and an embracing of Aboriginal identity as an adult. After finding her family, Donna visits the place where she spent her first five years of life. She expresses surprise at finding that it is not like the negative media images of Aboriginal communities to which she is accustomed. Yet despite this, she feels like an outsider and onlooker. She is only able to resolve the question of her Aboriginality and embrace an indigenous identity at her Aboriginal mother's funeral when she finally comes to see Aboriginal people in new ways and to accept them for what they are. This is described as a moment of revelation, which finally leads to a sense of positive identity and belonging:

> The more I examined the faces, the more it made me cry. It was so wonderful. I felt something I had never felt before. I saw true beauty in each face I beheld . . .
>
> (Meehan 2000: 210)

> As I sat looking at their dark velvet skin, I knew that this, too, had been another barrier, as somewhere in my childhood I had adopted the view from white society that the fairer the skin the more acceptable the people were; but now the darker the skin, the deeper the love I had for them.
> I had an overwhelming sense of belonging.
>
> (Meehan 2000: 212)

By the end of the book she has embraced a new sense of identity grounded in what she calls a 'Black perspective'.

Conclusion

Aboriginal women's life writings offer testimonies to the experience of living under a racist, white Australian state, in a society that continues to marginalize the voices, history and present-day plight of the indigenous people of Australia. The proliferation of life histories and oral history testimonies since the late 1980s has produced resources with which to begin to address marginalization, yet the struggle to be heard continues. It involves material questions such as, access to those institutions that control publication and distribution, as well as inclusion in educational syllabuses, all of which are largely in the hands of white people. These are issues that also shape Aboriginal women's relationships to Australian feminism.

Over the last few decades, postcolonial critiques of Western scholarship, including history, have raised issues of immense importance for indigenous women in settler societies, for women in developing countries, and for women in the West. These issues – a focus of postcolonial feminism – include Eurocentrism, representation, the question of voice, history and the development of new forms of political activism and identity. They are concerns with a political and theoretical importance that extend beyond the boundaries of women's issues but which Third World and indigenous feminists have brought into sharp focus and placed on the broader political agenda.

Second-wave feminism in Western countries in the late 1960s and 1970s was marked by a variety of forms of universalizing theory – liberal, radical feminist and Marxist – that claimed to represent the interests of all women. They shared a tendency, seldom made explicit, to assume that white Western norms and practices were the measure of all things. The often unconscious legacies of colonialism and of nineteenth-century scientific racism informed the ways in which women outside the West were perceived.

Often this was as victims of traditional, highly patriarchal cultures and religions which, at best, had their roots outside Western modernity and were assumed to be static and unchanging. Powerful symbols and cultural practices such as the veil, arranged marriages and genital mutilation came to exemplify the plight of Third World women, who were assumed to lack the power and agency with which to bring about progressive social change.[6]

The rapid diversification of second-wave feminism, together with the powerful theoretical and political critiques of universalism coming from Black, Third World and indigenous women as well as from postmodern theory, put into question the universal assumptions underpinning Western feminisms, pointing to their blind spots and limitations. At issue were questions of unacknowledged and often implicit racism, the Eurocentric gaze, the perpetuation of colonial modes of representation and the institutional privileging of the voices and narratives of white, middle-class, Western feminists. These issues have been raised in the Australian context by Aboriginal women, where the marginalization of Aboriginal voices and history and the related question of representation profoundly affects indigenous women's relationship to the feminist movement. The implicit racism of a white feminism that does not take indigenous women's issues seriously has the effect of rendering feminist forms of identity inaccessible to Aboriginal women. A crucial issue here (as in many other contexts) is the failure of white women to address their complicity with social relations that oppress and marginalize Aboriginal people. Jackie Huggins comments, for example, that:

> Australian historiography has been notably silent about relationships between white women and Black women and, in particular, female employers and their Aboriginal servants. . . . In white feminist writings, a wall of silence invariably has been maintained on this issue. The focus has been on 'women' as an entity as constituting the oppressed. Yet this literature has never raised the question of whether women themselves are oppressors. Instead, there has been a tendency to equate the situation of white women with that of all women. When the complex factors of race and gender are considered, however, white women's activities have to be seen as part of the colonisation and oppression of Black women. Certainly sisterhood was not powerful enough to transcend such racial boundaries.
>
> (Huggins 1998: 28)

The political implications of this are far reaching:

> It would be a fair statement to make that many Black women do not want to know about white feminism. I can't say I blame them. There are a multitude of reasons why this is so: (a) a closed women's movement which has never addressed the needs of Aboriginal women, (b) inherent racism within feminist circles, (c) white women's unfamiliarity with the process of colonisation and how it has affected all Aboriginal people (that is, the non-support of Black men and families), (d) elitism

and the subordination of subjects and objects, (e) exclusion of black women by white women, (f) our struggle as Blacks first.

(Huggins 1998: 118)

The reasons that Huggins gives for Aboriginal women's indifferent relation to white feminism are symptomatic of problems that beset feminism, not only in Australia, but also throughout the Western world. At issue is the failure of white Western women to acknowledge their own privilege and to tackle their implication in and indifference to question racism and the legacies of colonialism. This includes a widespread failure to interrogate whiteness, both past and present, and to acknowledge both its structural and everyday effects on non-white women. The structural privilege that whiteness offers white women affects their positioning both institutionally and personally in relation to women of Colour. While other issues, such as class and sexual orientation are important, whiteness is most often the dominant factor. Failure to address racialized structural privilege can lead to behaviour that leaves Black women's position in relation to white women untransformed, except at the level of rhetoric.

A starting point for change is for white women to seek out and listen to the voices of non-white women – both experiential and theoretical – and to attempt to understand the world through their eyes. Here life writing, like other non-fiction and fiction by indigenous women has an important role to play. However, white women need to be wary of the tendency to appropriate indigenous voices in ways that maintain white power. As Jackie Huggins points out:

There are also lines of accountability and responsibility to uphold. Questions which need to be asked are: Who has responsibility for what and whom? Who does what? Who takes responsibility for saying things for whom? Who does the saying and the writing? Who gets the feedback and benefit? White women must realise 'where to get off' in the Aboriginal struggle.

(Huggins 1998: 116)

Aileen Moreton-Robinson identifies a further problem in white women's relation to indigenous women – a problem that also transcends the boundaries of the Australian situation. It is the white tendency not to engage with women of Colour directly but through texts and in contexts where women of Colour are rarely in a position to answer back and contest the ways in which they have been read and appropriated. She argues that 'White feminist academics engage with women who are "Other" pre-dominantly through representations in texts and imaginings. This "Other" offers no resistance and can be made to disappear at will' (Moreton-Robinson 2000: 183). This form of engagement both allows for the perpetuation of colonial modes of representa-tion and the unquestioned normative status of whiteness. Moreton-Robinson suggests that it is the failure to interrogate whiteness that leads to the avoidance of 'an engage-ment with the Indigenous critical gaze on the white racial subject who constructs and represents the "Other"' (Moreton-Robinson 2000: 181). This produces partial readings of indigenous women's writing that do not challenge white subjectivity. Thus it is not just a politics of inclusion that is called for, but also a thorough questioning of the terms of that inclusion. Moreover, changing the terms of inclusion will require the relinquishing of power by white women. As in any contemporary relationships shaped by the legacies of colonialism, white women need to know and acknowledge the past and take responsibility for the present. This present – itself a product of history – must include their own privileged positions within society and the structural power of whiteness to marginalize and oppress. History has given white women that voice and representation that indigenous women are seeking through their life writings, the task for white women and men is to listen and learn from it.

Further reading

Huggins, J. (1998) *Sister Girl: The Writings of Aboriginal Activist and Historian Jackie Huggins*. St Lucia: University of Queensland Press.

Huggins, R. and Huggins, J. (1994) *Auntie Rita*. Canberra: Aboriginal Studies Press.

Kartinyeri, D. (2000) *Kick the Tin*. Melbourne: Spinifex.

Meehan, D. (2000) *It is no Secret: the Story of a Stolen Child*. Milsons Point, NSW: Random House.

Moreton-Robinson, A. (2000) *Talkin'up to the White Woman: Indigenous Women and Feminism*. St Lucia: University of Queensland Press.

Morgan, S. (1988) *My Place*. London: Virago.

NARRATIVES OF IDENTITY AND DIFFERENCE: VOICING BLACK BRITISH HISTORY

> Britain continues to be disfigured by racism; by phobias about cultural difference; by sustained social, economic, educational and cultural disadvantage; by institutional discrimination; and by a systematic failure of social justice or respect for difference. These have been fuelled by a fixed conception of national identity and culture. They are not likely to disappear without a sustained effort of political will. Is it possible to reimagine Britain as a nation – or post nation – in a multi-cultural way?
>
> (Parekh 2000: 36)

> Is it only a matter of unearthing that which the colonial experience buried and overlaid, bringing to light the hidden continuities it suppressed? Or is a quite different practice entailed – not the rediscovery but the *production* of identity. Not an identity grounded in the archaeology, but in the *re-telling* of the past?
>
> (Hall 1990: 52)

One answer to calls to rethink narratives of Britishness and British history, discussed at length in Chapter 2, is recent cultural production by British Black and South Asian writers and filmmakers. This includes historical and autobiographical fiction, poetry, comedy, documentary cinema and television. This chapter focuses on Black British writing and looks at how these texts offer a challenge to hegemonic constructions of British identity and their grounding in history. It asks how this fiction repositions Black Britons in relation to hegemonic white-centred narratives of Britishness and how this process might challenge common processes of othering non-white Britons.

Fiction is an important medium for exploring questions of identity and belonging. It is also effective in giving readers some sense of what it is like to be the subject of racism, made other in negative ways by white society. Fiction has played an important role in the cultural politics of race and racism, particularly in the United States. Telling and reading stories are key ways in which people make sense of their lives and imagine modes of living different from their own. Fiction allows for the exploration of emotions that are important in understanding racism both from the perspective of its perpetrators and its victims. Through processes of empathy and identification with fictional characters, novels, life stories and other such texts can initiate the development of new forms of identity for readers. They are important sources of ways of understanding both contemporary society and history and serve as repositories of social and cultural values.

Narrative – the telling of stories – is central to everyday communication between individuals. In narrating our experiences we attribute meanings to them and in the process assume the position of knowing, apparently sovereign subject. We become subjects through the process of interpellation that involves both being addressed and speaking. Yet the discursive construction of subjectivity most often remains invisible. Similar processes are at work in fictional narratives. In realist narratives, for example, the narrator is positioned as knowing subject, able to communicate to readers his or her interpretation of social life. We learn the conventions of narrative from an early age from the stories that we hear, read and watch. These conventions govern not only the structures of story-telling, but also our expectations about appropriate characterization and narrative resolutions. To narrate is to assume the position of a speaking subject. It involves the exclusion or marginalization of other possible subject positions and other meanings. Whereas much canonical British fiction speaks as if it were addressing the individual, the values that it represents most often position its narrator and reader as implicitly white. The effect of this can be to marginalize non-white readers, whose experiences are likely to be very different from this assumed norm. Recognition of shared values and experience is important to identity and identification with fictional characters or narratives can be affirming. Inequalities of race affect access to the discursive field of literary production in predominantly white societies. Non-white people are absent in any great numbers from those powerful cultural institutions that both facilitate and validate literary production, acting as gatekeepers within the discursive field. Thus, for example, the fiction discussed in this chapter, although arguable powerful in its evocation of Black lives and Black history, has for the most part remained on the margins when arguably it should be highly visible, particularly in education.

The year 1998 saw celebrations among Britain's African-Caribbean population to mark the 50th anniversary of the arrival of the *Empire Windrush* at Tilbury Docks on the Essex coast in June 1948, with its 500 passengers from the Caribbean who had come to find work in Britain. The *Empire Windrush* was the first of many ships to transport African-Caribbean migrants to Britain over the next two decades, and it marked the beginning of a flow of migration that would bring more than 500,000 settlers to the UK until, in the course of the 1960s, the government introduced legislation to restrict immigration. (For more on the history of Black people in Britain see

Fryer 1984.) Although many West Indian migrants initially saw themselves as coming to work, not to settle, most of them would stay permanently. The history of this major migration, which helped to change the face of Britain, remains largely unknown to Britain's white population. The process of documenting the migrants' stories, and making this hidden history widely available, has only just begun. A major step in this direction was the four-part series made by Mike Phillips for BBC 2 on the history of Black people in Britain since the Second World War.[1] Beginning with West Indian participation in the war effort, the documentary traces post-war migration and settlement and the racism, discrimination and social deprivation suffered by the 'Windrush generation' and their children. Using oral history and archive footage, the programmes covered the decades up to 1998, years which saw the re-emergence of the extreme right, protests and riots and the beginnings of acceptance as Black Britons achieved wider positive visibility particularly in music, sport and the media.

In the 1950s and 1960s people of Colour, both those settled in Britain for generations, mostly in London and port cities such as Liverpool, Bristol and Cardiff, and the influx of new immigrants, predominantly from the Caribbean and the Indian sub-continent, found themselves confronted on the one hand by overtly racist rejection and discrimination and on the other by discourses of assimilation that rejected their difference, implicitly asserting the superiority of the white British 'way of life'. In the immediate post-war decades there was a climate of overt, racial discrimination in all areas of life: housing, the workplace and leisure, as well as among state institutions such as the police, education and the health service. At this time, before the rise of discourses of multi-culturalism and cultural diversity, ideas of assimilation – according to which people of Colour should adapt and become just like the white British – were accompanied by a liberal humanist ideology of 'colour-blindness' which effectively denied difference and asserted that we are all the same. The claim not to see colour masked wide-ranging practices of discrimination even among those who thought themselves liberal and progressive.

Yet discourses of sameness and assimilation did not go unchallenged, especially in the arena of parliamentary politics where immigration control was repeatedly mobilized as an issue that would win votes. Politicians, most notoriously Enoch Powell MP, who was Member of Parliament for Wolverhampton in the West Midlands could call for the repatriation of Black and South Asian people, even those who were British born, explicitly suggesting that they were foreign bodies with no right to be in Britain (see in particular his infamous 'Rivers of Blood' speech (1968) extracts of which are available at *www.sterlingtimes.co.uk/powell_press.htm*.) It has been a long and painful struggle over the last fifty years to shift official discourses in the UK towards tolerance of difference and diversity. This does not, of course, mean that things have necessarily changed in the institutional practices and social relations of everyday life. Changing day-to-day practice is a much more difficult issue. Thus, for example, in his forward to the official publication detailing the second round of Home Office *Connecting*

Communities Race Equality Support Programmes, published in March 2003, Home Secretary, David Blunkett, wrote:

> This government is committed to creating a cohesive society, where we promote equality and diversity alongside a common vision and sense of belonging, where every member of our society is able to fulfil their potential, where racism is unacceptable and counteracted, where everyone is treated according to their needs and rights, and where cultural diversity is celebrated.
>
> (Blunkett 2003: Foreword)

Social statistics on ethnic minority participation within all aspects of British life would suggest that Britain is only at the beginning of this process. While such statements can be read as supportive of cultural diversity and equality, they are being produced alongside much less tolerant language and policies on asylum seekers. The treatment of the issue of asylum seekers by government, opposition and the media, not to mention white communities where asylum hostels have been located, suggest that they have become a new 'other' to be targeted and excluded, alongside other minority groups. This would tend to support the conclusions of the Parekh Report that this struggle for a non-racist, diverse yet cohesive society still has a long way to go, even in the area of policy.

The tenacity of resistance to racial and ethnic diversity in contemporary Britain has long established and deep roots in the discursive field of racialized thought and practice. Racist and ethnocentric ideologies, derived from earlier eras of racial science and colonialism, continue to inform commonsense thinking among many white Britons about Britain's non-white populations. During the colonial period Englishness, Welshness, Scottishness and Britishness were all, in part, defined in opposition to non-white others and this legacy has also shaped popular knowledge about race in Britain. Scientific racism reached a high point in Western Europe and the USA in the nineteenth century, yet many of the ideas about race and culture proposed by scientific racism still inform stereotypes of people of African, South Asian or Middle- and Far-eastern descent. Primitivism and classical orientalism continue to surface in signifying practices such as advertising, pornography and pop music videos and the negative language of classical racism in its nineteenth-century form has been taken up untransformed by extreme right-wing fringe organizations (see Daniels 1997). These racist organizations continue to target working-class urban communities in Britain, as well as specific groups such as football supporters.[2] If anything they are better organized nationally and internationally than ever before, expanding their reach through the internet.

For a long time the mainstream response to the language of the racist right in Britain was the liberal language of colour-blindness, according to which colour does not matter. As a discourse, it tends to ignore the material social relations and forms of institutionalized racism that precisely make colour and phenotype matter and it was powerfully critiqued among others by the Black American feminist Audre Lorde: in her classic essay 'Age, Race, Sex and Class: Women Redefining Difference' (Lorde 1981). In practice, as Lorde suggests, liberal colour-blindness leads to a disavowal of material differences and has often been allied with practices that precisely construct and maintain difference as inferiority. This, for example, was the experience of modernist artists of Colour who came to Britain from Commonwealth countries in the 1950s and 1960s. Trained though they were in Western modernism, their work was interpreted by white art critics not as modernism but as either imitation or expressions of their 'race' and/or ethnicity, irrespective of whether ethnic factors were in play. Moreover, the ideas of race articulated by art critics in their supposedly objective appraisals of the work of artists of Colour echoed the forms of primitivism so prevalent among major European modernists (for example, Picasso and the German Expressionists) at the turn of the nineteenth century (see Jordan and Weedon 1995: 315–488). The reception of modernist artists of Colour suggests that the art establishment would not allow them to join the ranks of international modernism which were, by implication, explicitly white. Rather it wished to contain them within a category of what would become known as 'ethnic art' (see Jordan and Weedon 1995: 473–88).

In all areas of life, colour-blindness has served as a screen for continued forms of prejudice and discrimination. It belongs to discourses of racism that tend to see it as an individual phenomenon rather than as structural and institutional. It is only recently that institutional racism has been put on the mainstream British agenda in the wake of the Stephen Lawrence case. Moreover, while the Race Relations Act in the UK dates from 1976, it was only extended to cover the police in the year 2000.

Attention to the cultural needs of ethnic minority communities was perhaps the first stage in the shift towards multi-culturalism and cultural diversity. This was a response both to demands made by ethnic minority communities themselves and to the social unrest produced by racism, poverty and what has recently been termed 'social exclusion'. Thus, for example, the Scarman Report on the Brixton Riots, published in 1981, suggested cultural provision as a way of diffusing social unrest, much as Matthew Arnold had done in the 1860s, in the face of growing working-class activism. (For a discussion of Arnold and social control see Jordan and Weedon 1995: 23–37). In the years that followed the Scarman Report, money was channelled by the central and local state into ethnic minority community centres and arts in an attempt to combat widespread alienation that had its roots in racism and material discrimination. Sometimes the source of funding was the Home Office, that is to say that government department responsible for immigration, police and prisons, a move that emphasizes the explicit connection made by the state between cultural provision and social control. That this continues to be the case is illustrated by the Home Office's *Connecting Communities* grant scheme, which targets ethnic minorities particularly in deprived urban areas but also insists on the involvement of white communities in its project areas.

The limits of early forms of multi-culturalism were that they tended to define, ghettoize and contain Black and South Asian culture in much the same way as the fine art establishment had ghettoized modernist artists of Colour. The cultural forms that were and are funded are often those associated with 'traditional' culture such as classical Indian dance or African drumming. Similar moves could be found in the schools in multi-cultural education, which would include the teaching of aspects of other religious and cultural traditions without necessarily dislodging the hegemony of Christianity and white British culture. Where this is thought to be under threat by leaders of the established church they tend to respond defensively. So, for example, in Autumn 2003, the Church of England called for a centralized national curriculum in religious education which would secure a privileged place for Christianity throughout the country, even in schools where the majority of students are of other faiths.

Despite shifts in policy, it has proved extremely difficult for writers and artists of Colour to move out of the category of 'ethnic art' into the mainstream.[3] As Stuart Hall argued in his keynote address to the Manchester conference on heritage in 1999, attention needs to be paid to the wide discrepancies between policy and practice. We must ask how the concept of 'British Heritage' 'is being – and how it should be – transformed by the "Black British" presence and the explosion of cultural diversity and difference which is everywhere our daily lived reality' (Hall 1999: 13). This chapter is concerned with one answer to this question.

While early moves into a discourse of multi-culturalism worked with notions of ethnic art, very different things were happening in the non-state subsidized sectors of popular culture. The increasing, postmodern commodification of difference and the success of Black cultural forms has had profound effects on popular culture. At the forefront of this development was the influence of Black American music (for example soul and rap) and Jamaican reggae. This led to the growth of an indigenous Black and South Asian British music scene producing new hybrid forms, for example, the British South Asian music known as Bhangra. As South Asian filmmaker Gurinder Chadha comments, these new forms of cultural production were important to the formation of new diasporic and hybrid forms of identity.

> Bhangra music gave us back something for ourselves, it had nothing to do with English people or white society. It also consolidated the debate about whether we are Black, British or Asian. . . . What I am saying is that we are not one thing or the other – we're everything when it suits us and one thing when it suits us, it is not exclusive or mutual.
>
> (Gurinder Chadha, Interview quoted in Ross 1996: 33)

Important, too, was the globalization of forms of youth culture that have their roots in US Black ghetto culture and include modes of dress and speech. Yet the commercial diversification of the broader 'cultural' marketplace has not been restricted to music and youth culture. The postmodern market in so-called 'ethnic' culture has reached both specialist shops, importing goods and artefacts from West Africa, Bali and other parts of the Third World, and the mainstream department stores. Whether you visit tourist shops in west Wales or Turkey, you will find the same types of imported articles, mainly from Bali.

If official policy on race, ethnicity and culture in Britain has gradually shifted since the immediate post-war years to a positive embracing of difference and diversity, this has had much to do with the interventions of a new generation of mostly British born and educated writers, filmmakers, academics, artistes and musicians. It is predominantly in the work of these writers and artistes that the wide discrepancies between official discourses of cultural diversity and the lived experience of ethnic minorities are documented and explored. In the process, questions of culture and identity are being raised and outmoded ideas of 'Britishness' challenged, together with persistent white stereotypes of non-white Britons. The history of Black contributions to the development of Britain is being rewritten through the media of history, fiction and television documentaries. Even the museum sector is beginning to take Black history seriously with new attention to colonial history, the slave trade and exhibitions and events to mark Black history month. Moreover the experience of living in racist, post-war Britain is being documented. In this body of work we find accounts of living in contemporary Britain when one is not white. Yet much of it goes unacknowledged by the gatekeepers of the hegemonic cultural institutions.

The history of African- and Asian-Caribbean migration and settlement in the UK after the Second World War has been largely invisible in post-war Britain. The half a million people who came to settle in Britain from the Caribbean in the decades immediately following the war arrived largely in response to government advertising campaigns that were aimed at attracting workers, particularly to industry and the public sector. In the mid-1950s, for example, the then Conservative government health minister, Enoch Powell, toured the Caribbean making speeches encouraging people to come and work in Britain. Subsequently Powell would become the main proponent of anti-immigration policies and repatriation. The closing off of employment possibilities in the US and the harsh economic conditions in the Caribbean, caused by under investment and neglect and intensified by particularly bad weather in 1944, which devastated the sugar cane plantations, were a further incentive to leave the islands for Britain.

Brought up within a colonial version of the English education system, migrants from the Caribbean had high expectations of life in what they had been taught to regard as the 'Mother Country'. Indeed many early immigrants had fought for Britain and seen their compatriots die during the Second World War. Testimonies by these migrants, collected for the four-part Windrush television documentary, repeatedly express their sense of shock at the poor and depressing reality they found upon arrival in Britain, an impression accentuated by the after-effects of war (*Windrush*, Part 1, BBC Television 1998).

The experience to which the new settlers in the 1950s and 1960s testify was one of discrimination and overt hostility on the part of white Britain. Itself ambivalent about immigration, the Conservative government did not inform the British people about the reasons for African-Caribbean migration and the immigrants were widely regarded as unwelcome competition for housing and jobs. The effects of the unexplained presence of large numbers of new and mostly male Black settlers on the indigenous white population was to consolidate more general fears of the Black 'other' and link them to questions of material interest ranging from jobs and housing to sexual partners. Racist forms of white identity were further strengthened by right-wing attacks on immigration, which served to legitimate individual hostility based on fear and ignorance. The effects of white hostility and of everyday racism on Black people came to the fore nationally in 1955 when the BBC screened a path-breaking documentary *Does Britain have a Colour Bar?* in which television cameras followed a well-dressed African-Caribbean immigrant around London in his futile search for accommodation.[4] Until 1966 it remained legal to discriminate in all areas of life on the grounds of race, and Black, Asian and Irish people often found themselves excluded not only from acceptable housing, but also from skilled employment and, in the case of Black people, even churches.[5]

This history of migration and life in a hostile, racist 'Mother Country' remains largely unknown to those who were not directly involved in it, yet it is a history that is crucial to the development of contemporary Britain. One place where it is being articulated is in fiction and poetry of Black and South Asian writers and I want to turn now to examples of work by writers of African- and Asian-Caribbean and African descent and to examine how their work is helping to reclaim the history of Black people in the West and, in the process, challenging and transforming exclusively white discourses of Britishness, and related conceptions of race and ethnicity. It is doing this by creating narratives that challenge the ethnocentrism of mainstream white British society, question hegemonic notions of difference and identity, and deconstruct traditional white notions of Britishness and otherness and the versions of history on which they are based. Important in this process is the act of testifying to the experience of migration and of adapting to a greater or lesser extent to life in a racist, post-war Britain.

Migration to Britain: the *Windrush* generation

As we saw in the previous chapter, having a voice and being heard are central to identity and subjectivity. Recognition by the wider society of the experience of migration is important, precisely because this experience is often negative. In this section I take the example of work by one writer from the *Windrush* generation of migrants. These writers included C.L.R. James, George Lamming, Wilson Harris and V.S. Naipaul. The early experience of migration and settlement features strongly in the London-based novels of Sam Selvon, who came to settle in Britain from the Caribbean during the war or immediately afterwards. Sam Selvon (1923–94) was of mixed Indian and Scottish descent and came to London from Trinidad in 1950. He had served as a member of the Royal Navy Reserve during the Second World War, and then worked as a journalist in Trinidad. In London he was employed as a civil servant while establishing himself as a writer. His first London novel, *The Lonely Londoners*, was published in 1956, at a time when more than 25,000 migrants from the Caribbean were coming to settle in the UK each year. It is the first of three novels that document aspects of the experience of West Indians who settled in London. It was followed in 1965 by *The Housing Lark* and in 1975 by *Moses Ascending*.

Written in what Mervyn Morris describes as 'a literary version of Trinidad speech', which uses 'creole not in dialogue only but also as the language of narration' (Selvon 1984: xi), *The Lonely Londoners* is a fictional account of life among working-class, male migrants. The explicitly Trinidadian mode of address establishes both the difference and the specificity of the voices in the text. Told by a third person narrator, it relates episodes from the life of Moses Aloetta, who has been settled in London for ten years, and Henry Oliver – known as Sir Galahad – who arrives at Waterloo Station from Trinidad in the opening pages of the novel. The narrative also depicts aspects of the lives of the other African-Caribbean men with whom they associate. The text is structured as a set of episodes from everyday life – some contemporary, some flashbacks – which the narrator refers to as 'ballads' and which give the text a feel of the Trinidadian oral tradition upon which it draws. Yet the novel is much more than a series of episodes about early migrant experience. Focused on Moses, one of the immigrants who has been longest in Britain and whose basement flat serves as a regular meeting point for the various characters, it contrasts Moses' view of life in Britain after ten years' experience of life in London with that of the newcomers. Moreover, the narrative gives a vivid picture of the poverty, loneliness and racism that the men experience on a day-to-day basis. Most are employed in factories, paid less that their white counterparts and have to work nights to make a living. They live in damp, unpleasant rooms for which white landlords charge exorbitant rents. The novel details the experience of the labour exchange, the search for accommodation, living and working conditions and social life. It also tells of the sexual exploits of a variety of single male characters, who, in a world largely bereft of Black women and family life, concentrate on 'hunting down' as much 'white pussy' as possible. Although the text contains much humour, its overall message is of the poverty of life on the margins of white society. It makes clear the impossibility of the male characters being accepted as part of mainstream white society and evokes the outsider identities that they are forced to adopt.

Selvon's 1975 novel *Moses Ascending*, also features Moses as the central character. It tells of how he buys a decrepit house with a five-year lease, due for demolition by the council on expiry, and becomes a landlord. In a reversal of usual roles, Moses employs a white 'man Friday', Bob, to look after the tenants and retires to the penthouse flat to write his memoirs. The Moses of this text is depicted as an apolitical man who is in search of a quiet life. Yet inadvertently, in his role as a landlord and in his quest for material for his book, he finds himself involved both with members of the Black Power movement, who organize from his basement, and with Pakistanis who trade in illegal South Asian immigrants, using his house as a staging post. On two occasions he experiences police brutality at first hand and the combined effect of both these episodes forces him to reflect on police behaviour and abandon his 'philosophy of neutrality' that marks him off from younger and more radical Black people (Selvon 1984: 97). His first violent encounter with the police is at a Black power demonstration in Trafalgar Square that he comes upon by chance. When a fight breaks out the police descend on the crowd:

> A set of Blacks was being towed, propelled, and dragged across Trafalgar Square. The place like it was full up of police as if the whole metropolitan force was lurking in the side streets waiting for signal. Blue lights flashing, radio-telephones going, sirens blowing, Alsatians baring their teeth for the kill, and Black Maria waiting with the doors fling wide open in welcome.
>
> (Selvon 1984: 36)

Commenting on the experience Moses betrays important aspects of the effects of racism on Black subjectivity, combining references to Black history with images from Hollywood cinema.

> I do not know about you, but it is a shuddering thought for a Black man to be locked up by the police. Once you are in, it is foregone conclusion that they will throw away the key. There was no protests from any of the passengers saying that they was innocent and shouldn't be here, nobody struggling to get out like me, nobody saying anything at all. Like we was all in the hold of a slave ship. I remember them stories I used to read, how the innocent star boy get condemned to the galleys. Next thing you see him in chains, with beard on his face, wrestling with one of them big oars like what stevedores have in Barbados when they loading the ships.
>
> Any minute now the timekeeper was going to crack a whip in the Black Maria. I wonder if I play dead if they would jettison me in the Thames. And I could make my escape.
>
> (Selvon 1984: 36–7)

On the second occasion, Moses is present when the police break up a peaceful Black power meeting and people leave the hall in panic. In trying to understand what is going on, he is forced to realize that the police are far from neutral:

> I try to rationalize the situation. Okay. So it must have had some wanted criminals in the hall, in spite of the respectable aspects of the meeting. Right? So the police make a raid and bust up the gathering. Right? That was it, simple and plain. Right?
>
> I catch a bus 52 in Ladbroke Grove and went to Notting Hill Gate and catch a 88 and went home, but I still couldn't convince myself that it was a simple as all that. I was beginning to get vex now; my dignity was affronted as I imagined myself pelting down the road terror-stricken when I didn't do nothing at all, not even spit on the pavement or smoke in a non-smoking compartment. Was all of we in the hall criminals that we had to jump up and flee for our very lives? There we was, sitting down, and I was just writing down the words of the Party anthem,

when we was so rudely interrupted. My blood begin to boil. I had half a mind to get back there and ask the Inspector himself what was the meaning of this outrage? 'How dare you intrude on this peaceful gathering,' I would say, 'and strike terror into the hearts of these innocent people.' And I would ask him for his name, number and rank, and report him to the Chief of Scotland Yard.

(Selvon 1984: 95–6)

Moses is forced to begin to see society in the way younger Black people do, that is as fundamentally racist and this puts into question his preferred identity as respectable, non-political retired landlord. Reflecting on his life he has to conclude that his experience of Britain, of the 'Mother Country', has been far from positive:

I don't know if I can describe it properly, not being a man of words, but I had a kind of sad feeling that all Black people was doomed to suffer, and that we would never make any headway in Brit'n. As if it always have a snag, no matter how hard we struggle or try to stay out of trouble. After spending the best years of my life in the Mother Country it was dismal conclusion to come to, making you feel that one and one make zero. It wasn't so much depression as sheer terror really, to see you life falling to pieces like that.

(Selvon 1984: 35)

Second generation writers and the migrant experience

That the younger British born and/or educated Black people who followed the Windrush generation should be more radical is unsurprising. Whereas first generation migrants had grown up and developed a strong sense of identity in the Caribbean and continued to see themselves as Jamaicans, St Lucians, Bajans and so on even after moving to Britain, their children's experiences were very different. Schooling brought them up against white racism at an early age and they were definitely British whether or not white society wished to accept them as such. Identity was thus a difficult issue and many young Black people turned to alternative sources of positive Black identity, mostly imported from the US and the Caribbean in the face of white racism. These included Black power and Rastafarianism.

During the 1960s and 1970s, everyday life for Black people was marked by increasing levels of racism and, from the late 1950s onwards, there was a rise in right-wing, anti-immigration groups that culminated in the founding of the National Front in 1966. From their inception, these groups found particular support in the West Midlands, where large-scale Black and South Asian settlement occurred in a heavily industrialized region with a particularly severe housing shortage. Local MP Enoch Powell exploited the situation to the full, whipping up sometimes violent hostility to immigration throughout Britain. His speeches urged an end to immigration and the repatriation of Black people. On 20 April 1968 he went so far as to predict future violent racial conflict if his policies were not implemented: 'As I look ahead, I am filled with foreboding. Like the Roman, I seem to see the River Tiber flowing with much blood' (*www.sterlingtimes.co.uk/powell_press.htm*).

The second generation of writers includes well-known writers such as Caryl Phillips and David Dabydeen who are published by mainstream presses and other less well known writers, such as Joan Riley and Vernella Fuller, published by the Women's Press, who are either British born or the children of immigrants who have been brought up and educated in the UK from an early age. It is in the work of this second generation that questions of culture and identity are raised most sharply and racism documented in its full brutality. These writers mobilize recent history in support of the postcolonial project of decolonizing Black identities, producing new forms of Black British identity and reshaping ideas of British culture and nation. They use fiction to articulate silenced voices, to explore inter-cultural and cross-generational conflicts, and to produce new hybrid identities and cultural forms. They challenge those forms of white subjectivity and ideas of history and nation that allow racism and ethnocentrism to flourish and refuse to acknowledge white complicity in and responsibility for the position in which Black people find themselves in today.

Joan Riley and Caryl Phillips, both born in the Caribbean but educated in Britain, offer particularly bleak pictures of the experience of post-war migration to the Mother Country. Phillips' novel, *The Final Passage* (Phillips 1999), published by Faber & Faber in 1985, and dedicated to his parents, describes the experience of their generation as they move from the Caribbean to Britain around 1960. The central protagonist, Leila, is the 19-year-old, mixed-race daughter of a Black mother and a white father whom she has never known. Leila enters into a disastrous marriage with Michael, who already has a relationship and a child by another woman whose own husband has gone to America. Leila's mother, a mere 40 years old, is seriously ill and leaves for England to seek medical treatment. Leila follows her once her first child is born, hoping that she and Michael can make a new start there. Michael looks to a better life than cutting cane.

In London the couple learn the reality of migrant life. They find that Leila's mother's letters home bear no resemblance to the terrible conditions under which she has been living. Now in hospital, she dies and is buried in a grave with two other coffins. Forced to live in degrading conditions in London, the couple are unable to make a success of their marriage and Michael leaves Leila, once more pregnant, to live with a white woman. Ill and emotionally disturbed, Leila resolves to return to the Caribbean.

The Final Passage covers many of the issues facing new immigrants to Britain in the post-war decades. It gives a vivid picture of the hostile reception that new migrants received from white Britain and covers issues such as stereotyping and the interplay of racial and sexual issues as they affect Black people. Michael has been warned by a migrant who has returned to the Caribbean that: 'England don't be no joke for a coloured man' (Phillips 1999: 105). Leila's best friend Millie warns her: 'I hear the white women do anything to get their hands on a piece of coloured man' (Phillips 1999: 114) and that 'home is where you feel a welcome' (Phillips 1999: 115). Yet letters home from emigrants tell a different story: 'They say every coloured man in England have a good job that can pay at least $100 a week' (Phillips 1999: 104). The new arrivals soon come up against the reality of everyday racism: in London the signs in the houses say: 'No Coloureds', 'No vacancies' and 'No children'. Landlords in houses without signs make excuses, so that Leila feels grateful for the honesty of the explicit 'No Coloureds' signs. The house that they rent through an agent turns out to be a dirty, damp slum. Edwin, Leila's mother's landlord, warns Michael: '[T]hey treat us worse than their dogs. The women expect you to do tricks with your biceps and sing calypso, or to drop down on one knee and pretend you're Paul Robeson or somebody . . . and you going to behave like a kettle, for without knowing it you going to boil. It's how the white man in this country kills off the coloured man. He makes you heat up and blow yourself away' (Phillips 1999: 168).

The racism, indifference and hostility of much of white Britain, documented in these texts, gave rise to the growth of self-help organizations among African-Caribbean settlers. Unwelcome in mainstream institutions, they developed social networks based on their homes and eventually founded their own churches, clubs and social centres. For example, the pardoner system, brought from Jamaica, enabled the purchase of houses in a climate where racism made it difficult to find decent rented accommodation. This involved a group of people paying a weekly amount into a fund, which was then lent to one individual to form the basis, for example, of the deposit on a house. Some of these strategies for survival figure in Joan Riley's second novel, *Waiting in the Twilight* (1987) which tells the story of one woman's life from her childhood and early adulthood in Jamaica, where she worked as a seamstress, to her death in Britain. The central protagonist of *Waiting in the Twilight*, Adella, migrates to Britain to join her husband and is eventually reduced to life as a disabled council cleaner, abandoned by her husband, but with children some of who, at least, are proving successful. Class, racism, ethnicity and gender all play their part in her bleak and unhappy life story.

Waiting in the Twilight draws on many aspects of the collective experience of migrants to Britain focusing on questions of identity and self-respect. It details the treatment that working-class, Black women received from whites, for example, Adella in her job as a council cleaner:

'Johnson!' The insolence ran through her and she gripped the mop tighter with her feeling hand, forcing back anger that still bubbled up after so many years. 'Thou shalt rise up before the hoary head,' she muttered under her breath, 'No wonda yu treat yu old people dem so bad.'

'Yes, mam . . .' she said aloud, turning to see a young white girl, not more than seventeen years old. Her feet had left a fresh trail of mud, and Adella's mouth thinned. This one had been working less than six months and already she had learnt how to treat the cleaning staff. Adella wanted to ask if this was how she was at home; bit back the words. Of course, this was how they all behaved: everybody knew what white people were like.

(Riley 1987: 2)

An appeal to cultural difference, in this case the treatment of old people, in the face of white racism, serves to sustain some form of positive identity for Adella. The narrative moves between her perspective on her life in Britain and flashbacks to Jamaica which throw light on how she has become what she is. The depiction of Adella's Jamaican experience highlights the cultural differences between the two societies and sets the scene for her subsequent life in Britain where class, gender, poverty, disablement and lack of family support magnify the effects of racism. Adella's early life as a seamstress in Jamaica is marred by her seduction by a married man, who forces her to live as his mistress in return for support for herself and their children. These flashbacks help the reader to understand Adella's attitude to her life in Britain. Gender relations in Jamaica are depicted as patriarchal. Women have little power outside the structures of the family but the extended family offers an important material and emotional support network that is absent in Britain. On moving to Britain, the novel suggests, African-Caribbean women become exposed to much harsher patriarchal oppression within the isolation of the nuclear family and Black men are likely to become more emotionally and physically violent and less responsible because of their own experience of racism in the wider society. Moreover cultural difference, the difference between the family, religion and codes of respectability in Jamaica and Britain make it impossible for Adella to explain, even to her British-born children, why she cannot return to live in Jamaica.

Identity and belonging

Being 'black' in Britain is about a state of 'becoming' (racialized); a process of consciousness, when colour becomes the defining factor about who you are. Located through your 'otherness' a 'conscious coalition' emerges: a self-consciously constructed space where identity is not inscribed by a natural identification but a political kinship. Now living submerged in whiteness, physical difference becomes a defining issue, a signifier, a mark of whether or not you belong. Thus to be black in Britain is to share a common structural location; a racial location.

(Mirza 1997: 3)

A key form that the reclaiming of history takes in Black British writing is the first person narrative, which functions as an apparently transparent testimony to experience. The 1980s saw the publication of novels by David Dabydeen and Joan Riley – both born in the Caribbean and relocated to Britain as children – that testify to the experience of migration and growing up in the UK. They deal with themes of the dislocation associated with migration to Britain, questions of identity and belonging, alienation, prejudice and racism. Riley's debut novel, *The Unbelonging* (1985) focuses in particular on how racism shapes identity. Written as a first person narrative, the novel tells of the experience of coming to Britain as a child, suffering abuse from a violent father and growing up as the only Black child in an English children's home. Here, the protagonist, Hyacinth, is subject to racism and deprived of any sense of Black identity, family or community. The novel depicts a Britain that many white people would wish to forget, graphically demonstrating the effects of practices that are at once racist and officially colour-blind. It is only when Hyacinth reaches university that she comes into contact with other Black people. Yet by now she has internalized white standards and values and sees other Black people through white eyes. The novel shows how her fruitless search for a sense of identity and belonging takes her back to her family roots in Jamaica which she had left behind as a young child. Here she finds a world radically different from that of her early childhood memories and subsequent dreams. Her experience is one of displacement: she finds that she belongs to neither world. Hyacinth becomes a diasporic subject in a negative sense, unable to root a positive form of identity in either Britain or Jamaica and unable to occupy those hybrid and plural identities that postcolonial critics tend to celebrate.

Yet, cultural difference can be a source of positive forms of identity from which to resist racism. This is made clear in Joan Riley's third novel, *Romance* (1988), which tells the story of two sisters who come to London from Guyana as small children. The novel traces the women's difficult paths to liberation based on the acquisition of a strong individual sense of identity and purpose. For Desiree, liberation means the transformation of her oppressive marriage and a redefinition of herself as something other than just wife and mother. For Verona liberation means the slow and painful process of coming to terms with sexual abuse, her fear of Black men and her flight from reality into romantic fiction and over-eating. As in *The Unbelonging*, Black men are presented as a source of fear, something for which Joan Riley has been criticized, since it raises questions of the politics of representation in a society where Black men are often seen in negative racist terms. In the case of both sisters, the support of other Black women and the influence of Jamaican cultural values are depicted as crucial.

Joan Riley's novels suggest that subjectivity and identity are socially constructed by the society within which one lives. In her novels, predominantly white racist societies, offer no positive subject positions or identities for Black people who are forced to look to each other and to Black cultural traditions for alternatives. Yet the very process of unmasking racist and patriarchal power relations and their implications for subjectivity – a major theme of the novels – helps to create conditions for developing positive forms of identity.

David Dabydeen's novel, *The Intended*, first published in 1991 in many ways parallels Riley's novel, *The Unbelonging*. It is the story of a young boy's life from his arrival in London from Guyana at the age of 12 to his departure for Oxford to study literature. Guyanese Asian, like Dabydeen himself, he is brought up by his mother in

New Amsterdam until his father, who is living in London, sends for him. After a few months, his father abandons him to social services and he grows up in a children's home, moving out at 16 to rent a room from an Asian landlord. The narrative moves back and forth between the London of his teenage years and his childhood in his grandparents' village, Albion, in Guyana. It is focused on the protagonist and his groups of friends and is set outside of the school context. As in Riley's work, identity in a racist society is the central issue in the novel. Other themes include teenage masculinity, sex, the police, violence, the effects of colonialism in Guyana, the boy's relationship to England and his desire not to be an eternal immigrant, that is, to belong.

The novel depicts how, from his first day at school in Britain, racial divides in the playground force the narrator to make contacts with other boys from the Asian diaspora with whom he has little else in common:

> The white boys were howling and spinning around a football, or lashing out with cricket bats, whilst Shaz and Patel stood against a wall watching. It was my first week at an English school and feeling isolated from the gang warfare I gladly sought out their company. Nasim, recently arrived from Pakistan, also gravitated in their direction and the four of us found ourselves together each school break. It was a regrouping of the Asian diaspora in a South London school ground. Shaz, of Pakistani parents was born in Britain, had never travelled to the sub-continent, could barely speak a word of Urdu and had never seen the interior of a mosque. Nasim was more authentically Muslim, a believer by upbringing, fluent in his ancestral language and devoted to family. Patel was of Hindu stock, could speak Gudjerati; his mother, who once visited the school to bring her other son, wore a sari and a dot on her forehead. I was an Indian West-Indian Guyanese, the most mixed up of the lot. There we were together in our school blazers and ties and grey trousers, but the only real hint of our shared Asian-ness was the brownness of our skins. Even that was not uniform.
>
> (Dabydeen 1991: 5–6)

The sense of vulnerability in the face of white racism, which creates alliances between boys from very different backgrounds, also creates a violent rejection of victimization in which the victim is blamed, rather than the oppressors. The text offers insights into the psychological damage that racism causes its subjects. Thus, when Nasim is hospitalized after being run over while trying to escape a racist attack, the narrator visits him in hospital and instead of sympathy, he feels hatred:

> I hated him. A strange desire to hurt him, to kick him, overcame me. . . . I watched him, not knowing what to say, distressed, feeling a bitter contempt, especially at the sight of his stupid, helpless eyes peeping out between the bandages. He was a little, brown-skinned, beaten animal. His wounds were meant for all of us, he had suffered them for all of us, but he had no right to. It was Nasim's impotence which

was so maddening, the shamefulness of it. I knew immediately that Patel, Shaz and I could never be his friend again, because he had allowed himself to be humiliated. We would avoid him in school because he reminded us of our own weakness, our own fear.

(Dabydeen 1991: 14)

His sense of identity is also negatively shaped by the fear of white censure, which provokes a desire to distance himself from other South Asians. When Nasim's family arrive at the hospital bedside, he is embarrassed by their difference of dress, language and culture and wants to escape all association with their Asianness. Racism is shown to permeate not only the narrator's sense of self, leading him to deny his origins, but his everyday life. This ranges from racist imagery on rides at Battersea Funfair, to abusive customers in Patel's father's video shop. He describes how the 'World Cruise' ride depicts, among other things:

A black woman with full breasts and gleaming thighs carried a pot on her head. Another sat on a donkey so oddly – her buttocks merged into its flank – that it seemed she was having some kind of bizarre sex with it.
Someone had scrawled 'nigger out' on her body and had drawn a fat penis pointed at her mouth.

(Dabydeen 1991: 78)

Yet, the text suggests that such racism is not restricted to white attitudes to Blacks and Asians, but also affects South Asian attitudes to Black people. When their African-Caribbean friend Joseph fails to switch on his stolen camera while filming Shaz shouts:

'You're just like one of those savages chewing on bone on the river bank and scooting off whenever the white man blows the steamer horn'.

(Dabydeen 1991: 106)

'You're like a monkey playing with all those dials, and you don't have a clue what they mean. The white man has got to regret the day he took you people out of the bush and showed you science.'

(Dabydeen 1991: 107)

The narrator describes how white norms and prejudices affect his own reaction to young West Indians on the late night bus who are talking loudly, swearing and drinking beer from cans:

I wished they would behave, act respectfully, keep quiet, read a book, anything, instead of displaying such vulgar rowdiness. No wonder they are treated like animals, I heard myself thinking, distancing myself from all this noisy West Indian-ness, and feeling sympathy for the outnumbered whites. They should send them back home. All they do is dance and breed. Not one 'O' level between the bus load of them and yet they complain they've got no jobs, no proper housing, no future. If they stayed home and studied, they'd get somewhere. But no, it's dance hall and shiny shoes and expensive clothes. I'm different really. I come from their place. I'm dark-skinned like them, but I am different, and I hope the whites can see that and separate me from that lot. I'm an Indian really, deep down I'm decent and quietly spoken and hard-working and I respect good manners, books, art, philosophy. I'm like the whites, we both have civilisation. If they send immigrants home, they should differentiate between us Indian people and those Black West Indians. I was glad I was sitting next to Shaz, one of my own, with brown skin and straight hair.

(Dabydeen 1991: 177–8)

Ironically here anti-Black racism in the face of white censure causes him to identify with South Asianness, but above all he envies what he perceives as the uncomplicated sense of belonging reserved for white people. When his white friend Janet shows him photographs of the Kent village where she grew up, he fingers them 'in a mood of sullen envy':

Our lives were messy by contrast: families scattered across the West, settling in one country or another depending on the availability of visas; we lived from hand to mouth, hustling or thieving or working nightshifts and sleeping daytime; we were ashamed of our past, frightened of the present and not daring to think of the future. When I looked at the images of her mother and father in their neat house and manicured garden the first instinct was to inflict pain, to shatter the security of their lives, for in some vague way I felt they were responsible for my own disordered existence . . .

(Dabydeen 1991: 168)

Deep down I preferred to believe in her photographs, I wishes I belonged to her family and the village she came from with all its protections and confident virtues . . .

(Dabydeen 1991: 169)

I didn't want to be an eternal, indefinite immigrant.

(Dabydeen 1991: 243)

New forms of resistance

As the decades progressed and second-generation children grew up in often unsupportive and openly racist school environments, there was a marked growth in resistance to the racism and discrimination that Black people experienced on a day-to-day basis. Powellism and the growth of the National Front brought with them national demonstrations against immigration and increased attacks on Black people and their homes. In response, protests, even riots, became the order of the day. The targets of attacks by teddy boys in the 1950s and right-wing groups in the 1960s and 1970s, Black people found little help or support from the police with whom they increasingly came into conflict. The police themselves operated racist practices which ranged from failing to investigate crimes against Black people to harassment through raids on Black premises and the repeated use on stop and search on the streets under the so-called 'sus' laws.

Police treatment of young Black people is a central theme of Diran Adebayo's first novel *Some Kind of Black* (1996) which depicts being Black and British in the 1990s and takes up many themes similar to those found in Selvon's *Moses Ascending* some two decades earlier. The novel contrasts the very different racisms of university life in Oxford and the everyday life of young Blacks – African and African-Caribbean – in London. Set in 1993, the story tells of a few months in the life of a young British Nigerian Dele, brought up in London, in a traditional Nigerian family, currently in his final year of study at Oxford. It depicts his life, in London and Oxford, before and after a police beating injures him and nearly kills his sister who has sickle-cell anaemia. Like Selvon, Adebayo offers a picture of working-class hustling and Black politics. Dele's encounter with the police leads to his involvement in a campaign for justice for his sister and a rejection of his Oxford experience where he had been feted by rich white students as a token Black:

> Dele wasn't necessarily talented or beautiful either, but up here there just wasn't a big enough supply of brothers to go round. Well, there were the bloods who laboured at the British Leyland plant and lived on the big estates down Cowley way, on the east side, but they didn't count in the student scale of things. Up here, Dele was what you'd call a Mr Mention. A player. X amount of invites to events and launches littered his college pigeon-hole.
>
> After three years of sharing his sense and flexing across the city, Dele was now the undisputed number one Negro.
>
> (Adebayo 1996: 19)

The novel depicts a radical contrast between Dele's Oxford experience and life in London where he is forced to confront the everyday experience of less privileged Black people, including police harassment and drug culture. The picture of Black radicalism is both detailed and at times negative, suggesting that individual self-interest leads some Black activists to exploit other members of the Black community. Yet it is not only various forms of white racism, Black politics and police brutality that are shown to shape Dele's identity, it is conflict with his father who is determined that he should grow up a proper Nigerian not the hybrid, bi-cultural Black Britain that he has become. The novel offers a graphic picture of student life in Oxford, politics among Blacks in London, police brutality and the world of disaffected young Blacks.

Mixed-race identity

If African-Caribbean and African origins cause identity problems for British-born Blacks subject to racism, being mixed-race is no less complicated. Growing up mixed-race in Britain in the late 1950s, 1960s and 1970s is the central focus of Lucinda Roy's first novel *Lady Moses* (1998). It recounts the first thirty-six years in the life of a mixed-race woman, Jacinta Louise Buttercup Moses, born and brought up in Battersea, London. Jacinta is the daughter of a white English former actress, Louise Buttercup and a West African father, Simon Moses, who works in a Brillo Pad factory and writes stories about Africa that only receive acclaim long after his death. He dies when Jacinta is 5 and the narrative focuses on mother-daughter relationships, placed within the wider immediate community with its poverty, social deprivation and everyday racism.

After her father's death, Jacinta lives with her mother and the lodgers in her parents' house, where she becomes a victim of her mother's inability to come to terms with Simon's death. Although very poor, Jacinta is educated at the local Catholic convent school and goes on to study English at university. Keen to escape a childhood and adolescence overdetermined by racism, she marries a white American, Manny, and emigrates to the US. Here she has a daughter who is born missing an arm and her marriage begins to founder when Manny rejects his daughter. He is subsequently killed in a car accident while the couple are living in West Africa where Jacinta has insisted that they go to enable her to find her own roots.

Lady Moses focuses on questions of identity and belonging shaped by poverty, social class and racism. It explores the issue of mixed-race identity through a search to belong in a world not overdetermined by questions of race. Like Riley's Hyacinth in *The Unbelonging*, and the narrator of the Dabydeen's *The Intended*, Roy's central character looks beyond Britain to an imagined world for a positive identity. For Jacinta it is the world of her father's stories of Africa. The search to belong takes Jacinta back to Africa and her father's family, an experience which is at once both affirming and a source of realization that here, too, she is different, namely of dual heritage:

> I hadn't thought enough about my mother's race and my own. I was mixed race; Louise Buttercup was white, my father was African. Yet I wasn't simply the bringing together of two opposites. I was me. Distinct. A race apart . . . I wanted to know other people like myself. It would be a luxury to talk with someone who understood what Blackness meant from a white perspective and what whiteness meant inside the dark.
>
> (Roy 1998: 300)

Rewriting history

Recent Black British writing not only deals with post-war history and experience, but also with the little known history of Black people in the West. Perhaps the most widely acclaimed second generation Black British writer, Caryl Phillips, tells the long history of people of African descent in the West since the slave trade. David Dabydeen, too, has written historical novels about the colonialist creation of the Caribbean South Asian diaspora (*The Counting House*, 1997) and of Blacks in London in the eighteenth century (*A Harlot's Progress*, 1999). Phillips' novels cover the slave trade and plantation life (*Crossing the River*, 2000; *Higher Ground*, 1989 and *Cambridge*, 1991), and the subsequent experience of Blacks after the end of slavery. He also deals with the history of the Jews in *Higher Ground*.

These novels not only bring to life a little known history, drawing on period source materials, but also raise the complex question of culture and identity in an historical context. For example, Black history and subjectivity are at the centre of Phillips' novel about the slave trade and plantation life *Cambridge* (1991), which also details white attitudes to the treatment of Black people. This novel tells the story of the visit by an absentee planter's daughter, Emily, to his estate in the Caribbean. It details her voyage from England to the island and her stay on the estate. The novel gives details of the workings of the plantation from a white perspective, drawing on period sources and incorporating nineteenth-century white racist ideas about African and Creole slaves. Set in the years between the abolition of the slave trade and the abolition of slavery in the West Indies, the novel raises questions about the nature and legitimacy of slavery from the perspective of the period in which it is set and juxtaposes the planter's daughter's narrative with that of an educated African slave, Cambridge, who had been freed by his master in Britain and re-enslaved by the trickery of the captain transporting him back to Africa as a missionary.

The text cleverly juxtaposes competing narratives, consisting of a prologue in England, Emily's journal, the local press version of the murder of the plantation manager, Brown, by Cambridge, Cambridge's lifestory and an epilogue in which Emily gives birth to the stillborn child of the manager. It shows how context moulds both subjectivity and identity. When Emily sets out for the Caribbean, her motives are philanthropic: 'Perhaps my adventuring will encourage Father to accept the increasingly common, though abstract, English belief in the iniquity of slavery' (Phillips 1991: 7–8). Her perspective is shown to change as she becomes more familiar with plantation life and forms a relationship with the harsh and incompetent plantation manager. She becomes complicit in white justifications of slavery and concludes: 'It would appear that Mr Wilberforce and his like have been volleying well wide of the mark, for the greatest fear of the Black is not having a master whom they know they can turn to in times of strife' (Phillips 1991: 37).

Cambridge's narrative is written in prison as he awaits execution. It tells his life story from his capture as a 15-year-old in Africa to the killing of Brown. The narrative informs the reader of aspects of the slave trade and attitudes towards slavery and Blacks in Britain. It details the capture of slaves and the middle passage. Olumide, as Cambridge was originally called, is transported to South Carolina and then straight on to England to become the house servant of the now retiring captain. He is renamed Thomas on the ship and taught the rudiments of English. He lives happily for ten years in the captain's house, receives an education and becomes a Christian called David Henderson. With the blessing of his master, he has a short-lived marriage with a white servant who dies in childbirth. On his return to London, after his master's death, he finds he has been left 400 guineas by the captain and sets out as a missionary to Africa but is re-enslaved by the ship's captain and a fellow cabin passenger who steal his money. He is transported to a plantation in the Caribbean, where he gains the respect of the other slaves and lives in the hope that he will be freed from slavery. His identity remains that of a devout Christian and a wronged free Englishman, not an African, nor a slave.

In another example, Phillips' novel *Crossing the River* (2000), the text portrays episodes of Black life over 250 years. The text delivers detailed fictive episodes from Black history that seek to connect the position of diasporic Black people today with their history. The individual stories are framed by a brief prologue and an epilogue. Here a West African tells of how he sold his two sons and daughter into slavery when the crops failed and how he has been mourning them ever since. The characters in the sections that follow the prologue bear the names of these children: Nash, Martha and Travis. Part One is the story of freed slave Nash Williams, sent by his master as a missionary to Liberia, and Edward Williams, his former master who travels to Liberia to find him. Part Two, 'West', is the story of Martha, a slave who is sold on after the plantation owner dies, and who loses both her husband and her daughter who are bought by others. Part Three, 'Crossing the River', comprises the journal of the captain of the slave ship the Duke of York on its voyage to West Africa in 1752. This is the trip on which the African in the prologue sells his sons and daughter and the story gives graphic details of the slave trade, based on original sources. Part Four, set 'Somewhere in England', tells the story of Joyce, a working-class northern girl, and Travis, an American GI posted to a village somewhere in the north of England. Through these various narratives, Phillips raises important cultural and political questions, central to the Black experience and throws light on how the past has shaped the present. In the epilogue the African, who sold his children into slavery, reflects on the following 250 years of the African diaspora and on the importance of history and collective memory to survival:

> For two hundred and fifty years I have listened. To voices in the streets of Charleston. (The slave who mounted this block is now dying from copping a fix on some rusty needle in an Oakland project.) I have listened. To reggae rhythms of rebellion and revolution dipping through the hills and valleys of the Caribbean. I have listened. To the saxophone player on a wintry night in Stockholm. A long

way from home. For two hundred and fifty years I have listened. To my Nash. My Martha. My Travis. *Joyce. That was all he said. Just, Joyce. I could now see the gap in the middle of his teeth. At the bottom. And then he reached out and pulled me towards him. I couldn't believe it. He'd come back to me. He really wanted me. That day, crying on the platform, safe in Travis's arms.* For two hundred and fifty years I have listened. To the haunting voices. Singing: Mercy, Mercy Me. (The Ecology.) Insisting: Man, I ain't got no quarrel with them Vietcong. Declaring: Brothers and Friends. I am Toussaint L'Ouverture, my name is perhaps known to you. Listened to: Papa Doc. Baby Doc. Listened to the voices hoping for: Freedom. Democracy. Singing: Baby, baby. Where did our love go? Samba. Calypso. Jazz. Jazz. Sketches of Spain in Harlem. In a Parisian bookstore a voice murmurs the words. Nobody Knows My Name. I have listened to the voice that cried: I have a dream that one day on the red hills of Georgia, the sons of former slaves and the sons of former slave owners will be able to sit down together at a table of brotherhood. I have listened to the sound of an African carnival in Trinidad. In Rio. In New Orleans. On the far bank of the river, a drum continues to be beaten. A many-tongued chorus continues to swell. And I hope that amongst these survivors' voices I might occasionally hear those of my own children. My Nash. My Martha. My Travis. My daughter. Joyce. All. Hurt but determined.

(Phillips 2000: 236–7)

Conclusion

Writing of contemporary African-Americans, bell hooks suggests that:

> resistance struggle must be rooted in a process of decolonization that continually opposes re-inscribing notions of 'authentic' black identity. This critique should not be made synonymous with a dismissal of the struggle of oppressed and exploited peoples to make ourselves subjects. Nor should it deny that in certain circumstances this experience affords us a privileged critical location from which to speak, this is not a reinscription of modernist master narratives of authority which privilege some voices by denying voice to others. Part of our struggle for radical black subjectivity is the quest to find ways to construct self and identity that are oppositional and liberatory.

(hooks 1991: 29)

History is crucial to the process of decolonizing identities and showing them to be complex, located and contingent, rather than fixed, authentic and true. History is important since it has made the present what it is and how we understand the present will depend, in part, on the versions of history to which we have access. Phillips' work marks a highly accessible attempt to retell the history of Black people in the West in ways that challenge the hegemonic narratives of history on which Britishness is founded. Historically grounded fiction is a powerful tool in the evocation of the past. It offers a way into history that brings it alive and can deal not only with past events, but with imaginative reconstructions of complex forms of subjectivity and identity and how they were shaped by changing forms of racism. Literary texts can evoke what past social relations meant and felt like to those involved. They can engage the emotions of the reader in an empathy that can give a sense of what it was like to be the subject of racism or slavery and a victim of oppression. They can voice the experience, views and perspectives of those groups not usually heard in the pages of history books. They can evoke the role of white people in the history of colonialism and its legacies and show the complexities of Black and white relations.

In talking to Black people who came to Britain as part of the *Windrush* generation, it became clear to me that it is the unwillingness of white Britons to acknowledge the past that is found most disturbing by Black people. The selective amnesia about racism in Britain in the post-war period, and the histories of slavery and colonization that preceded it, desperately need remedying in the interests of a contemporary Britain in which diversity is welcomed not merely tolerated. Recent Black British writing is making an important contribution to this process. It is beginning the process of repositioning Black Britons in relation to hegemonic white-centred narratives of Britishness and British history, challenging racist processes of othering non-white Britons and creating narrative that allow for positive forms of identity.

Further reading

Arana, V. and Ramey, L. (eds) (2004) *Black British Writing*. New York: Palgrave Macmillan.

Black, L. (1996) *New Ethnicities and Urban Culture: Racisms and Multiculture in Young Lives*. London: UCL Press.

Bryan, B, Dadzie, S. and Scafe, S. (1985) *The Heart of the Race*. London: Virago.

Fryer, P. (1984) *Staying Power*. London: Pluto.

Procter, J. (2003) *Dwelling Places: Postwar Black British Writing*. Manchester: Manchester University Press.

Wasafiri (Quarterly Journal) London: University of London, Queen Mary College.

IDENTITY, ORIGINS AND ROOTS

. . . And Still I rise!

On the West Coast of Africa, where millions of slaves saw their homeland for the last time, African-Americans now search for the memories of their ancestors. With a new millennium, many African-Americans are sensing that the ancient wisdom of the past should be re-discovered. They feel the calls of the ancient sacred places growing stronger.

That is what our company is all about – Heritage, knowledge, culture and fun. The development of self and spirit through the discovery of one's origins at special sites and countries scattered throughout our world.

The difference between an 'African-American Journey' and traditional tours is the difference between visiting a destination and experiencing it. Travelers don't only want to understand the social, cultural and religious aspects of a society, but they want to discover that place in their consciousness. They want to become an intimate part of that experience. To 'feel' it, not just 'see' it.

Most important, they want to share the entire experience with other like-minded travelers. To travel with those who understand and believe in learning about the past and sharing a vacation of a lifetime. To be greeted with a warm friendly smile, 'my brother' or 'my sister' and then an embrace.

(*www.africanamericanjourneys.com*, copyright © 2000 montauk-online.com)

The desire to be from somewhere, to have a sense of roots and a feeling of belonging are key features of the quest for positive identity in postmodern, post-colonial societies. The current popularity of genealogy and family history point to this need, as does the marketing of family names, crests and the like. It is also manifest in the popularity of tourism concerned with roots and heritage. For diasporic peoples, this concern with roots often leads to a quest for the place from which their forebears originally came and sometimes even for an original, authentic identity (see Hall 1990). Often 'roots and heritage' tourism is organized and marketed with reference to histories that include the slave trade, colonial displacement, transportation or migration for economic reasons. Thus, while many Irish-Americans trace their roots back to an Ireland that their ancestors were force to leave during the famine, African-American and African-Caribbean peoples look to West Africa for their roots.

The quotation that introduces this chapter comes from publicity posted on the website of *africanamericanjourneys.com*, a company specializing in tours aimed at African-Americans that offers 'the opportunity to travel with like-minded people to some of the world's most sacred sites'. The promotional language used is in its own way quite remarkable. It evokes a sense of a long and distant past, which is a source of wisdom, memory and spirituality. It assumes that the place of origin of one's forebears is etched in one's consciousness. It stresses a search for the memories of one's ancestors and for ancient wisdom. The emphasis in the company's marketing is on culture, history and emotional and spiritual well-being: 'Our custom-designed itineraries include the rich culture and ancient history of these countries, as well as their diverse spiritual heritage. They are led by authors and recognized authorities in the wellness, spiritual and metaphysical fields. Local guides will escort your group.' The appeal of West Africa in the marketing of this company is to a search for roots that link African-Americans to a past rooted in the slave trade and the slave experience.

The need to connect with a pre-colonial past has become an important and widespread feature of contemporary multi-ethnic societies. In another, rather different example of 'roots tourism', various places in Ireland market themselves as ideal starting points for tracing one's forebears. Indeed the Genealogical Society of Ireland, in its Tourism Policy Review of March 2003, argued that the search for ancestry should be cultivated as a major source of national income:

> Genealogy and heraldry are undoubtedly important tourism assets in Ireland with a sizeable percentage of our overseas visitors choosing to come to Ireland in search of their roots and, almost certainly, purchasing a souvenir or two bearing their 'Family Coat-of-Arms.'
>
> The ancestral link to Ireland shared by millions throughout the world is the most important resource on which to develop a sustainable tourism development plan and, indeed, these 'ancestral links' provide the basis for this Society's sizeable and increasing overseas membership. . . .
>
> With an estimated seventy million people world wide claiming Irish ancestry and thereby, feeling a special affinity with Ireland, we have a resource that would be the envy of many of our neighbours in the European Union.
>
> (*www.gensocireland.org:* 1 and 3)

The desire to be from somewhere where one would unambiguously belong and the related search for roots in contemporary Western societies is, in part, a product of the ethnocentrism and racism experienced in the societies in which diasporic peoples now live. Part of the appeal of that other place to which diasporic people look for their roots is often the belief that, there, one would not be treated as different or as an outsider. As we saw in Chapter 4, this is a key theme in writing by Black writers in Britain for whom the imagined place of belonging most often proves illusory or its reality more complex than anticipated.

The theme of belonging and a search for roots have received insightful, critical treatment in a recent autobiographical text, *Sugar and Slate* (2002), by the mixed-race, Black Welsh writer and academic, Charlotte Williams. Writing of the search for roots, Williams recounts how she visits the graves of young Black men, known as the 'Congo boys', who were trainee Black missionaries in Colwyn Bay on the North Wales coast and who, having died prematurely, were buried there. Williams reflects:

> As I stood one Sunday morning in the overgrown graveyard at Llanelian I remembered that long ago Ma had told me that there used to be a college for Black fellows in Colwyn Bay, but at the time it hadn't registered. Now it has become one of those ancient trails I retrace over and over again as if to print myself onto it.
>
> I regard it as my own mini version of the Pan-Am pilgrimage only all I have to do is take a right at the roundabout at Old Colwyn and walk up the road. When I visit the graves of the Congo Boys I feel just like those pilgrims to the slave fortresses at Elmina in Ghana who stand in the ancestral spaces and recreate the past in the present. It is as though through each retraced step the slave experience is owned by them. They have to go back to make sense of themselves in the present. In one single moment they are the past, the present and the future all rolled into one – the recollection, the recreation and the restatement of the whole thing gives them a profile. I once read that diaspora peoples without a collective historical event to refer to invent one in order to define their presence in their inherited country. It took me a long journey to understand why the Congo boys are part of my Elmina. A hundred years separate me from the Congo boys, a small cargo shipped from the Dark Continent to little Wales.
>
> (Williams 2002: 26)

For Charlotte Williams, like the Black and mixed-race British writers discussed in Chapter 4, growing up visibly different from the rest of the people in her small Welsh town has profound effects on her identity and sense of belonging. The othering to which she is subject by white society is shown to precipitate both a sense of alienness and a search for origins and roots that might compensate for this sense of non-belonging. Charlotte Williams, like the main protagonist of Lucinda Roy's novel *Lady Moses* discussed in the previous chapter, finds that being mixed-race complicates the process of achieving a positive identity and sense of belonging, as she is marked as different by both white and Black societies.

In her autobiography, Williams tells how she spent her early years in Lagos, where she was not regarded as Black: 'There are no brown skins in this place. Peanut brown we are. Roasted peanuts from another land. In Africa we were white and in Wales we weren't' (Williams 2002: 37). Once she moves back to Wales, she is seen as 'coloured':

> There was no such thing as 'black' where I grew up; Llandudno wasn't that kind of place. We were 'the coloured family' in polite English . . . I grew up coloured, half-caste, and it took me a long time to realise that to be half-caste wasn't to be half of anything. It took me even longer to realise that to be mixed was not to be mixed up, or was it? How would I have known? You have to have knowledge of a wider experience to make sense of your own and that just wasn't available . . . We lived in a respectable town, in a very respectable road and 'race' was one of those dirty words nobody would dream of bringing to their lips.
>
> (Williams 2002: 48–9)

The racism that Williams experienced from the town's inhabitants while growing up took forms that most of the white people involved would probably not have recognized as racist:

> Are you from Africa? I bet it's hot in your country. Are you feeling the cold? Do you eat this sort of food where you come from? Are you that colour all over? Can you speak English? You people are so good at dancing. Is that your father? He's a proper gentleman isn't he? What part of Africa is he from? Can't tell when you're dirty can we? You don't need to wash so often I suppose? That's some suntan you've got there. Have they all got small ears like you? Let me feel your hair. People like you don't blush do they? I mean, there's no point.
>
> (Williams 2002: 49)

Charlotte Williams comments: 'You mean I spent all those years with my cheeks burning and nobody knew any different' (Williams 2002: 49).

On returning from Africa to primary school in Wales, Williams attempts to deal with being marked as different by conforming as much as possible. Her aim is to become invisible and she describes how she did not dare openly acknowledge her two older sisters, since to recognize them was to see those aspects of herself that made her feel so shamefully different.

Williams analyses how low level, everyday, small town racism has profound effects on her identity and sense of self-worth, since it combines both a measure of acceptance and rejection, visibility and invisibility. It is the terms on which she is accepted that are deeply problematic:

> 'We never really noticed you were coloured,' they would say in condescending tones, or 'You're not really black, you're just brown,' and we would all be relieved of the onerous impoliteness of being black. We would trade bits of ourselves for their white acceptance, denying ourselves to provide reassurance against the intrusion of difference. But it was the background assumptions embodied in

the questions that caught me so unawares. The everyday assumptions of inferiority that eventually ground me down until I didn't know who or what I was.

(Williams 2002: 49–50)

It is this internalized sense of inferiority, fed by a lack of contact with other mixed-race people, that leads Williams to look for alternative roots.

In her search for roots, Williams travels to Guyana, the home of her father. Here she learns to reappraise the effects of her upbringing in an all white community on her sense of self, her attitudes to other Black people and to whites: 'second class citizenship was my inheritance in a way that these people just didn't accept' (Williams 2002: 125). While this recognition helps her develop a new sense of self, in Guyana she finds herself once again marked as different. Roots and a sense of belonging prove not to be necessarily linked. When she tries to befriend a Black woman with whom she shares an office in an aid agency, she is politely treated as an outsider and forced to recognize that 'We were different although I didn't want us to be. I knew that my great-great grandmother had the experience of slavery like hers, and I thought of the generations of Negro women who were my ancestry. Somewhere we were joined at the root' (Williams 2002: 133).

Through her journey to find her roots, Williams comes to see both her position as mixed-race and her need to identify with her father's people critically. She quotes the words of another Welsh woman, Cardiff-born, mixed-race Suzanne, who has grown up in an ethnically and racially mixed community where belonging has been less of a problem: 'there are roots and roots. . . . Ever see any of our kind go searching out their white roots?' (Williams 2002: 167). Williams' Guyanese experience teaches her the limits of the search for roots and she comes to realize that the diasporic experience is precisely one that involves claiming a home where one lives and reworking aspects of dual heritage: 'We may look to Africa or the Caribbean for our inspirational cues, we may inherit fragments of a traditional culture from our parents, but these we reformulate and reinvent and locate in our home places' (Williams 2002: 191).

If the diasporic experience, combined with racism and ethnocentrism in the country in which one lives are important motivations behind the search for origins and roots, so too is the colonialist experience in formerly colonized countries, and the more recent effects of processes of modernization which are often perceived as Westernization. Here 'true' identity becomes a question of returning to an imagined pre-colonial state, but this return inevitably privileges particular interests over others. Stuart Hall reminds us that 'We should not, for a moment, underestimate or neglect the importance of the act of imaginative rediscovery which this conception of a recovered, essential identity entails' (Hall 1990: 52). Indeed it can have far-reaching consequences, as for example, in the case of contemporary India, where the rise to prominence in recent years of the Bharatiya Janata Party (BJP), with its philosophy of *Hindutva* or cultural nationalism, has had marked effects on society. Among other things these have included attempts by the BJP to rewrite educational syllabuses and in particular, as Uma Narayan has pointed out, Hindu cultural nationalists are rewriting the meaning of aspects of Indian history to assert a specific conservative discourse of true Hindu womenhood and women's role in society (Narayan 1997). These moves are justified by the BJP as a return to the authentic traditions of true Hinduism, to true Hindu identities and lifestyles, which are, of course, themselves cultural constructions. Moreover they are being used to motivate and justify attacks on Indian Muslims, who find themselves defined as alien others. Commenting of the implications of BJP cultural nationalism in relation to women, Narayan argues that Indian feminists need to include within the scope of their struggles

> not only contestations of *particular practices and institutions* detrimental to women, but additionally to include challenges to the larger pictures of Nation, National History, and Cultural Traditions that serve to sustain and justify these practices and institutions. These are often 'pictures of History' that *conceal their own historicity and their own status as representations* – suggesting that the nation and its culture are 'natural givens' rather than the *historical inventions and constructions* that they are.
>
> (Narayan 1997: 20–1)

When origins and roots are invoked to justify contemporary social and political developments, the cultural political interests at stake will vary massively. In the Welsh case, with which Charlotte Williams is concerned in her autobiography, questions of roots and origins have played an important role in the development of modern Welsh identities. This includes those grounded in the Welsh language, English-speaking Welsh identities and those of the long established mixed-race communities, mostly located in the port cities of Cardiff and Newport in South Wales. The Welsh case clearly shows that the search for roots does not only effect mixed-heritage, colonized and diasporic peoples. It is also important in the case of ethnic groups and nations that have been both colonized and assimilated into larger units. The Welsh identity with which Charlotte Williams has a conflictual relationship is itself a multiple and fought over phenomenon. Much cultural political struggle around Welsh identities focuses on the question of language in a country in which according to the 2001 census, just over 20 per cent of the population have 'one or more skills' in the Welsh language. The struggle over Welsh culture and identity has a long history and was, in part, provoked by the effects of the assimilation of Wales into the English crown. From the fourteenth century, Wales was totally governed from London, until a measure of devolution was introduced in 1999, with the founding of the Welsh Assembly. With industrialization, beginning in the eighteenth century in South Wales, an influx of labour from across the English border and from Ireland, helped turn large areas of the country into English-speaking areas. This anglicization of culture was compounded in the second half of the nineteenth century by the effects of the Royal Commission into the State of Education in Wales, published in the so-called 'Blue books', which outlawed the use of the Welsh language in state schools. As large areas

Plate 3. Complex Cardiff Black Welsh Identities, 1959.
(Butetown History & Arts Centre archive.)

of Wales lost their Welsh-speaking character, they also lost their indigenous oral traditions.

The invention and re-invention of tradition is a phenomenon that can be found in many cultures at different moments of history. For example, much of the pomp and ceremony associated with the British Crown was developed in the Victorian period. The case of Wales provides a particularly interesting example that in many ways resembled what was happening in other small European countries in the eighteenth and nineteenth centuries and which is detailed in an article entitled 'From a Death to a View: the Hunt for the Welsh Past in the Romantic Period' (Morgan 1992). Here Prys

Morgan describes in some detail how in the eighteenth century, with the demise of much traditional culture, Welshness was effectively reinvented, largely by (ex-patriot) London Welsh, and given many of the features still identified with popular images of Welshness in the twenty-first century: 'In this period Welsh scholars and patriots rediscovered the past, historical linguistic and literary traditions, and where these traditions were inadequate, they created a past that had never existed. Romantic mythologizing went to quite extraordinary lengths in Wales, leaving a permanent mark on its later history' (Morgan 1992: 43–4). Among the Welsh cultural phenomena that were re-invented were the musical festival, known as the *Eisteddfod* and neo-Druidism, both of which had ancient or mediaeval precursors. Prys Morgan described how:

> The Druid underwent a sea-change in the early years of the eighteenth century from the archane obscurantist, who indulged in human sacrifice, to the sage or intellectual defending his people's faith and honour and the Welsh began to see that they had a special relationship with him that was different from Druidism in England.
>
> (Morgan 1992: 63)

> The revival of Druidism was a movement of considerable significance, all in all, because it involved myths which showed the cultural tradition of Wales to be older than any other in Western Europe, and it made the scholar or poet or teacher central to that culture. To some extent it restored the bard to his primary place in Welsh life.
>
> (Morgan 1992: 66)

Here claims to authenticity rooted in the far distant past are paramount. Among the other features of Welshness, that developed from the eighteenth century onwards, were celebrations of the language, the creation through heroic literature of national heroes with origins in the Mediaeval period, the casting of Wales as a land of song, the invention of a national costume and flag, a romantic re-visioning of the harsh Welsh landscape in terms of romantic beauty and the designation of rugby as a national sport. In each case Wales was marked as different from England and Welshness defined in opposition to Englishness.

In the museums, heritage and the tourist industries of the twenty-first century, Wales and Welshness continue to be defined by what Prys Morgan has called this 'invention of tradition'. Institutions concerned with history and national identity draw on eighteenth- and nineteenth-century traditions to project Wales to the populations living within its borders and to the outside world. In doing so they help to define who the Welsh are and what it means to have a Welsh identity. At the centre of many of the narratives in question is a concern with ancient Celtic roots and origins that pre-date those waves of invasion, from the Romans onwards, that are seen as creating England, but not Wales, Scotland or indeed England's own Cornish Celtic fringe. In the popular imagination, Wales traces its roots and origins back to pre-Roman Britain when pre-

Christian Celtic culture, language and religion defined Britain as a whole. For example, the video produced by the Museum of Welsh Life at St Fagans, which is the most popular museum and tourist attraction in Wales, situated on the outskirts of Cardiff, describes Wales as follows:

> Though small, it is a country with a positive identity and its own widely used language, a diverse landscape with rugged mountains, trout-filled rivers, smooth rounded hills and peaceful pasture. And above all, Wales is a country of tradition populated by the descendants of the warlike but creative Celts, a race now confined to the Atlantic fringes of Western Europe.
>
> (Museum of Welsh Life Video 1995)

One implication of this narrative of Welshness is its implicit exclusivity. Its emphasis on ancient roots is at the expense of developments in Wales since the industrial revolution. These included the development, from the 1850s onwards, of substantial non-white and mixed Welsh communities, mainly along the South Wales coast, as a result of the growth of the coal industry. Writing of the position of Black and mixed-race people in Wales, Charlotte Williams comments on how Wales is one of the geographical spaces in Britain where to speak about race is outlawed: 'That the idea of black Welsh wasn't really lodged in the cultural consciousness or in fact in the cultural memory. It was one of those sickening pieces of cultural amnesia that had conveniently managed to disassociate the Welsh from any implication in the facts of black history and in doing so rendered us with an invisible present' (Williams 2002: 177). The exclusivity of definitions of Welshness grounded in Celtic origins thus works to exclude Welsh-speaking Black and mixed-race people from Welshness (see Jordan 2004). This has not, however, prevented some Black Welsh people from engaging in a Black nationalist project to create what Foucault calls a 'reverse discourse' that involves claiming Wales for the Black Celts (see Ali and Ali 1992).

Biblical and 'scientific' myths of origin: the white identity movement in the United States

The search for identity, roots and belonging is not always positive or benign in its objectives and effects. It takes extreme and racist forms in the wide range of organizations in the United States that come under the broad umbrella of the White Identity Movement. Such organizations include white supremacist political organizations such as the Ku Klux Klan, the American Nazi Party; the Church of Jesus Christ Christian, the Aryan Nations; the Confederate Hammerskins; Jubilee, the National Association for the Advancement of White People; the Order; radical modern offshoots of the original Posse Comitatus; Scriptures for America, White Aryan Resistance (WAR) and White Separatist Banner. (For more on the White Identity Movement in the USA see

Aho 1995 and Barkun 1997a,b) Other small white supremacist groups come and go. Many of these organizations articulate supremacist ideas through what has come to be called the Christian Identity Movement, and some of them have discursive and organizational roots that can be traced back to the nineteenth century. The Christian Identity Movement is a loose network of organizations that ground white supremacist objectives in discourses of roots and origins that claim to go all the way back to Adam and Eve and that echo debates from the first half of the nineteenth century about the Bible and the status of different races. In their white supremacist Christian narratives of origins and roots, white people (rather than the Jews) become God's chosen people.

The website of religioustolerance.org offers a compact account of the Christian Identity Movement: 'Included within the Christian Identity movements are: Anglo-Israelism, British-Israelism, and some White supremacists, anti-semitic and other hate groups.' It suggests that term 'Christian Identity' signifies, among other things, the belief that

> The Anglo-Saxon, Celtic, Scandinavian, Germanic and associated cultures are the racial descendents of the tribes of Israel. Thus, by extension, Americans and Canadians, are composed of the descendents of the ancient Israelites of the Hebrew Scriptures (Old Testament). . . . The Christian Identity movement is a movement of many extremely conservative Christian churches and religious organizations, extreme right wing political groups and survival groups. Some are independent; others are loosely interconnected.
>
> (*www.religioustolerance.org*)

While the white Christian Identity Movement had its origins in British-Israelism which was founded around 1840 following the publication of John Wilson's text, 'Lectures on our Israelitish Origin' (see Barkun 1997a), today, it is

> composed primarily of conservative Christian groups who all believe to some extent that white, Anglo-Saxons are the true chosen people of God. People holding these beliefs do so in different ways; some simply provide information such as literature, videotapes, and lectures for people wishing to learn more about the movement. Others have set up their own congregations or organizations where these Identity beliefs are taught and practiced.
>
> (*www.religioustolerance.org*)

In his study, *Religion and the Racist Right* (1997a), Michael Barkun suggests that the Christian Identity Movement encompasses some 50,000 people in the United States, and is the glue that holds right-wing extremist groups together. All groups share very conservative interpretations of the Christian Bible, a belief that Adam and Eve were white, a hatred of homosexuals, strong anti-semitism and a belief in the superiority of the white race, the 'Adamic race' or 'True Israelites'. More extreme groups consider non-whites sub-human and these beliefs are grounded in readings of the Bible. As *religioustolerance.org* explains, 'As a minimum, they call for racial separation; some call for extermination of what they call the "*mud races*" (non-white races). . . . The Commandment which forbids adultery does not refer to extra-marital sexual relationships. Rather, it forbids "racial adultery"; i.e. inter-racial marriages.' Acts of violence and terrorism have been attributed to these groups including the bombing of abortion clinics, arson attacks on synagogues, and the murder of gays and Jews:

> These terrorist acts appear to be planned and executed by individual Christian Identity followers, and not by Identity churches or the movement itself. Because of the freedom of speech and religion guaranteed in the 1st Amendment of the Constitution, the FBI is prohibited from general monitoring and infiltrating of Christian Identity and similar groups.

> (*www.religioustolerance.org*)

If Biblical narratives are one discursive mode commonly used to assert authenticity and a connected supremacy, the language of far right organizations in the United States is also often framed by mainstream discourses of cultural diversity which are turned on their heads in ways which can be seen as an extreme form of a more widespread backlash against multi-culturalism. For example, the website of *Stormfront.org*, which I initially chose at random from an internet search for sites connected with white identity, and which proved to be a particularly extreme right-wing supremacist organization, tackles the issue of diversity head on. *Stormfront*'s graphic self-presentation on the worldwide web uses iconography and typefaces that immediately link it to those of Nazi Germany and other Neo-Nazi groups. Its logo is 'White Pride World Wide' and it describes itself as: 'a resource for those courageous men and women fighting to preserve their White Western culture, ideals and freedom of speech and association – a forum for planning strategies and forming political and social groups to ensure victory'. It argues that whites are the group most discriminated against in the United States. For example, in an article entitled *What is Racism?* published on the *Stormfront* website, Thomas Jackson argues that:

> Today, one of the favourite slogans that define the asymmetric quality of American racism is 'celebration of diversity'. It has begun to dawn on a few people that 'diversity' is always achieved at the expense of whites (and sometimes men), and never the other way round. . . . Let us put it bluntly: To 'celebrate' or 'embrace' diversity, as we are so often asked to do, is no different from deploring an excess of Whites.

> (*www.stormfront.org/defaultnf.htm*, updated 12 July 2003)

Jackson goes on to argue that this call to celebrate diversity involves forms of discrimination that no other ethnic group or nation would endure. He asks:

> Would Mexico – or any other non-white nation tolerate this kind of cultural and demographic depredation? Of course not. Yet white Americans are supposed to

look upon the flood of Hispanics and Asians entering their country as a priceless cultural gift. They are supposed to 'celebrate' their own loss of influence, their own dwindling numbers, their own dispossession, for to do otherwise would be hopelessly racist.

Among the assumptions underpinning this discourse is the belief that the United States belongs to its *white* inhabitants. Diversity is thus seen as entailing loss of influence and dispossession. Moreover, *Stormfront* argues, white consciousness has been duped by arguments supporting diversity:

> No, it is the White enterprise in the United States that is unnatural, unhealthy, and without historical precedent. Whites have let themselves be convinced that it is racist merely to object to dispossession, much less to work for their own interests. Never in the history of the world has a dominant people thrown open the gates to strangers, and poured out its wealth to aliens, never before has a people been fooled into thinking that there was virtue or nobility in surrendering its heritage, and giving away to others its place in history. Of all the races of America, only whites have been tricked into thinking that a preference for ones own kind is racism. Only whites are ever told that a love for their own people is somehow 'hatred' of others.
>
> (*www.stormfront.org/defaultnf.htm*, updated 12 July 2003)

In a gesture typical of racist appeals to the way things naturally are, Jackson suggests that it is 'sick' and 'unnatural' to prefer other races over one's own and that this inevitable 'fact of life' is not motivated by hate. In his narrative, one's 'race' becomes one's natural family:

> All healthy people prefer the company of their own kind and it has nothing to do with hatred. All men love their families more than their neighbors but this does not mean that they hate their neighbors. Whites who love their racial family need bear no ill will towards non-whites. They only wish to be left alone to participate in the unfolding of their racial and cultural destinies.
>
> (*www.stormfront.org/defaultnf.htm*, updated 12 July 2003)

Jackson further argues that ' "Black pride" is said to be a wonderful and worthy thing, but anything that could be construed as an expression of White pride is a form of hatred.' This discursive move which also underpins much of the mainstream back-lash against positive action, disavows the both the history of racism in the United States, and the existing structural relations of inequality that govern race relations today. It speaks particularly powerfully to those white people who find themselves disadvantaged by often unacknowledged class relations.

For white supremacists, the answer to cultural diversity is White nationalism. Although the numbers actively involved are small in proportion to the population of the United States, their influence extends into the wider society, helping to fuel both the belief that whites are disadvantaged and the widespread backlash against positive action programmes. In its web page of frequently asked questions about White Nation-alism, *Stormfront* offers a series of definitions that both stress separatism and deny its supremacist aspirations. White nationalism is described as motivated by the 'need to create a separate nation' as a necessary form of self-defence against exploitation:

Q. So how is it that Whites are exploited?

A. It is a long list. Burdensome racial preference schemes in hiring, racial prefer-ence schemes in university admissions, racial preference schemes in government contracting and small business loans. Beyond quotas there is the denial of rights of free speech and of due process to Whites who are critical of these governmental policies. We have special punishments for assaults committed by Whites if the motives might be racial. In addition, Whites pay a proportion of the costs of the welfare state that is disproportionate to what they receive in benefits.

But the most exploitative aspect of the situation is that neither the racial quotas, the business preferences, the loss of freedom of speech, nor the dis-proportionate contributions to the welfare state have managed to sate the appetites of non-Whites living in the United States.

The more Whites sacrifice, the more non-Whites demand. Many Whites are beginning to believe that no amount of tribute, other than mass suicide, would satisfy the non-White demands.

If our presence stirs up that much hatred in the hearts of non-Whites, then the only sensible course of action is to separate ourselves from them.

(*www.stormfront.org*, Yggdrasil, *White Nationalism FAQ*.)

Here the terms of the arguments that usually address the relations between whites and non-whites are reversed. Whites become the exploited victims and the subjects of hate on the part of non-whites. In a break with classical racism, Yggdrasil claims that White nationalists neither feel superior to other races nor wish to dominate them, they just want separation.

White nationalist culture may go largely unnoticed in the everyday life of main-stream America, where some of its ideas about positive action and the social position of whites vis-à-vis other groups have become aspects of common sense and an everyday part of white identity and subjectivity. Beyond the mainstream, however, it is there to be seen. Here, for example, is a conversation with Rochelle Gladden, an African-American parole officer, working in California:

RG: My title is Parole Agent 1 with the Department of Corrections. The main purpose of my job is to 'protect the community'. The second purpose is to help felons re-integrate back into society.

CW: In what context do you come across white people wearing white nationalist emblems or tattoos?

RG: When a parolee comes to the office, upon release from prison, the Parole Agents are required to take pictures of all identifying scars, marks or tattoos. As part of our training we have been made aware of what different institutional and street 'gangs' exist and the tattoos that represent association with or membership of those gangs. Some white guys will have 'WHITE POWER' tattooed across their back, stomach or chest. Some will have 'WHITE' tattooed down the back of one arm and 'POWER' (sometimes substituted with the word 'PRIDE') tattooed down the other arm. Some will have swastikas tattooed all over them. More and more I have found more acceptable tattoos (flowers, scenery, faces, etc) with various white power, neo-nazi symbols intertwined into the tattoo.

In my position as an African-American Parole Agent, when white guys are asked to take off their shirts to have the tattoos photographed and I see 'White Power' or 'White is Better' or 'White Pride,' I will ask them to tell me what it says. Not many of them sound real proud to repeat it. When asked if it is gang related or what does it mean, I often hear 'Oh, Ms Gladden, it's just something I had done in prison, it doesn't mean anything.'

In Rochelle Gladden's view, the White nationalist tattoos are more often than not acquired strategically by inmates as signifiers of an identity that will aid survival in the prison environment:

I believe that while in prison, some of these guys need to feel important or need protection. California prisons are very much into segregating the races. Everyone is separated (or put together) by race. So when they are put in a situation where they need protection or importance, they associate with whatever group they feel best with. Some do it with tattoos, others do it with illegal acts in prison. I feel there are very few that actually leave prison and begin life with some kind of White nationalist gang or group.

Yet though for many people White nationalist and White supremacist identities, and the discourses and organizations that produce them, may be used strategically, their effects are much wider and more insidious. They have helped turn the tables in the struggle for equal opportunities. Asked to explain White nationalism, Parole Agent 1 replied as follows:

I believe the fact of oppression suffered by Blacks and Jews throughout the world had been lost to these people. That somehow they have come to believe that there is a time limit on how long you should be acknowledged for your oppression, and the time limit is up. Interestingly enough, you don't hear these groups ranting on about hatred for the Japanese who were oppressed through the internment camps. But they have chosen to suffer quietly and have not demanded much.

The big word is racism. The concept of racism and oppression is not only lost on these people but is slowly being lost with the general population of white people in this country. Racism is being interpreted as allowing privileges to some people but not all people, When I hear whites talk about how Equal Opportunity Laws are racist, and how getting a job, getting enrolled into school and getting loans, etc. should be based on your abilities, that all sounds well and good, but the reality is so far from that, it lets me know that the word racism, when used in those contexts and when used by white people is an excuse. These whites seem to feel as though Blacks and Jews are getting something 'extra' and they want it too.

By and large I don't take these groups lightly, they can be dangerous just as any group of people who believe they have been wronged can be dangerous. But I just can't take their cause seriously. It's people like them who have been able to poison the minds of so many into believing that people who have been oppressed in America and are still oppressed in America, have had their opportunity to make it and now it is the oppressor's time to shine again.

Commenting on the multiply effects of racism in the United States, Gloria Anzaldúa argues:

The people who practice Racism – everyone who is white in the US – are victims of their own white ideology and are impoverished by it. But we who are oppressed by Racism internalize its deadly pollen along with the air we breathe. Make no mistake about it, the fruits of this weed are dysfunctional lifestyles, which mutilate our physical bodies, stunt our intellects and make emotional wrecks of us.

(Anzaldúa 1990b: xix)

The battle for the meaning of the flag

I want to turn to a final example from the United States of the rooting of white identity in a particular version of American history that has become focused in recent years on cultural political struggles in the southern states over the Confederate flag. The histories of the Old South, the Confederacy and the Civil War are major features of both popular southern, white identities and of the tourist industry in the southern states. Shops selling confederacy memorabilia: T-shirts, baseball caps, ties, beach towels, car bumper stickers and all manner of other items, are widespread as are internet retail outlets. The confederate flag is perhaps the predominant symbol in this merchandise. For many white southerners, the Confederate battle flag, called the 'Southern Cross' or the cross of St Andrew, symbolizes a lost but one time great southern heritage. For Black Americans and other whites, it is most often regarded as a shameful reminder of slavery and segregation. As Borgna Brunner comments:

In the past, several Southern states flew the Confederate battle flag along with the U.S. and state flags over their statehouses. Others incorporated the controversial symbol into the design of their state flags. The Confederate battle flag has also been appropriated by the Ku Klux Klan and other racist hate groups. According to the Southern Poverty Law Center, more than 500 extremist groups use the Southern Cross as one of their symbols.

(*www.infoplease.com/spot/confederate1.html*)

In 2001 Governor Jim Hodges of South Carolina signed a law in front of the media removing the flag from the statehouse in the state capital Columbia. It had been flying there since 1962, two years before the Civil Rights Act was passed by Congress. This was in part in response to a National Association for the Advancement of Colored People (NAACP) tourism boycott that started on 1 January 2000. This did not, however, resolve the situation. As Aaron Page of the Public Broadcasting Service explains:

> The bill that orders the flag [to be] taken down also orders – as a compromise – a new Confederate flag to be raised on a 30-foot pole at the nearby Confederate Soldier Monument. The monument is on the Statehouse grounds – in other words, the flag is still flying on government property. The NAACP says this is unacceptable, and plans to continue its boycott. Even if an agreement is reached in South Carolina, the debate continues elsewhere in the South. For example, the Confederate flag is incorporated into the design of the Georgia and Mississippi state flags, and many people think those flags should be redesigned to remove the Confederate symbolism.
>
> (*www.pbs.org/newshour/extra/features/jan-june00/flag.html*)

Commenting on this controversy, Page reflects that 'a history of slavery is a difficult legacy to overcome. The debate continues – in words, in the law, and in symbols.' An example of this extensive cultural political struggle over symbols of white identity in the context of a history, governed by white supremacy was reported on 4 May 2001 by the Associated Press:

Confederate T-shirts spark debate

RICHMOND HILL, Georgia. – Zane Dunn wore a banned T-shirt to school and became a rebel with a Confederate cause. Like six other students at Richmond Hill Middle School, 14-year-old Zane was suspended for a day because of the Confederate flag on the shirt. More than a century after Lee surrendered at Appomattox and a few months after defenders of Confederate symbols lost battles in the Georgia and South Carolina statehouses, the fight over Southern heritage has moved to schoolhouses.

'My Confederate ancestors, they died for this flag,' said 14-year-old Zane, whose mother bought him the shirt after another student was suspended. 'I was born and raised in the South and I have to stand up for it.'

(The Associated Press, 15 April 2001)

While school staff said they had banned Confederate symbols not out of political correctness but in order to prevent racial violence, parents dressed in Confederate shirts and bandanas, protested against the suspensions at school board meetings.

> 'School folks are in a very precarious situation,' [Cairo High principal Wayne] Tootle said. 'If they don't do something to try to prevent, and something happens, then the parents and news media will just lambast them for what they didn't do.'
>
> (The Associated Press, 15 April 2001)

Whereas, according to school officials, bans on Confederate emblems had been in place for years, 'the flag fight prompted students and parents to violate them deliberately'. This had also caused a major increase in Confederate memorabilia sales[1]:

> The classroom clashes have been a boon for Dewey Barber and his T-shirt company, Odum-based Dixie Outfitters, which has more than 200 shirt designs that incorporate the Confederate flag. 'When they tell them they can't wear the rebel flag, they say, "By gosh, we have the right of free speech and to our heritage!" And they buy more,' Barber said. Dixie Outfitters shirts are so popular that some schools have banned them by brand name. Zane and his six fellow students all wore Dixie Outfitters shirts. Zane's shirt depicted a snarling, wild boar, with the Confederate emblem as a backdrop. Another Dixie Outfitters design shows just the flag's corners peeking from a basket of sleeping puppies. A third shirt depicts slaves working in a cotton field beneath the words 'The Land of Cotton.'
>
> (The Associated Press, 15 April 2001)

In this discourse, 'standing up for the South' equals standing up for the flag. At the heart of the controversy is the argument that the flag symbolizes a past governed by slavery, racism and white supremacism. As such, it is an affront to African-Americans and to other Americans wanting to put this past behind them. In an internet debate and poll on the Confederate flag controversy, the following arguments were among those published on the web page in support of the proposition that the Confederate flag is a symbol of racism.

> Raising the Confederate Flag during the civil rights movement was a slap in the face to those fighting for equal rights. Now the flag is a constant reminder of that struggle and the fact that we have not overcome the hatred and divisiveness of that period of our history. Several attempts to take it down have failed, including a lawsuit by business leaders.
>
> A former racist-in-denial who was the National Campaign Director for George Wallace's organization, has said. We used all things Confederate to glorify 'Dixie' and mask the slave-owning, racist culture that created that white supremacist

state. The Confederate Battle Flag has become emblematic of white supremacy from rebel flag waving, Nazi Skin Heads in Germany to church burning Klansmen in South Carolina and the Aryan Nation in Idaho.

Maybe confederate flags wouldn't have such a bad rep, if they weren't flown at hate rallies, by the 'boys in the hoods'. This is not dogmatic, it's factual. How 'bout a flag that will draw people together instead of apart?

The main argument against the proposition was that:

The NAACP crowd sees the Confederate battle flag as a flag of slavery. If that's so, the United States flag is even more so. Slavery thrived under the United States flag from 1776 to 1865, while under the Confederate flag a mere four years. The birth of both flags had little or nothing to do with slavery. Both flags saw their birth in a violent and proud struggle for independence and self-governance.

(Confederate Flag Debate and Poll)

At issue in this debate and in the widespread battle over the meaning of the Conferderate flag are questions of the history and meaning of symbols that are strongly linked to questions of identity. In his essay on new Caribbean cinema, 'Cultural Identity and Diaspora' (1990), Stuart Hall argues that cultural identity is often defined in terms of

one shared culture, a sort of collective one true self, hiding inside the many other, more superficial or artificially imposed 'selves', which people with a shared history and ancestry hold in common. Within the terms of this definition, our cultural identities reflect the common historical experiences and shared cultural codes which provide us, as 'one people', with stable, unchanging and continuous frames of reference and meaning, beneath the shifting divisions and vicissitudes of our cultural history.

(Hall 1990: 51)

It is arguably this understanding of cultural identity that white southerners are attempting to define and fix in the battle over the flag. The problem, of course, is that the American south is not composed of 'one people' with 'one history' or 'stable, unchanging and continuous frames of reference and meaning'. Moreover, as Foucault has shown so clearly, both frames of reference and meaning are effects of power. What is most striking about the widespread quest to ground identity in narratives of roots and origins that claim truth status is the powerful attraction that they hold for a wide range of different groups and individuals who perceive themselves to be in some way marginalized, excluded, deprived or oppressed. It points to the need to address both the material and discursive conditions under which different people live in multi-ethnic, postmodern societies. If the celebration of difference is a much valorized aspect of postmodernity, difference is often also mobilized to exclude and oppress.

Further reading

Barkun, M. (1997a) *Religion and the Racist Right*. Chapel Hill: University of North Carolina Press.

Hall, S. (1990) 'Cultural Identity and Diaspora', in J. Rutherford (ed.) *Identity: Community, Culture, Difference*. London: Lawrence & Wishart.

Hobsbawm, E. and Ranger, T. (eds) (1992) *The Invention of Tradition*. Cambridge: Cambridge University Press.

Williams, C. (2002) *Sugar and Slate*. Aberystwyth: Planet.

6 | DIASPORIC IDENTITIES: SOUTH ASIAN BRITISH WOMEN'S WRITING

I was born in India, when India was under the British Raj. As a teenager I grew up, spent my early youth and was educated in Pakistan. At the age of 29, inspired by the West's achievement in art in the 20th century, and to fulfil my own aspirations to be a modern artist, I left my country to live in Europe. I have now lived and worked in London for 27 years. I often travel to Pakistan to see my mother, brothers and sisters and also some friends. I can say I'm Asian, Indian, Pakistani, British, European, Muslim, Oriental, secular, modernist, postmodernist, and so on. . . . But what do these mean? Do they define my identity? Can I accept all of them as part of my life, or must I choose one thing or another according to someone else's notion about my identity? I have no problem in saying that I am all of these things, and none of these things at the same time.

(Araeen 1992: 89)

Cultural hybridity, the fusion of cultures and coming together of difference, the 'border crossing' that marks diasporic survival, signifies change, hope of newness, and space for creativity. But in the search for rootedness – a 'place called home' – these women, in the process of self-identification, disidentify with an excluding, racist British colonizing culture. They articulate instead a multi-faceted discontinuous black identity that marks their difference.

(Mirza 1997: 16)

One of the main legacies of Western colonialism and the slave trade has been the creation of significant diasporic communities of people of African and South and East Asian descent. There are, of course, also many white populations, both in settler colonies and throughout the developing world. Diasporic communities often display multiple and hybrid identities that draw both on relatively fixed ideas of traditional culture and new hybrid identities and cultural forms – particularly among subsequent generations – that emerge from engagement with the culture and society in which the original migrants settled. These new cultural forms, practices and identities in their turn often challenge both assumptions based on ideas of traditional culture and those of the hegemonic white societies within which non-white, diasporic subjects are located.

Yet predominantly white societies, especially former colonial powers, have themselves been shaped by a history of contacts with their colonial others. The current meanings of ethnic and racialized difference are often inflected by this legacy. Recent critiques of Western cultural traditions – poststructuralist, feminist and postcolonial – have each pointed to how meanings in Western culture are organized according to sets of binary oppositions that imply hierarchies of value.[1] For example, Western Europe's image of itself as the most developed and modern political, social and cultural order is based on a set of binary oppositions between Europe and its 'Others', that is to say, people of Colour. Colonialism is increasingly seen as the unspoken but necessary counterpart to Western European culture. Thus, for example, Robert Young in his book *White Mythologies: Writing, History and the West* draws on the work of Aimé Césaire, Frantz Fanon and Jean-Paul Sartre to argue that European claims to universalism developed at the expense of colonial others. Taking the example of literature, a cultural form, still exported to former colonies via education, he argues: 'Every time a literary critic claims a universal ethical, moral, or emotional instance in a piece of English literature, he or she colludes in the violence of the colonial legacy in which the European value or truth is defined as the universal one' (Young 1990: 124). To make European or North American meanings and values universal is at the same time to render all other cultures merely particular and by implication inferior.

In Britain, liberal humanist traditions of cultural theory and policy long sought to define those literary and artistic texts and cultural practices which were said to be representative of universal values and which might serve as the basis for a common, shared, national and (post)colonial identity and culture. (For a fuller discussion of the liberal humanist cultural tradition in Britain see Jordan and Weedon 1995: 23–64.) These traditions were until recently almost exclusively male, white and middle-class. Yet the last three decades have seen significant challenges from a variety of sources. Key among them have been feminism and the work of writers and filmmakers of Colour. This chapter examines examples of such work that address questions of identity, race and ethnicity in the context of contemporary Britain. It looks at examples of how recent British South Asian women's writing handles questions of gender, ethnic and racialized difference and what has come to be known as 'hybridity'.

Over the past few decades, feminist writers and scholars have offered comprehensive critiques of traditional cultural canons, uncovering a multitude of works by women that had been marginalized or lost. Feminists of Colour, critical of the white bias in much feminist research, have brought a wealth of texts by women of Colour to critical attention. (For an account of feminist cultural politics see Jordan and Weedon 1995:

177–216.) Moreover, the impact of the Women's Movement on contemporary culture and the creation of new markets has helped to promote new writing by women of Colour. One of the key concerns of this writing has been to redefine hegemonic versions of women's 'Otherness', whether this be constructed in sexist and/or racist terms. The effect of this abundance of fictional, historical and critical work has been to contest the apparently universal criteria of value in the liberal humanist tradition and to strengthen mainstream commitments to what has recently become known as 'cultural diversity'.

Recent work by British South Asian women writers is part of this larger project. It is deconstructing patriarchal models of femininity, questioning heterosexism and racial stereotyping. It has begun to articulate new forms of subjectivity and identity using both postmodern and realist literary forms. In the recent debates on hybridity, Homi Bhabha (1990) and Gloria Anzaldúa (1987), among others, have argued for hybridity as a 'third space', which offers the possibility of moving beyond those binary oppositions that constitute differences in hierarchical ways. They have argued for hybridity as a space from which it is possible to deconstruct and reshape the dominant hierarchies, be they of gender, sexuality, race or colonialism and to create new forms of identity. This chapter looks at how identity and difference are textually constructed in representations both of the South Asian and white communities in the UK. It asks whether difference is envisioned as a source of enrichment, choice and liberation, or rather of confinement, contradiction and oppression. It further asks: what is the cultural political potential of this writing in the struggle towards a more egalitarian society in which identity and difference are no longer structured through long established ethnocentric, colonial and racist oppositions, stereotypes and assumptions?

Language is central to racism, colonialism and notions of identity and hybridity. Colonialism imposed not just a language, in this case English, on South Asian peoples, but with it, sets of meanings and values. The language used to justify the colonial enterprise was one of civilizing, Christianizing, developing and modernizing. Implicit in this language was the assumption that the peoples in question were less civilized, less developed, pagan and either primitive or pre-modern. These stereotypes became part of a widely shared commonsense thinking in imperial Britain and they persist into the present. Both South Asian and Black British culture is engaged in challenging these stereotypes.

The last twenty years have seen the development of a new South Asian women's writing in Britain. Its themes span life in the Indian sub-continent, migration to Britain and the experience of living in contemporary Britain. It is a writing marked by the legacies of colonialism and the overtly racist attitudes of dominant forms of white British culture. It is also a body of writing concerned with the largely generational problems of difference and conflict between South Asian culture and religions and the society and culture of contemporary Britain. These differences and conflicts have profound effects on the identity, aspirations and lifestyles of British-born South Asian people.

Two factors were particularly important in establishing the beginnings of British Asian women's writing: the growth of feminist publishing outlets, particularly the Women's Press, with its policy of encouraging work by new women from minorities, and the establishment of the London-based Asian Women Writers' Workshop in 1984. Writing from this workshop was written and published in English, whatever the mother tongue of the writer concerned. Among the effects of writing in English is to locate such writing indisputably in the Western world, making it accessible to a wide readership. Another is to forge new forms of South Asian culture that transcends the boundaries of particular South Asian communities in Britain, encompassing women from all over the Indian sub-continent and the South Asian diaspora. In the introduction to *Flaming Spirit*, the second anthology published by the Asian Women Writers' Collective, Rukhsana Ahmad and Rahila Gupta comment:

> English may have been the coloniser's language and a mark of privilege and class in our home countries but here it also enabled us to break out of our regional identities and make common cause with the other black communities and, for that matter, the different cultures that inhabit the term 'Asian'.
>
> (Ahmad and Gupta 1994: xiii)

Writing in English has, the editors argue, enabled the formation of alliances against oppression on all fronts. Yet it also opens the texts' concerns to a large potential white readership, a move that has broader cultural political implications.

South Asian women were until recently one of the most silenced groups in Britain. There are many reasons for this. They include different religious and cultural norms – particularly for Muslim women from less developed and poorer area of India, Pakistan and Bangladesh. They further include problems of language and literacy, the lack of sympathetic publishers and the lack of established traditions of writing in the UK and of role models. As a result of this, it took many years for a new generation of immigrant women to begin to write about their contemporary experience and to be published.

It was the very difficulty of finding a voice as Asian women writers in Britain that led a group of women to found the Asian Women Writers' Workshop. As founder members recall:

> The workshop was formed in 1984, originally the result of lone efforts by Ravi Randhawa, who had managed to get the support of Black Ink and funding from the Greater London Council. Now [1994] we are getting financial support from Greater London Arts and Lambeth Council. The workshop was the first of its kind for Asian women writers in Britain, and was meant to draw out any isolated woman who wanted to write but needed a supportive environment to achieve this. The need for this kind of group was poignantly expressed in one of our early meetings when a younger woman, born in Britain, confronted an older woman who had just finished reading a moving story with the question, 'Where were you

when I was growing up?' Did it take that long for 'immigrants' to feel settled and strong enough to want to express, re-order and interpret their reality for themselves and society at large? We were also working in a vacuum; there seemed to be no precedents to which we could refer. A few Asian women had been published, but not enough to set up parameters which we could break or work within. Organising as a group gave us visibility, credibility and access to institutions, publishers and other groups in the community. The workshop gave us the confidence to approach publishers, which as individuals we might never have done. It answered the vital question that haunted all of us: is my writing of any interest or use to anyone else?

(Asian Women Writers' Workshop 1988: 1–2)

The workshop – or collective as it later renamed itself – was important in encouraging, supporting and publishing work by Asian women. Its first publication *Right of Way*, was published in 1988 and is a beautifully written anthology that uses poetry and prose, realism, myth and fantasy, to explore the variety of South Asian women's culture and experience. In addition to encouraging Asian women's writing, the collective also ran workshops in the community. It was committed to promoting writing in a supportive and collective context – writing which testifies to the problems and concerns of an otherwise silenced minority within British society.

Whatever their feelings of marginality, ten years of work – marked in 1994 by the publication of a second anthology *Flaming Spirit* – was a testimony to the achievements of the collective. *Flaming Spirit* was published by Virago and in the foreword to the book, the two editors – founder members Rukhsana Ahmad and Rahila Gupta – looked back over ten years of the collective's work:

As we celebrate our tenth anniversary, the Asian Women Writers' collective continues to be a safe and supportive space for Asian women writers. Our greatest wish is to encourage new writers both in developing their own writing skills as well as in feeding into wider networks of, for example, performance poetry, radio and TV scriptwriting, journalism, visual arts, etc. *Flaming Spirit* is an important achievement in an on-going process of recognition of Asian women's writing in Britain. Some of us have been commissioned to write for TV and radio, some are well respected in national performance poetry circuits, whilst others are becoming published novelists. For many of us, however, writing is not a professional activity, and the collective is just as valuable for sharing our views, experiences and ideas. Within our network women have collaborated formally and informally on various creative projects and we have all benefited from a camaraderie and friendship which enriches our lives as well as our writing.

(Ahmad and Gupta 1994: vii)

The themes and issue taken up in the South Asian women's writing that emerged from the collective are many. They include the importance of knowing one's history, roots and heritage, that is to say, of knowing about life, history and culture before emigration. They further include the importance of contesting the colonial and racist attitudes and assumptions confronted in the media and in everyday life and of articulating and affirming South Asian experience in both its positive and negative aspects, for example the experience of racism and of problems within the different South Asian communities. Related to these are the need to negotiate difference, crucially that between South Asian cultures and religions and contemporary British society and to achieve positive identities in the face of racism.

Many British South Asian families who are originally from the Indian sub-continent still have links with families and communities in India, Pakistan and Bangladesh. These links are often renewed and strengthened by arranged marriages. Ties of religion, language and culture, together with patterns of immigration, have helped sustain communities within the urban areas where most South Asian people have settled. The establishment of institutions such as mosques and temples on the one hand, and cultural, advice and support centres on the other, as well as the flourishing of shops and other small businesses and a South Asian press, have provided communities with an infrastructure. This has enabled cultural norms and practices, derived from the Indian sub-continent to survive, sometimes with fewer changes than in India, Pakistan or Bangladesh.

Recent Asian women's writing raises questions of culture and identity in the context of immigration, racism and the bi-culturalism of second generation South Asian Britons. In novels, short stories and poems, writers look at family life and work both in Britain and in the Indian sub-continent. They offer both positive images of South Asian culture and critiques of aspects of the norms and values of the different communities. They explore the problems that South Asian women face in Britain and examine the negative aspects of traditional religions and culture for women.

Among the key themes represented in both *Right of Way* and *Flaming Spirit* are the problems and conflicts that result from moving from the Indian sub-continent to Britain. Coloured by the legacy of colonialism in which Britain was portrayed as the Mother of Empire, emigration is imagined as the move to a better life. The reality depicted in the fiction tells a different story. The narratives testify to the difficulties faced by divided families where the wives and children wait to join husbands and fathers in Britain. They wait years for visas and are subjected to humiliating investigations into their sexual status and kinship ties. In 'Sisters' by Sibani Raychaudhuri, for example, the wife and children have to wait so long for a visa that when it finally comes through, the eldest daughter is denied access to Britain because she is 18 and no longer officially dependent (Ahmad and Gupta 1994: 16–28). The experience of emigration can be both harrowing and destructive, as it is for the central character in 'The Nightmare' by Ruhksana Ahmad. This story describes the fate of an Indian woman who comes to Britain with her children to join her husband from whom she has been separated for ten years. It opens in a mental hospital where Fariha has been taken by her husband, Salim. She has suffered a nervous breakdown after Salim forced her to have an abortion following contact with rubella (Asian Women Writers' Workshop 1988: 19–25).

Fariha's identity is shown to be grounded in traditional Indian attitudes to motherhood and marriage. Like her mother before her, she sees a woman's value in her children and her duty in adapting to her husband. 'A man is like a vessel, hard and unchanging, and a good woman should be like water, flow and adapt herself to his shape' (Asian Women Writers' Workshop 1988: 20). Fariha's relationship with her husband has not been happy. For ten years he worked in England before bringing his family over. He sent money home, but not regularly. By the time he sends for her his own expectations have been changed by his life in Britain:

> It was a shock when he saw them arriving at the airport; talk about the reality betraying the dream. She looked . . . 'fat' . . . his mind had hesitated over the word then. And so much older than she ought. And the children, too. They looked so dark and, for some reason, poverty stricken. Much darker than he remembered them. Yes, the sun bakes, he reminded himself. They were toddlers when he'd left.
> (Asian Women Writers' Workshop 1988: 22)

The children adapt quickly, but Fariha does not. In the mental hospital she is given heavy drug treatment and at the end of six months she is released, only to be told by Salim that he has a job in the United States and she cannot accompany him because of her history of mental illness. He plans to send her back to her family in India and take the children with him to the America. 'The Nightmare' shows the consequences of immigration for a woman whose husband has become assimilated to Western norms while she clings to her Indian cultural values and identity in a foreign and hostile environment. It powerfully evokes the pain of her life in a loveless marriage away from family support and traditional values. For Fariha no negotiation is possible with her new life.

Conflicts of culture and identity arising from the experience of immigration are shown to affect not only first generation immigrants but their British-born children. Generational differences are intensified for second generation South Asian women by the experience of growing up in British society where gender norms and expectations are not only different, but also in conflict with parental values. 'Leaving Home' by Rahila Gupta, for example, looks at the problems of the younger generation of Pakistani women who are attempting to negotiate two cultures (Asian Women Writers' Workshop 1988: 32–45). Zara, a 21-year-old, unemployed and desperate to go to art school, lives a schizophrenic life. She dresses differently in and outside the home, transforming her public, Punk image – spiked hair with pink tips, skin-tight, shiny, black trousers and boots – into something more acceptable to her traditional family before returning home each day. To escape her dual life and to go to art college, she plans a marriage of convenience to a Muslim man (Ahmad) from the same tiny village in Pakistan from which her family has come to Britain. Ahmad has had two applications for political asylum rejected.

Zara's plans go wrong from the day of her marriage. She has saved to go to college and organized a housing association flat. After the wedding, however, Ahmad refuses to leave her flat and attempts to rape her. While she defends herself successfully, Ahmad continues to pursue her. Helped by a Black women's centre, she is reconciled with her family who respond supportively to her situation, asking only that she pretend still to be married. The problems of cultural difference and aspirations incompatible with tradition Muslim life are not resolved, but the story suggests that even traditional families can be tolerant.

If the problems of what has come to be called 'hybridity' and of bi-culturalism or the lack of it are important themes in the anthologies, so are the less attractive aspects of modern Britain – particularly its racism. One powerful and disturbing story from *Flaming Spirit*, Tanika Gupta's 'Rebecca and the Neighbours', depicts the experience of racial abuse and the consequences of one teenaged girl's resistance to it (Ahmad and Gupta 1994: 67–79). Rebecca and her younger sister Savitri live with their parents on a housing estate. Rebecca is lively and rebellious. The appearance on the estate of an extreme right-wing family transforms their lives into one of racial harassment and perpetual fear, which Rebecca seeks to resist. She collects evidence of racial harassment and is successful in persuading the council to evict the family. Before they leave, however, she is gang-raped in a lift and left in a pool of her attackers' urine. Found by other neighbours, she is unable to tell her family what has happened and as a result of the incident suffers a complete change of personality. She is transformed into a depressed and unhappy teenager, who never speaks and is finally sent to stay with her family in India. Eventually her parents go to join her, leaving Savitri alone, now a student at university. In this story one sister survives racism, the other is its total victim.

I want to turn now to look in some detail at the novel, *A Wicked Old Woman*, by one of the founder members of the Asian Women Writers' Collective, Ravinder Randhawa.[2] *A Wicked Old Woman* tells a familiar tale, the story of Kulwant (Kuli) Singh who came to Britain as a young child with her mother and sister to join a father she had not seen for many years. As the narrative opens, Kuli, now a divorced grandmother, assumes the cover of a poor, crippled, bag lady – someone beyond the limits of both respectable British and Asian society – in order to explore life in the broader Asian community. The novel sets out to contest the idea voiced by a white nurse at the beginning of the novel that 'We all live in the same world' (Randhawa 1987: 3) and to explore the various worlds in which South Asian people live in contemporary Britain. These worlds encompass those of poor, retired, elderly men; the successful Asian middle classes; Asian working-class life; self-help and support groups; mixed marriages; and young people who have joined originally white sub-cultures or dropped out completely. It is a varied picture of a multifarious set of lives, lifestyles and identities that white discourses usually lump together indiscriminately as the so-called 'Asian community'.

Through a series of loosely linked, unnumbered vignettes of life in Britain, the novel traces moments from the central character's past and present, moulding them into an overarching narrative about cultural difference, racism and identity. The short episodic chapters cover a wide range of issues. These include the patronizing treatment of Asian people by white professionals and by liberal do-gooders and the experience of racism ranging from abuse on the streets to murderous arson attacks on Asian homes. They further include dominant notions of Asian women which range from Orientalist ideas about female sexuality to women as passive victims of restrictive cultural norms and the pressure to conform to British norms and to criticize and reject Indian and Pakistani culture as some how traditional and more primitive. The novel depicts the work of Asian advice centres and self-help groups and the problems caused for families by the bi-cultural pressures on second generation children. It vividly evokes the impossibility of successfully choosing to be either Indian or British when one is by circumstance a 'hybrid'. These issues are raised through accounts of the lives of Asian characters who range from the very old to young adults and are loosely linked through extended families and the formal and informal structures of the South Asian community.

The second chapter of the novel, which recounts a defining episode from Kulwant's childhood, sets the framework for many of the themes which structure the text as a whole. While still a teenaged schoolgirl, Kuli is forced to confront the question of who she is and where she belongs. Chosen as girlfriend by much desired Michael, Kuli finds herself living a double life. Michael views her in Orientalist terms as his sensuous Eastern princess. Meanwhile she hides his existence from her family. The desire to be accepted by her white school friends forces her to confront white definitions of her culture as more primitive. When Michael proposes marriage she feels compelled to choose between the two cultures rather than negotiate a bi-cultural existence. She refuses Michael and demands an arranged marriage instead of the higher education that her parents want her to pursue. Her choice results in a failed marriage with a man from India who eventually leaves Kuli for a much younger woman. The ensuing divorce has profound and destructive effects on the family as a whole.

The novel traces the question of identity and belonging through the different generations and characters in the text. Both Kuli's brother and her own children are torn by the conflicts and contradictions between South Asian and British culture. These are particularly pronounced for Kuli's son and daughter-in-law Avind and Shirley, who are in a 'mixed marriage'. Shirley is determined to enable her children to belong to both traditions by seeing that they are taught their father's language and culture. The couple come up against negative attitudes towards difference in both the white and Asian communities as they confront negative attitudes to mixed marriages.

In *A Wicked Old Woman* the extreme effects of the failure to negotiate both cultures and resolve issues of identity and belonging in ways that allow one to live a positive life are illustrated by the desperate story of story Rani/Rosalind, an Asian teenaged girl who chooses to live white, drops out, lives rough and ends up in a mental hospital after killing a white man in self-defence. All the different and divided members of the South Asian community come together in a defence campaign for Rani. The novel suggests that whatever the internal problems and conflicts in the Asian community, differences become insignificant in the face of white racist oppression.

Among the other sub-plots which raise the question of community solidarity vis-à-vis white power is the story of Maya. Maya is employed to do research for a television programme on mental illness in the Asian community to be made by two white men. The story raises questions of control of the means of representation, meaning and the need for positive images. It is resolved by Maya's acquisition of editorial control over the programme.

This theme of media representations of ethnic minority communities also figures in more recent work by British South Asian writers, for example, in the novel *Life isn't all ha ha hee hee* by Meera Syal. Published in 1999, this text deals with the lives of three very different women from the South Asian community of East London: Tania, Sunita and Chila. The novel develops a number of themes, most of which can be seen as the product of a community, well established and self-confident enough to turn its attention to its own internal dynamics rather than focus predominantly on the problems caused by white Britain. A woman-centred novel, the text follows the lives of three childhood friends who live their South Asianness in very different ways. Tania is a programme maker for television who negotiates two worlds with increasing difficulty as she begins to address South Asian issues in her work. Sunita is a former student radical who, after meeting her future husband at university, becomes pregnant, has an abortion and fails her law exams. She marries only to become a downtrodden housewife and mother who, in the course of the narrative, once more emancipates herself. The third character, Chila, is a woman widely perceived as having neither beauty nor academic accomplishments. She eventually marries a man considered a good match by her family and she dedicates herself to domesticity. Despite her constant efforts to please her husband, she finds that he rekindles a former love affair with Tania, while Chila is pregnant with his child. She leaves the relationship determined to raise her son as a single parent. Through the depiction of the lives of these three women, *Life isn't all ha ha hee hee* raises questions of cultural difference, identity, family expectations and traditional cultural practices, illustrating how they are negotiated in different ways by second generation British South Asian women.

As this discussion of recent South Asian British women's writing suggests, difference as depicted in short stories and novels is very far from postmodern notions of free choice, celebration and play. Difference is shown to be socially constituted by both the dominant and minority cultures within which the writers' work is located. Dominant forms of British culture construct Asian people as 'other', in ways that fail to do justice to the reality of their lives. In doing so they draw on long established colonial stereotypes, racist assumptions and monolithic notions of so-called traditional Asian culture. Women are seen as both sensual and passive, as desirably erotic and as the victims of rigid patriarchal regimes. Moreover, the consequences of being different in a racist society are hammered home by the constant threat of verbal and physical attack, violence and arson.

The images of white people in the fiction range from the patronizingly liberal and paternalistic – itself a mild form of racism – to the most brutal forms of far right racism (see Gupta 1994). There are positive images of white people in the texts and they are marked out as different from the norm by a non-hierarchical acceptance of difference and mutual respect. Yet it is not only dominant white British culture that defines identity and difference for Asian women writers. It is also the Asian cultural contexts in which their characters live. For some these are set in the Indian sub-continent, for others in Britain's Asian South communities. The depiction of these communities is far from romantic. We see forms of oppression that relate to caste, class and religion as well as the positive aspects of family and community. The position is most difficult and contradictory for characters who are second generation or of mixed parentage. Women and girls, in particular are subject to irreconcilable contradictions and, as *A Wicked Old Woman* suggests, choosing between poles is rarely a satisfactory solution. What is called for is a life of negotiation that leads to a redefinition of boundaries. Hybridity, here, is far from liberating, yet cultural difference only matters because of the hierarchical power relations which constitute and structure it. This must surely be one of the main messages for white readers of this fiction. Another important message is one that is also central to Chandra Mohanty's influential essay on Western feminist treatments of 'Third World' women, 'Under Western Eyes' (1991). Mohanty demonstrates how the Western gaze, including the Western feminist gaze, tends to construct Third World 'otherness' in ways that deny the differences and specificity of other cultures. Similarly British South Asian cultures, in which a wide range of different types of people are living lives in which they are active agents not just passive victims, become reduced to monolithic, stereotyped and ethnocized categories such as the 'Asian community'. In much British discourse this construction of the Asian community is characterized by its victim status – victim often not only of white racism but of a set of so-called traditional norms and values. South Asian women's writing resists this strategy, offering testimonies not only to oppression and exploitation, but also to resistance and negotiation. It affirms a plural South Asian experience that goes beyond narrow racist boundaries and oppositions and offers hope for a better future.

Recent fiction by British women of South Asian descent suggests that Britain is not only multi-cultural but is reshaping notions of culture and identity, producing hybrid forms that draw on both so-called 'ethnic' and white British identities, cultural forms and practices. It is in this work that hegemonic racist and ethnocentric white British ideas of otherness are being made explicit and challenged. It is in this work, too, that the history of Britain is being rewritten to foreground the history of people of Colour in Britain and the importance of empire to the making of British society and culture. It is here that ideas of Britishness as white, and of traditional so-called 'ethnic' culture as static and unchanging are being subverted. The production of new, hybrid forms of culture and identity are explored, together with the problems and experience of living in a racist Britain that is in the process of shifting towards an acceptance of cultural diversity. It is in this work that the radical discrepancy between official discourse on multi-cultural, culturally diverse Britain is explored and ideas produced about how this gap might be narrowed.

Further reading

Ahmad, R. and Gupta, R. (eds) (1994) *Flaming Spirit*. Stories from the Asian Women Writers' Collective. London: Virago.

Asian Women Writers' Workshop (1988) *Right of Way*. London: The Women's Press.

Brah, A. (1996) *Cartographies of Diaspora: Contesting Identities*. London and New York: Routledge.

VISUALIZING DIFFERENCE: SOUTH ASIANS ON SCREEN

When I'm with Asian people, like at weddings, I act Indian. And when you're at work or when you've got mixed people there, you act British, you talk in English and everything. You have like two different characters.

Asian, female, London, 25–30 age group.

. . .

I fell off the seat when that Asian family took over the corner shop in *Coronation Street*, but you can't recognise them as an Asian family because they are not, culturally – that's not there, it's just them, it's just the colour of the skin what's there. There is nothing about them being Asians, any traditions.

Mixed heritage, male, Birmingham, 16–24 age group.

. . .

When you go on holiday and they say where are you from, I say Britain or England. I wouldn't say I'm from India, no way.

Asian, male, London, 25–35 age group.
(Parekh 2000: 41)

The exploration of the experience of emigration and of living and growing up in Britain's South Asian communities has not been restricted to writing by women and men of South Asian descent. The cinema and television, too, have begun to explore these areas with rise of a new generation of British South Asian scriptwriters and film and programme makers.[1] Television and cinematic representations are never arbitrary, they are scripted constructions – whether fiction or documentary. They invite interpretation and that create meaning through audience negotiation of specific uses of image, sound and editing. In the case of television, they are governed by both broadcasting and programme scheduling policies. Moreover, both television and cinema films have to attract funding in order to be made and distributed. Much South Asian television has been restricted to 'ethnic minority slots' (see Ross 1996: 119–30). Moving out from these into the mainstream can prove difficult if the potential audience is judged by funders to be small. This has meant that South Asian film and television programme makers wishing to do so, have had to address a broader audience that is largely white. Ethnic minority film and programme making is often also constrained by the burden of representativeness. Whatever communities they depict, individual programmes inevitably privilege particular voices and perspectives. Yet the paucity of representations of non-white people on British television, as in the cinema, has meant that those programmes that are broadcast become invested with more importance and authority than they would otherwise be expected to bear. They are often read by white audiences as representative of ethnic minority communities and they are subject to specific expectations within ethnic minority communities themselves. These expectations include style, subject matter and approach. Many of the issues of representation that have been identified by critics in relation to Black filmmaking, also hold for South Asian British film and television. Thus, for example, in her book on Black and Asian film and television, Karen Ross argues that:

> Much of the work from contemporary black filmmakers has emerged as a critical response to the historical denial of authority to control images of their own communities and many of their efforts have generated intense debates around both aesthetics and content. While there are continuing arguments over the appropriate use of realist or modernist styles, the broader problematic revolves around the issue of representation and whether texts should only portray 'positive' images and/or deal with the race relations discourse, or whether they can concern themselves with micro and specific interests and issues which speak *from* a black perspective but not *for* the black community.
>
> (Ross 1996: 50)

Like filmmakers of African and African-Caribbean descent, British South Asian writers, directors and producers are constantly faced with tensions over representation. They inevitably find themselves working in a field that is overdetermined by a long history of racialized stereotyping. At stake are issues of the control of imagery, but also the impossibility of controlling how images are read. This has lead to calls for positive images rather than films and programmes that explore the complexities of South Asian communities and may include less than positive representations. Mainstream, white perceptions of the South Asian 'other' have been shaped by a long history of colonial and racist modes of representation that include now classic 1980s popular cinematic and television representations of the Raj such as *Heat and Dust*, *Gandhi*, *A Passage to India*, the *Raj Quartet* and the *Far Pavillions*.[2] Repeated showings of these often lavish productions continue to recycle images of the colonial native as other, even if their portrayal of white colonial subjects and their exercising of power has become more differentiated than previously. For a white British public, this body of cinematic and fictional television representations of colonial South Asians is compounded by fifty years of familiar, negative, racist stereotypes of South Asian migrants to Britain.

Given the small number of films and television programmes that are made depicting British South Asian life, questions of content and modes of representation figure more prominently than they would if white audiences were constantly exposed to a varied range of images of British South Asian life. As Black filmmaker Isaac Julien and critic Kobena Mercer have argued: 'If only one voice is given the "right to speak", that voice will be heard, by the major culture as "speaking for" the many who are excluded or marginalised from access to the means of representation' (Julien and Mercer 1988: 4). Thus a crucial issue for both Black and South Asian filmmakers is the problem of being expected to represent an entire community. Moreover, there is clearly a need to contest hegemonic assumptions about ethnic minority communities in the media, for example that they are a 'problem'. This issue is linked to the potential dangers of showing images that might reaffirm racist views in white viewers, since it is impossible to control how texts are read.

The visual is central to the cultural politics of representation. Whereas written texts may engage the non-South Asian reader using techniques promoting empathy or enabling the reader to 'see' the world through South Asian eyes, it cannot insist on an engagement with characters as visibly other. Reading novels and watching film versions of them are very different experiences. While films inevitably tend to reduce the degree of complexity that is found in novels, they insist on an engagement with that visual difference that is fundamental to racism. Often the juxtaposition of the visual and the aural can undermine common assumptions about ethnic others. For example, Gurinder Chadha's first film: *I'm British but . . .* (1989 BFI Films), which was a British Film Institute production with additional funding from Channel 4, voices the views of four young South Asians from different parts of Britain and Northern Ireland: the Rhondda Valley in South Wales, Belfast in Northern Ireland, Glasgow in Scotland and Birmingham in the English West Midlands. They speak about being Asian in Britain in strong regional accents that sound quintessentially British or Irish, while their appearances undermine the assumption that to be British is to be white. The interviews are interspersed with bhangra rhythms and rap vocals that insist on hybridity.

In the 1990s South Asian film and television began to move from ethnic minority slots, often broadcast in a mixture of English and South Asian languages, into the mainstream. Recent films have raised questions of gender, cultural difference, hybridity, generational conflicts, identity and racism. A significant landmark in this shift was the film *Bhaji on the Beach* (1993), written by Meera Syal and Gurinder Chadha, which was shown on television and in 'arthouse' cinemas and released on video. It is now often taught on film and media studies courses. *Bhaji on the Beach* – a fiction film –

raises questions of the politics if representation, and was criticized by some British South Asians for not restricting itself to positive images of South Asians. It is explicitly feminist in its approach to its subject matter, offering a series of insights into the lives of a group of South Asian women from the Midlands, who range in age from teenaged girls to elderly ladies. They come together for a day trip to Blackpool organized by the local Asian women's centre. The film raises issues of white racism and ethnic stereotyping, problems within the South Asian community, including cross-generational conflict and domestic violence as a response to the changing role of women. It also looks at the community's reaction to interracial relations, in this case, a young South Asian woman and a Black man.

Bhaji on the Beach is centrally concerned with questions of culture and identity. From the older women who cling to traditional values, brought with them from the Indian sub-continent, to the teenaged girls anxious to experience 'a bit of the other' – in this case white boys – ethnic and gender politics are played out against a racist white society. Subjectivities and identities are portrayed as both fractured and complex and no attempt is made to create homogeneous positive images. Indeed the only character who is completely at home with herself in the film is the middle-class, westernized visitor from Bombay, who chides the older women over their outmoded notions of tradition.

A major theme in the film is the changing role of South Asian women who are no longer ready to conform to subordinate roles within the family. While older women are shown to exercise power, it is very much in the form of power behind the throne. The younger generation are no longer willing to settle for this and their challenges to oppressive patriarchal practices produce family tensions and even domestic violence. Yet because these issues are rooted in storylines and characters with which white viewers can empathize, they do not become issues peculiar to South Asians. The social realism of the film is interrupted by the visions of one of the characters, Ashe, which vividly express the clash of cultures and her unhappiness at her traditional role and her critical attitude towards those younger women who do not conform to parental and community values.

Racism in the film takes many forms ranging from grafitti on shop fronts and verbal abuse by young white men, to the orientalist stereotyping of Asian women by white men, a stereotyping that restricts them just as much as unchanging notions of tradition. It is against these white preconceptions, as much as ideas of traditional culture, that the women have to fight for identities with which they can live.

If the distribution of *Bhaji on the Beach* was mostly restricted to art house cinemas and television, Gurinda Chadha's film, *Bend It Like Beckham* (UK/Germany 2002) was a mainstream commercial success. It examines conflicts that arise for a second generation South Asian girl from the clash between her own aspirations and her parents' expectations. Jesse is the 18-year-old daughter of a British Sikh family, who are immigrants from East Africa. She is in the process of taking A levels with a view to studying law at university, but her secret passion is football and her hero, the captain of the English team, David Beckham. At the opening of the film her football career is restricted to playing with Asian boys in the park. A member of the local girls' team, Jules, notices her footballing skills and recruits her for the team. Jesse does not tell her parents, and after they have discovered it, she goes to great lengths to hide the fact that she continues to play. Her cover is finally broken when her father sees her photograph in the local paper when the team goes to Hamburg. The plot reaches crisis point for Jesse when the most important game of her life, attended by American College talent spotters, clashes with her elder sister's wedding. Her father allows her to leave the wedding to play in the second half of the match and both she and Jules are offered full sports scholarships in Santa Clara, California. The narrative is made more complex by a subplot, in which both Jules and Jesse are in competition for the affections of their young Northern Irish coach. The sub-plot ends with the promise of another broken family taboo as Jesse looks outside the Sikh community for a sexual partner.

Bend It Like Beckham focuses on the strong differences between Jesse and her sister who is about to enter into a traditional Sikh marriage, though one based on love rather than family arrangement. Style of dress, body language and behaviour mark the differences between the sisters. Both parents worry about Jesse's failure to conform to traditional modes of femininity. Their protectiveness is shown to be motivated by the desire to keep their daughter away from the racism that they assume she will come up against if she moves outside of her own community.

The film works by emphasizing both difference and sameness. It parallels two families: that of Jesse and her white footballing friend Jules, and emphasizes the shared problems that the girls face. For example, both experience difficulties with their mothers, who do not approve of football for girls. Indeed Jules' mother is so worried about her daughter's apparent lack of appropriate femininity that she comes to believe that the girls are lesbians. In both cases it is the fathers who come to support their daughters in their aspirations to be women footballers. Similarly, by developing a sub-plot in which both the South Asian and white central characters are in competition for one man, sameness is emphasized. Yet in the depiction of Sikh family life, including a traditional wedding, cultural difference is put on colourful display for white audiences and what might be read as over-protectiveness is explained in terms of the need to protect Jesse from the racism that her parents suffered. The filming of cultural difference is embedded in familiar problems, recognizable to the audience whatever their ethnic background. Questions of identity in the film focus on the difficulties for second generation girls – both Jesse and her sister – of living forms of identity that are hybrid, in a familial climate in which they are expected to conform to traditional cultural values and expectations.

Similar issues emerge in another mainstream success released in 2002, *Anita and Me*, written by Meera Syal and directed by Metin Hüseyin. The film is based on a novel of the same name by Meera Syal, that tells the story of two years in the life of a young South Asian girl, who is being brought up in a former mining village in the Black

Country near Wolverhampton in the English West Midlands. Meena is the daughter of the only non-white family in the village and the only family who are explicitly middle-class, though this difference is over-ridden by ethnic difference. Both the novel and the film look at questions of class, gender, race, identity and belonging. However, the film version simplifies the plots, reduces the time period and downplays or omits some of the important elements in the novel that are central to Meena's acquisition of a positive identity, placing more emphasis on the role of Meena's relationship with Anita. Both texts are structured as first person narratives with the film version using a voice-over to reveal to the viewer Meena's inner thoughts.

Anita and Me offers a humorous portrayal of working-class rural, Black Country life. Set in 1972, the film has a cast of strong women who bond on the basis of hardship. In addition to the Kumars' immediate neighbours, further characters include Uncle Alan, the local minister, Hairy Neddy, who plays in a pop band and Sam Lowbridge who becomes a skinhead. The film depicts Meena's relationship with her 'bad girl' friend, Anita, who is older than Meena and eventually become Lowbridge's girlfriend and goes 'Paki-bashing' with him. This leads to a break in their relationship, which, though irrevocable in the novel, is bridged in the film by Anita reading Meena's diary, just before the Kumar family move away. Among the central issues raised by the film is Meena's struggle for a positive identity as the only South Asian child in a village where life is governed by low-level racism which takes both exoticizing and more vicious forms. She spends her time with white children and indulges in the same early teen pursuits as the white girls. She is fluent in both the local dialect and mainstream teenage culture. The hybrid qualities of her identity come into full focus when she is placed in situations in which she is measured against the children of South Asians visitors from the town who have been brought up in accordance with other South Asian cultural norms. A further important issue in the film is how white people do or do not negotiate difference.

South Asian difference is visually manifest in the depiction of family life, including Meena's grandmother's visit from India, regular social visits by other South Asian families and a trip to the temple in Birmingham. Meena's contact with white children is much more extensive than the white children's with her family. Although her mother teaches at the local primary school, Anita is the only white person to enter the family home and then only once. Meena draws her own comparisons between her parents and those of the white children as she learns something of her parents' experiences in India before coming to the UK. For example, when she asks her father if he fought in the war, she is told that he had different battles to fight in India where Britain was the enemy. She comes to learn that she cannot simply be white, as she sometimes wishes, nor simply South Asian in any traditional sense. She is of necessity a hybrid subject with plural identities.

Gender, ethnic stereotyping and questions of identity are also raised in work by British men of South Asian descent. Perhaps the most successful of British born, second generation writers is Hanif Kureishi, who became well known for his film, *My*

Beautiful Launderette (1985), which deals with a gay relationship between a young South Asian man and his white childhood friend, a former member of the extreme right-wing National Front. The film raises issues of racism, sexuality, violence and bigotry in London in the early 1980s. Kureishi's novel *The Buddha of Suburbia* (1990) looks in detail at racism, identity, culture and politics in the previous decade, the 1970s and was filmed for BBC 2 and first broadcast in 1993.[3] *The Buddha of Suburbia* tells the story of a decade in British life that began with the legacy of the 1960s, saw the rise of punk rock and the Anti-Nazi League, and ended with Margaret Thatcher's election to government.

At the heart of both the novel and film are forms of racism and ethnic stereotyping which lead not only to violent attacks on South Asian individuals, homes and businesses, but to determine the terms on which Asians can access mainstream society. Thus the audience repeatedly sees how liberal and left-wing whites restrict Karim, an up-and-coming Asian actor, to so-called 'Asian' roles. The story line follows the lives of three interconnected families, that of Haroon and his English wife Margaret, that of Haroon's childhood friend Anwar and his wife Jeeta, and that of Haroon's mistress Eva, whose son Charlie, attends the same school as his son Karim. Karim is at the centre of the different narratives. He is the child of a mixed marriage. His father is a civil servant, born to an aristocratic Indian family and raised in India. Haroon studied law in Britain, settled there, and married an English woman. All the Indian characters in the film and novel become downwardly mobile in Britain, when compared to their social status in India. Thus, Anwar has a corner shop, and his son-in-law, an engineer who is not interested in shopkeeping, ends up on the dole. The film shows how racism and social exclusion have the effect of pushing Anwar towards embracing traditional cultural norms and practices to which he previously did not subscribe. Anwar goes on hunger strike in order to force his westernized daughter, Jamila, into an arranged marriage with Changez, who has been sent to Britain from India by Anwar's brother. Changez is used in the film to cast an outsider gaze on British South Asian life. While he is depicted as both overweight and ugly, with a deformed hand, he is also a very positive character with a critical but warmly human perspective on life. Jamila lives with her husband but never consummates the marriage. She becomes active in a left-wing political party (clearly based on the Socialist Workers Party, in particular its 1970s anti-fascist campaigns) and ends up in a lesbian relationship in a left-wing commune.

The Buddha of Suburbia is both the portrait of a decade, the 1970s, and a study in racist and ethnic stereotyping. Class plays a crucial role, both in the depiction of South Asian and British social circles. Class and locality dictate that Anwar, the corner shop keeper, and his family in Peckham are much more directly exposed to racism in its most violent forms. The middle-class, white, artistic and intellectual circles in which Haroon and Karim move as a result of Haroon's liaison with Eva perpetrate racial stereotyping in different ways. Thus, at the start of the plot, Haroon, a Muslim, is able to masquerade as a Buddhist wise man with no questions asked. Karim, who becomes an actor, finds himself restricted by ethnic stereotyping. From his first role as Mowgli in

The Jungle Book, to his success with a left-wing theatre group and his offer of a role in a television soap opera about Asian people, he is forced to conform to roles that depict images of Asianness as defined by the white people who control the theatres and television.

Questions of culture and identity are central to the different subplots. Brought into sharp relief by Haroon's mixed relationships, they are also raised by the contrast offered by Changez, newly arrived from Bombay, and are further framed by white stereotyping, other forms of racism and anti-racist politics. Karim's homelife is lived in mostly white environments, from the neighbourhood and school to his mother's extended family. His only access to South Asian culture, other than his civil servant father, is through his friendship with Jamila. Neither he nor his mother have any doubts that he is English not Indian, as she points out when he is forced by the director to 'black up' for his role as Mowgli in *The Jungle Book*. For white society, whether working-class or upper-middle-class, however he is a 'Paki' or Indian expected to play only such roles. For Jamila, he is a traitor to the Black cause in a climate where neo-Nazis are regularly attacking Black and Asian people. For Changez he is westernized to the point of having lost himself and any sense of morality. It is Karim's class position and the circles in which he moves that allows him to avoid the harsher realities of racism. Yet, while he moves between radically different social and political groups, assuming and discarding identities as required, he remains in his own mind a product of suburbia as he tell his friend and later stepbrother Charlie when they first come across punk rock. Charlie, an aspiring pop musician, sees Punk as his way forward. Karim replies: 'We're not like them. We don't hate the way they do. We've got no reason to. We are not from the estates. We haven't been through what they have' (Kureishi 1990: 132). Charlie, however, realizes early on that success is really only a question of playing at revolution or politics.

For Karim's father, Indianness is also something that he can play at, masquerading as a Buddhist holy man to meet white, middle-class expectations about the Indian other. Only Anwar is firmly rooted in an increasingly dogmatic and inflexible view of traditional Indian Muslim culture which he tries to impose on his only daughter. For Haroon and his son, identity is strategic and multiple.

Mixed relationships as a device for putting questions of culture and identity into sharp relief are frequently used in South Asian British culture. Other cinematic examples include the films *East is East* and *My Son the Fanatic* (discussed in Chapter 8). *East is East*, like the *Buddha of Suburbia*, is set in the 1970s, but this time in Salford in the north of England in 1971. It is based on an auto-biographical play by Ayub Khan-Din that he began in drama school and performed fifteen years later at the Royal Court theatre in 1996. In his introduction to the screenplay, Khan-Din writes:

It was important to me from the early stages that this shouldn't be just one son's story but the story of a whole family, and not just an excuse for Paki-bashing my father (although this would have been easy to do as he behaved monstrously at times). But the more I looked at my parents and their relationship, especially considering the times they lived in, the more admiration I felt for their bravery. This was not a time of mixed-race marriages, which were barely acceptable in the middle-class salons of London. Anywhere else in Britain a white woman with a black man would be considered a prostitute. It must have been very hard for them, the hatred and the bigotry that they would have faced.

(Khan-Din 1999: viii)

The family at the centre of the narrative, the Khans, live like their white neighbours in a crowded back-to-back terraced house with no bathroom and an outdoor toilet. Two sons are at work, one at college and the other children are at school. The Khans run a fish and chip shop in which the children are expected to help out. Ella Khan, the mother, is a white, local, working-class Catholic. Zaheer Khan, known to his family and neighbours as George, is a Muslim from Pakistan who settled in Britain in 1937. He attends the mosque regularly and attempts to bring his children up as what he considers good Pakistanis and good Muslims.

The opening sequence of the film points to the dilemmas that the family face. It shows a Catholic Whitsun procession in which the six sons and tomboy daughter Meenah take a full part, carrying a crucifix and a statue, while the youngest boy, Sajid, strews rose petals in the street. Their involvement in Catholic rituals is kept secret from their father and when they are warned of his early return from the mosque, we see them dodging in and out of the narrow streets with their statues and flower petals, to avoid their father's on-looker's gaze. Comic in its presentation, this sequence sets the scene for all that follows. It signals the double life led by the children, who see themselves as English, not Pakistani.

Both their father's commitment to Islam and the children's rejection of their Pakistani heritage are explained in cultural terms as effects of race relations in Britain. We see posters of Enoch Powell in a neighbour's house, publicizing Powell's forthcoming visit to Salford, and we watch the Khan children looking at Powell's repatriation speech on the television and joking about applying it to their father. They are called 'Pakis' by their neighbours and are subject to minor forms of discrimination and abuse. Yet, apart from Maneer, the one devout Muslim son, they do not identify themselves as Pakistani but also talk derogatively about 'Pakis'. While Tariq wants to insist that they are English, and passes at a disco that excludes Pakistanis as 'Tony', Maneer supports his father's line of argument: 'We're not! No one round here thinks we're English. We're the Pakis who run the chippy' (Khan-Din 1999: 44).

Once a month the family visit their Pakistani relatives in Bradford, where they are fed curry and attend a Bollywood film. While their English mother attempts to accommodate her husband's desire to bring up his children as good Muslims, the six children, with the exception of Maneer, all resist his attempts. Their resistance is only contained by their fear of their father.

The characterization of George is perhaps the most controversial aspect of the film.

George occupies an in-between position in the film. He is between cultures, something that is symbolized by his accepting half a cup of tea after arguments or moments of tenderness with his wife and children. He has been in Britain for decades, having left his first wife behind in Pakistan. He is both proud of his fish and chip business and ambivalent towards his English life and family. He seeks to be fully part of the local mosque-based Muslim community, but is set apart both by his marriage to an English Catholic and his children's unwillingness to conform to Muslim expectations. His relationship with his children is based on his assumption of absolute obedience on their part, yet they constantly resist, hiding from the minibus that will take them to the mosque, sitting bored and unengaged during their lessons in the mosque, failing to learn Urdu or eating bacon and sausages when George is out of the house.

It is, however, the issue of arranged marriages that brings things to a head. George's first attempt to marry off his eldest son ends in disaster when gay Nazir literally runs from his wedding ceremony and is disowned by his father. George takes the chance, offered him by the Mullah, of arranged marriages for his next two sons with unattractive but better off Pakistani women from Bradford. He believes that this will integrate his children into the community and make them good Pakistanis. Tariq, in particular, fiercely contests any form of Pakistani identity and the whole affair ends in discord and domestic violence.

More so than the *Buddha of Suburbia*, *East is East* has strong comic elements but these do not detract from the seriousness of the issues dealt with. While George is in many ways a tragic figure unable or unwilling to recognize that his children are mixed British, not Pakistani, the audience is encouraged to laugh at the ways in which his children elude his control. Despite his attempts to fashion them into his idea of good Pakistanis, they remain largely hostile to those aspects of Pakistani culture with which they come into contact. Their father's authoritarianism and failure to listen and understand is contrasted with their mother's pragmatic love and support for them against the outside world, whether brown or white. She is well aware of the prejudices and racism of white society and the attitudes of other South Asians to mixed marriages. Much of the humour of the film is at George's expense and the plot offers little scope for positive depictions of South Asian Muslim culture. Ultimately the characterization of George is rescued by its tragic elements, as he remains caught between two cultures and yet supported by Ella, even after episodes of domestic violence.

Much of the humour in the film can be read as, on the one hand, reinforcing stereotypes about Pakistanis, while suggesting that identity is a question of culture and background rather than what one looks like or who one's parents are. While it is the case that Salford working-class Catholic culture is also satirized in the film, arguably this does not serve to reinforce negative stereotypes in the non-South Asian Muslim viewer in the ways that as the portrayal of George and his Bradford connections threaten to.

The deconstructive potential of comedy

Comedy as a mode of critique is often ambiguous in its effects. It works as a double-edged sword, that may both deconstruct and reinforce stereotypes, depending on the viewing subject and position from which it is viewed. The second half of this chapter turns to the cultural politics of representation in comedy in more detail and considers how identities can be challenged and unfixed through one particular, controversial genre, television comedy. It examines comedy's effectivity in raising issues of cultural difference, racism and ethnocentrism and asks how powerfully it can challenge and transform the dominant, deconstructing identities, including those grounded in racism and ethnocentrism. A key question here is whether comedy can work to undermine stereotypes for white viewers and in the process put into question the certainty of the viewer as knowing subject.

My textual example, *Goodness Gracious Me*, began life as a radio comedy series in the 11pm spot on Radio 4, the BBC's talk-based network.[4] Radio 4 carries news, documentaries, drama, comedy, quiz shows and a range of informative factual programmes. The less than auspicious 11pm spot in the schedule is often used for comedy and, more particularly, to try out new types of programme. In 1998 the series, like other successful radio comedies before it, was transformed into a television series.

The programme's title, *Goodness Gracious Me*, was taken from the 1960s song of the same name, sung by the well-known comic actor, Peter Sellers in the role of a stereotypical Indian doctor in *The Millionairess*.[5] This was reworked into the signature tune of the series, which, like much of the programme is marked by self-aware references to pre-existing modes of representation that highlight long-established, commonsense British conceptions of South Asians. It has a regular format of short sketches using a familiar cast of characters many of whom reappear from week to week. The tempo is fast moving and many of the sketches are based on well-known existing BBC television programmes such as *The Book Programme*, *The Food Programme* and investigative journalism like *The Cook Report*. The sketches also reference other familiar genres, ranging from British cinematic and television representations of colonial India to previous television comedies, detective series, contemporary youth culture, film and popular music. The series is marked by a rich intertextuality and works on many different levels, depending on the ethnic background and prior knowledge of the audience.

Comedy is a necessarily controversial medium in which to tackle social and individual phenomena like racism, xenophobia and ethnocentrism. Race, class, gender and sexual orientation have long been mainstays of stand-up comedians in Britain, who, more often than not, continue to recycle familiar negative stereotypes for easy laughs (see Wagg 1998). Both racism and much comedy function through stereotyping and one crucial question in discussing *Goodness Gracious Me* is whether the reliance of both racism and comedy on stereotyping means that comedy is more likely to reinforce rather than challenge racist stereotypes. It is, of course, equally possible to argue that

the exaggerated reproduction of racialized stereotypes in comedy can work to deconstruct them, showing them to be absurd constructs rather than humorously distorted
mirrors of real life.

Most humour achieves its effects because it is to some extent grounded in popular
perceptions of everyday life. Thus the ubiquitous British mother-in-law joke may have
nothing to do with an audience's own experience of their mother-in-law, but it works
by referencing a long tradition within popular culture of negative stereotyping and by
evoking something that is popularly perceived as a problem within British culture.
Racism and the negative stereotyping of racial and ethnic others have a long history in
Western societies. As discussed in Chapter 1, they reached a high point in the nineteenth century with racial science and its construction of hierarchical categories of
different races. These categories were never simply descriptive of physiological difference. They attributed different moral, intellectual, sexual and cultural traits to
specific 'races'. Many of the social and cultural attributes that were linked by racial
scientists to phenotypic and skin-based differences became part of the collective consciousness of Western cultures producing stereotypical, racist assumptions about
'Africans', 'Asians' and so on. In Britain, these racist stereotypes received specific
inflections through the experience of empire and media and other popular cultural
representations of the colonized peoples in question.

If racism often works by creating stereotypes, it also allows for individual exceptions
who do not, however, undermine the general stereotype. The assumption that although
the person you know is fine, others in the same category, who remain unknown to you,
are a problem, is fundamental to racism. Humour is one way of exposing this practice
of token inclusion. For example, the successful Black British comedian Lenny Henry
makes substantial use of personal experience in his jokes and comedy sketches. In his
case, this is often an effective technique, given Henry's very positive relationship with
predominantly white audiences. As part of his *Live and Loud* tour (1994) he recounts a
conversation with a taxi driver who tells him: 'I hate them black bastards, except for
you Len because you're famous.' Henry adds a final line to the effect that the solution
to racism must therefore be for all Blacks to become famous, a joke that points to the
absurdity of particular forms of racism.[6]

Much comedy functions by rendering the familiar absurd. Yet absurdity and ridicule
can be read in different ways and in thinking about comedy we need to ask whether it is
always possible to distinguish between the caricature and the subject being carica-
tured. How does one ensure that this difference is recognized by the audience? In
evaluating the effects of comedy sketches, various factors need to be taken into
account. These include the question of who is speaking for or about whom – in other
words, who is the butt of the joke – and what power relations govern the positions of
speaker, subject of ridicule and audience. In looking at the racial politics of individual
comedy sketches, the question of the authority of the speaker is of crucial importance.
A second important question is what gives a comedian's voice its authority. In
analysing comedy, we need to examine closely not only where discursive authority lies,

but also how this authority is achieved. In the case of television comedy, it may be affirmed or undermined by use of camera and *mis-en-scene* as well as the actual verbal script and how this is delivered.

In *Goodness Gracious Me*, the sketches focus on a range of issues. These include many aspects of the experience of living as a South Asian British person in contemporary Britain. In addition to everyday life and the family, themes include the legacies of colonialism, stereotyping, acculturation and the overtly racist attitudes of dominant forms of white British culture. Further issues dealt with are the generational problems of difference and conflict between South Asian culture and religions and the society and culture of contemporary Britain. These differences and conflicts have profound effects on the identity, aspirations and lifestyles of British-born Asian people. The sketches span the generations from teenagers to their grandparents. The characters range from exaggerated portraits of an Indian nationalist to a family who want to be totally assimilated as English, and from teenaged rappers to traditional parents.

When looked at as a challenge to white British ethnocentrism, *Goodness Gracious Me* raises the question of the extent to which apparently progressive comedy is undermined by the long-standing reliance of mainstream comedy on racist stereotyping. For example, many of the sketches in *Goodness Gracious Me*, which seem to be addressed in the first instance to a South Asian British audience, satirize the Asian characters and play around with norms and stereotypes of Asian British life. Might this strategy not inadvertently lead to the reaffirmation of racist stereotypes among an audience that is predominantly white? White audience assumptions about Asian British people will, for the most part involve stereotypes, given the long history of demeaning comic representations in music hall, novels, cinema, television and so forth. With this in mind, I want to turn to some of the strategies that the programme uses to deconstruct or arguably sometimes reaffirm racial and ethnic stereotypes and how these strategies position the white viewer.

A common strategy in comedy is that of magnifying stereotypes and prejudice to absurd proportions. An example of this is a sketch from *Goodness Gracious Me* that directly addresses the widespread prejudice among white Britons that traditional Muslim families treat their daughters oppressively, denying them the freedoms enjoyed by non-Muslim girls and British women. 'Exposé', the sketch in question, is based on the recognizable genre of investigative journalism, exemplified by the successful BBC series *The Cook Report*. It opens with the image of a traditional Muslim man, recognizable by dress, hat and beard. Yet, despite his visible difference from the white British norm, he at the same time represents aspects of British normality. He is shown doing that quintessentially British thing: cutting the hedge in the well-tended front garden of his respectable suburban home. Stopped in his tracks by a reporter, Mr Ishak and his wife, are shown to be totally mystified by the questions that the reporter puts to them, questions which represent the widespread British view of Muslim families taken to extremes. The reporter suggests that Muslim parents lock up their daughters, beat them if they fail to achieve at school, prevent them from enjoying normal teenage pursuits and forcibly marry them off to distant, deformed and uneducated relatives from Pakistan. The Ishaks' responses signify total non-comprehension and non-recognition of the stereotypes to which the journalist expects them to conform. However, the sketch does not end here. In a move which may well make politically aware white and other non-Asian viewers feel distinctly uncomfortable, the sketch takes a radical turn. Asked by the journalist to stage a beating for the benefit of television viewers, the couple are immediately seduced by the prospect of being on television and readily agree. The effect of the sketch up to this point had been to render the reporter ridiculous and to undermine the familiar stereotype by subverting it. The final twist, which is at the expense of the Asian family, arguably weakens this effect in the interest of achieving a further comic impact which points to the political implications involved in changing the subject of ridicule.

Another technique employed by *Goodness Gracious Me* to highlight racism is that of reversing the roles in which South Asian people find themselves in relation to the white British population. The effect of this is to render the dominated dominant and the dominant 'other'. In the process the white viewer comes to realize what it feels like to be treated in the ways that whites commonly treat South Asians. An example of this technique is a sketch in which a white Englishman applies for a job in an Indian business. Reversing the situation in which many South Asian people find themselves in Britain, his new colleagues mispronounce his name and he is told that 'Jonathan' is far too difficult for them. Unless he Indianizes his name, the management adds, he will not go far in the firm. In response he assumes a much longer Indian name that he is still able to pronounce fluently. A similar tactic is used in a sketch about young South Asians having a Friday night out. Viewers are offered a reversal of the norm according to which young, white British males go out to the pub, drink too much, and then go off going for an 'Indian', in other words, a curry, and take pleasure in insulting the restaurant staff. The Asian youths in the sketch describe a typical night out: 'You go out. You get tanked up and then you go for an English. It wouldn't be Friday night if you didn't have an English.' The sketch shows them with their girlfriends, behaving drunkenly, calling for the blandest meals on the menu, mispronouncing the waiter's name (James) and the names of the English dishes, becoming aggressive when advised that they may be ordering too much food, mocking the waiter and then threatening him.

Linked to role reversal is the technique of portraying ethnic minorities in the style of the dominant culture. Thus the Kapoors, a suburban middle-class South Asian couple, who feature regularly in the programmes, are depicted as trying unsuccessfully to be more English than the English, anglicizing their names to the Coopers, despising everything Indian and denouncing their Indian heritage. Meanwhile their British-born son is on a trip to India in order to 'find his roots'. The effect of the sketch is to send up both white middle-class norms and lifestyles and the desire of the South Asian family to be accepted as part of the white middle-class group that devalues them. For all their extreme efforts to become English, their racist neighbours still throw bricks marked 'Pakis go home' through their windows and exclude them from the local golf club.

Much of the humour in *Goodness Gracious Me* works by surprising the viewer, undermining his or her expectations. A series of Guru sketches, for example, reverses the usual view of Indian holy men, showing a holy man who is clearly a charlatan. The joke, however, is at the expense of the white disciples who are taken in by him, despite his lack of knowledge of Indian myths and religious traditions. His evocation of Sanskrit consists, among other things of chanting the names of fashion designers such as Armani and his version of the life of Krishna draws heavily on *Star Wars*. Yet when it was broadcast, some members of the viewing public found this sketch sufficiently objectionable for them to complain to the Broadcasting Standards Commission, which upheld twelve complaints about the representation of the Hindu religion.

Crucial to any analysis of the success or otherwise of these techniques in contesting ethnocentrism, stereotyping and other forms of racism is the question of audience. The composition of the audience directly raises issues of race and ethnicity but also class, education and what Pierre Bourdieu termed 'cultural capital' (see Bordieu 1993). The meanings of comedy sketches and how they are read depends not only on the ethnic make-up of the audience, but also on their class and cultural knowledge. The producers of *Goodness Gracious Me* were quite clear about this, shooting the series in the presence of a South Asian studio audience. The ethnic composition of the audience meant that it found many of the sketches funnier than a white audience would be likely to. This access to humour depends on the cultural knowledge and experience of South Asian Britons. In addition to this, the use of a South Asian British studio audience serves to cue the majority white television audiences, watching the programme in their own homes, giving them a licence to laugh at things that they might be unsure about. This sense of insecurity – an undermining of the knowing subject – covers both the culturally unfamiliar and addresses the uncomfortable feelings felt, for example, by the educated, politically aware, student audiences with whom I have discussed the series.

Crucial to audience responses to comedy sketches is the question of audience positioning. In the case of students who were uncomfortable with various sketches, one of the key issues was the positioning of the audience in ways that provoked laughter at the expense of the South Asian characters. For example, in the series of 'Memories of the Raj' sequences, a British journalist interviews an elderly Indian woman about her memories of British India and is visibly disturbed by her wistful, nostalgic memories of violent colonial oppression. Her memories include beatings, rape and murder by the British army but in her accounts of these incidents she stresses how she cannot help remembering the soldiers' beautifully creased trousers and shiny boots as they beat or raped her, as well as the beautiful gardens of the governor's residence where she was chained to the railings and flogged. The sketch positions the audience with the white English journalist in his disbelief at her nostalgia for the Raj. This example leads directly to the question of where and how the white British figure in these sketches. In several sketches, South Asian characters play the fool to straight white programme presenters, as in those based on the BBC's *Book Programme* and *Food Programme*. In the 'Food Programme' sketch, a white television presenter discusses the elaborate main course dishes created by the guest South Asian chef. The comedy element comes when they move on to the dessert, which he says is the most popular among Asian families: fruit cocktail and Tip Top, that is to say, tinned fruit and cream substitute. For all his skill in creating the main courses, the chef plays what might be easily read as a negative Asian stereotype and there are arguably serious problems with the representation. The character of the chef maintains an imbecilic leer throughout the sketch and seems to be following in the footsteps of a tradition of white comic depictions of Asians such as Dick Emery and the television comedy series *It Ain't 'Alf Hot Mum*. This is set against the white woman presenter who plays her character straight. This structure is visible in a number of sketches, including the Raj interview where the audience is positioned with the white male journalist and in the 'Book Programme', where the discussion about Asian writing and questions of Eurocentrism are undercut by the nature of books that the authors are said to have written. What happens in these sketches is arguably a reassertion of a white British normality against which the South Asian 'other' is depicted as different in a range of negative ways.

Despite the more radical moments in *Goodness Gracious Me*, it could be argued that middle-class, white, British normality is often the implicit standard against which the depictions of South Asian characters are measured. White audiences are likely to read this normality as the uncriticized defining absence, as the humour targets things associated with traditional South Asian culture and aspects of everyday South Asian British life. For example, the well-known television series the Waltons is used as the vehicle for a critiques of the Asian family. American voices are heard talking, as they lie in bed at night while the screen shows a Walton-style house. The son asks questions about his future: Will he soon be able to leave home, marry and get a job? His parents reply that he will continue to live at home and work in the family business. The twist comes when we learn that he is already 43 and shares a bed with his grandmother. He asks: 'Mom, are we Asian?'

Where the comedy sketches take on British racial stereotyping many of the worst elements of British treatment of South Asians are absent. The forms of racist abuse of South Asians, which can range from name calling to physical attacks on individuals and arson attacks on Asian homes rarely figure. References to British brutality tend to be restricted to the colonial period, a strategy which probably accounts for some of the programme's popularity with its white audience, since they do not find themselves accused. Racism becomes part of history. In an interview in the British national daily newspaper, *The Independent*, published on 4 July 1998, Sanjeev Bhaskar, one of the writers and actors of *Goodness Gracious Me*, claimed: 'the first port of call is always "funny" rather than "political" ' (Bhaskar 1998: 14). Yet whatever writers may think, and whatever their intentions, it is impossible to detach the comic from the political, especially where questions of race and ethnicity are concerned.

This leaves us with the question of whether culturally and racially affirming comedy about oppressed groups is possible. Satire depends for its success both on the position-ing of the viewer and position from which the voice of authority emanates. It would seem that comic exaggeration can both reinforce stereotypes and, in other contexts, subvert them. Certainly comedy is helpful in encouraging white Britons to face up to racism and ethnocentrism, since laughter can release audiences from disabling feelings of guilt. Yet, it may also induce guilt or discomfort if it produces recognition and/or identification with the racist views presented.

There is rarely such a thing as a victimless joke. The key question is who is the victim? Jokes work progressively when they successfully encourage the audience to identify and empathize with the perspective of the victim of racism. Yet the question of identification in comedy also depends on the make-up of audiences and may well change between audiences, a point that returns me to the question of who is speaking for or about whom. Among the most progressive aspects of *Goodness Gracious Me* is the fact that it is an all-Asian show that depicts South Asian British people laughing at aspects of their own normality as well as the often oppressive behaviour of white Britons. If we were to ask whether white writers and performers could do these sketches without being read as racist, the answer, in most cases, would be 'no'.

Comedy is a form that allows both the illicit and the tabooed to be voiced. It facilitates taking on the 'bad form' of talking about race and raising questions of representation. It may serve to reinforce stereotypes and legitimate racist bigotry, an argument made, for example about the 1960s BBC television situation comedy *'Til Death Us Do Part*, whatever the intentions of its makers (see Ross 1996: 92–4). At its best, however, it produces sketches which can be read in different ways, introducing moments of undecidability and dislodging the sovereignty of the knowing subject. It is here that its strength lies when it come to challenging racist and ethnocentric modes of representation.

Further reading

Modood, T. (1997) ' "Difference", Cultural Racism and Anti-Racism', in P. Werbner and T. Modood (eds) *Debating Cultural Hybridity: Multi-Cultural Identities and the Politics of Anti-Racism*, pp. 154–72. London and New Jersey: Zed Books.
Moore-Gilbert, B. (2001) *Hanif Kureishi*. Manchester: Manchester University Press.
Ross, K. (1996) *Black and White Media*. Cambridge: Polity.

8 | COMPETING CULTURES, COMPETING VALUES

I felt quite comfortable within the liberal camp until the Salman Rushdie affair. I thought those who believed in religion were backward. The Rushdie affair changed all that. I was shocked by the way that liberals, who proclaimed their belief in freedom of thought and expression, were completely unwilling to listen to the voice of very powerless people who felt offended by the book . . . I knew the way all Muslims were being portrayed was quite unfair – these supposed dangerous people were my mum, my aunts and my uncles. My liberal associates were talking about them in terms of pure hatred. But it was not just the hatred which angered me. It was also the way liberals totally misunderstood people's continuing need for religion, particularly among members of Muslim groups who are still finding it hard to find their place in British society.

(Alibhai-Brown quoted in Runnymede Trust 1997: 28)

A mosque in lovely old English Chichester? No! No! . . . Thank God for everything English . . . They wouldn't want one of our churches funded by Chichester in one of their Muslim areas. During the Gulf War our lads had to refrain from taking part in Christian prayers etc, so what on earth is going on?

(Letter in the *Chichester Observer*, 16 May 1996
quoted in Runnymede Trust 1997: 55)

In Atlantic City on 7 September 1968, members of New York Radical Women, an early Women's Liberation group, demonstrated against the Miss America Pageant. This marked the first major Women's Liberation demonstration in the United States. Writing on the occasion of the demonstration, Robin Morgan explained:

The pageant was chosen as a target for a number of reasons: it is patently degrading to women (in propagating the Mindless Sex-Object Image); it has always been a lily-white, racist contest (there has never been a black finalist); the winner tours Vietnam, entertaining the troops as a mascot of murder; the whole gimmick of the million-dollar pageant corporation is one commercial shill-game to sell the sponsors' products. Where else could one find such perfect combination of American values – racism, militarism, capitalism – all packaged in one 'ideal' symbol: a woman.

(Morgan 1993: 25–6)

Within multi-ethnic Western societies, cultural practices, identities, meanings and values are often highly contested even among the white majority. For some, beauty pageants signify the celebration of apparently natural norms of female beauty – norms that are actually particular and tend to privilege hegemonic European and North American ideals of white beauty and hybrids derived from them. For others they signify a capitalist exploitation of women's bodies that reduces women to sex objects in the interests of profit. Beauty pageants, an early target of women's liberation, would remain controversial among feminists, but fade in importance as the contests gradually became less popular with the Western media, no longer televised on terrestrial TV, for example, in the UK.

Some thirty-four years after the Atlantic City protest, in November 2002, another beauty pageant, the Miss World contest, once again made the headlines. Following the success of Miss Nigeria in 2001, when Agbani Darego became the first *Black* African woman to win the title of Miss World, the contest was scheduled to take place in Abuja, Nigeria. Contestants from all over the world were gathered there in the Hilton Hotel when a storm of protest broke out. There was rioting in Kaduna and Abuja, in which, according to Red Cross officials, 250 people were killed and 3500 injured. The riots were the culmination of Muslim protests at the holding of the Miss World contest in Nigeria and, in the rioting, Christians were the main focus of attack. Commenting on the riots, the Chairman of the Christian Association of Nigeria, Archbishop Ola Makinde stressed that the pageant was a secular project, not supported by the Nigerian Christian Churches:

We were surprised, however, that Christians and their places of worship became the centre of attack and aggression in Kaduna metropolis. From the information we gathered, over 200 people, mostly Christians and pastors have been killed while several others were maimed, over 15 churches have been burnt and pulled down.
(Makinde, *ThisDay*, Lagos, 1 December 2002 (source: *www.allAfrica.com*))

The riots were a response to an article in the Nigerian newspaper *ThisDay* by a young journalist, described as a 'fashion writer recently returned from training in Britain', Isioma Daniel. Her article, which referenced Muslim calls for the cancellation of the pageant, and suggested that the Prophet Mohammed would have approved of the pageant, was regarded as blasphemous by Nigerian Muslims. The Sharia court in the northern province of Zamfar State issued a *fatwa* against Ms Daniel and although the newspaper apologized for the article, its offices were vandalized and burnt down in the riots that followed.

Nigeria's 120 million people are split fairly equally between Christians and Muslims. The north is mainly Muslim and the south Christian, although significant minorities live in each region. Zamfar State in northern Nigeria was the first of twelve regions in the north to introduce Sharia law and between its introduction in 2000 and the beauty pageant, two men and two women had been sentenced to death by stoning, though the sentences had not yet been carried out (Newswatch Online, 1 December 2002). These sentences are illegal under federal Nigerian law.

The riots led to the relocation of the Miss World contest to London. Yet the holding of the pageant in Nigeria was controversial long before the riots and not just among Nigerian Muslims. Christian leaders, too, objected to it on moral grounds and in the West various voices were raised against Nigeria as a suitable location for the pageant for other reasons. From the late summer 2002 onwards, a number of contestants announced that they were boycotting the pageant in protest against the sentence of death by stoning passed on an unmarried mother by a Sharia court in Zamfar State. On 6 September 2002, BBC News World Edition reported:

Miss World Nigeria Boycott spreads
Two more contestants in the Miss World contest to be held in Nigeria in November have announced that they are pulling out in protest at a Sharia death sentence passed on a woman convicted of adultery.

Miss France and Miss Belgium have joined a growing list of the world's beauty queens who have said that they will not be going to Nigeria.

Amina Lawal, 30, is due to be stoned to death after giving birth outside marriage. In August her appeal was rejected by a Sharia court.

Contestants from Denmark, Ivory Coast, Kenya, Norway and Togo have already announced that they will not go to Nigeria unless the death sentence on Ms Lawal is dropped.

(BBC News World Edition, 6 September 2002)

The Miss World contest, once the target of feminist protests, had now become a focus of controversy from a range of different standpoints. It became a vehicle for raising issues of Nigerian Muslim and Christian beliefs and values, and the ongoing conflicts between the different ethnic and religious groups within Nigeria. It focused both Western and secular Nigerian critiques of the status and perceived legitimacy of Sharia law. Moreover, serious economic questions were raised by the staging and last minute cancellation of a First World beauty contest in a developing country. Writing for Reuters on 12 November 2002, John Chiahemen reported that:

Pageant sources said organisers were battling to raise cash for everything from hotel rooms to air charters, including two jumbo jets that will fly equipment into a country with some of the world's poorest infrastructure.

'The stage to be used for the final in Abuja alone weighs 96 tonnes and must be flown in from London,' a pageant official said.

Because Nigerian promoters were unable to pay all five million sterling ($8 million) for hosting rights, they had to shoulder the 148 million naira ($1.2 million) hotel costs at Abuja's NICON.

(Chiahemen, REUTERS, 12 November 2002)

Newswatch Online reported that the Government of Rivers State, home of Miss World 2001 and co-host of the pageant, lost about 500 million naira on logistics alone, and that the overall losses were around 10 billion naira (*Newswatch Online*, 1 December 2002).

Within Nigeria, cultural and religious questions and conflicts, that also haunt post-colonial, multi-ethnic Western societies, take a sharper form. In large part an effect of the colonial process of drawing boundaries and constituting nations, Nigeria comprises three main ethnic groups and two main religions. The federal Nigerian state is secular, yet federal laws and values often conflict with those held by half the population, which is Muslim. The considered responses of various interest groups to the riots highlight the contradictions in play, but also the degree to which Nigerian Muslims were willing to come to an accommodation over the contest. In an interview with Phillip Oladunjoye of *Newswatch* entitled 'Let's Never Have Miss World Here Again', Lateef Adegbite, secretary-general of the Supreme Council for Islamic Affairs explained that:

The entire Muslim community of the country was against the staging of the contest in the first place. We think it is not a priority for the country. And, then, secondly, we feel that because of the form of the contest where people parade what they are supposed to modestly guard . . . You know, they just parade and in some cases in semi-nude action, which we feel is indecent and, of course, is against our religion. And we are concerned about the impact that such displays would have on the young ones. So, that was our general position because Islam has prescribed a way, particularly, of how women should guard their modesty. That is general. Then secondly, we felt that the timing was very wrong in the month of *Ramadan*. And it is the last 10 days of *Ramadan*, which is the holiest period for the Muslims in any year. Then, we led a protest publicly, well published, that the event should not come and that any event should not take place in the month of *Ramadan*. We also said the government facilities and government functionaries should not be involved in the exercise. Because anything that is considered unacceptable to a significant part of the population ought not to be financed with the government resources. And we published it. Then, of course the organisers, met us half-way and they continued with the contest but shifted the date of the grand finale, and, instead of November 30, shifted it to December 7. And they also made a concession in that the 'beauty queens' would not appear in semi-nude, they will appear in full dress or so. How that would have succeeded is a different matter. But then it appears that the Muslims were ready to live with the exercise until this irresponsible statement appeared in the *ThisDay* newspaper of 16 November blaspheming the person of the prophet, which is a very serious offence. And we protested and called for a retraction and an apology. And of course, some young people had moved to sack the office of *ThisDay* newspaper in Kaduna and that was the beginning of the problem.

> (Oladunjoye (2000), interview with Lateef Adegbite, Secretary-general, Supreme Council for Islamic Affairs. *Newswatch, www.allAfrica.com*)

The image of Nigerian Muslims that this response implies is far removed from the common Western picture of inflexible and dogmatic fundamentalists. *ThisDay*'s response to the riots was to claim that the newspaper practised 'responsible journalism'. Interviewed on CNN, chairman and editor-in-chief of Leaders and Company Limited, publishers of *ThisDay*, Mr Nduka Obaigbena said that the offensive portion of the article had been edited out of the story by the supervising editor, but 'the corrections were not effected in the main server in the heat of production deadlines. . . . We are very responsible journalists and we practice responsible journalism.' He went on to explain that:

> As responsible journalists we are very sensitive to the feelings of our readers in Nigeria, which is a multi-ethnic and multi-religious country. But the reporter who wrote the story is a young journalist who recently returned to the country, she is a British-trained journalist who had not practised in Nigeria before joining *ThisDay*. So as a young reporter, we attached her to Style Section where we thought she would not be faced with serious issues that could lead to any problem.
>
> (Djebah, *ThisDay*, Lagos (2002))

In response to the riots, the newspaper published apologies and, in its own words, 'deployed staff to the northern part of the country to explain the company's objective, balanced journalism policy' (*TheNEWS*, 3 December 2002). In an interview with the British Broadcasting Corporation, Mr Nduka Obaigbena, publisher of *ThisDay*, insisted that religion was important to *ThisDay*: 'Up to 30%, 40% of our staff members are Muslims on the editorial management boards. Our Group Executive Director is a senior Muslim, very devoted. He runs a page on Islam. So, we are very sensitive to religious feelings. It's just that this time we made a mistake and we are sorry for the mistake' (*TheNEWS*, Lagos, 3 December 2002).

A spokesman for the National Government, the Minister of Information and National Orientation, Professor Jerry Gana commented on the *fatwa* issued against the journalist who wrote the offending article to the effect that 'the Zamfara State government directive that Ms Daniel, who has since last week relocated to the United States, should be beheaded is "null and void"' (Oladunjoye, *ThisDay* (Lagos) 1 December 2002).

The contradictions

At issue in much of the conflict over the Miss World pageant was the uneasy status and composition of Nigeria as a nation state, drawn up by colonial British administrators without due consideration of the pre-existing territories of the different ethnic and religious groups. The contradictions between competing beliefs and values, apparent from reactions to the staging of the Miss World pageant, mirror broader conflicts between those desiring a secular pluralism and those wanting Islamic government. In a speech in Lagos, two weeks after the riots, Nigerian writer, Wole Soyinka expressed the view that the Federal Government should take responsibilities for the deaths and destruction of property, since it was responsible for protecting the federal character of the nation and 'the right of every individual in this pluralistic society'. Soyinka also criticized officials' complacency in allowing what he described as 'an inciting call for murder' (*fatwa*). For him secularism and pluralism are paramount and Muslim Nigerians should be subject to the rule of (Federal) law:

> We have worked hard to put this nation together, but for those who want to separate it, let them understand that we can no longer go down as second class citizens in this country . . . there has also not been demand for punishment for those plunging this country into the unbelievable path of disintegration. I do not understand what is going on. The sacrifices we made were not to turn this country into a theocratic state.
>
> (Soyinka, *ThisDay*, 2 December 2002)

The incidents surrounding the 2002 Miss World competition highlight the question of competing and conflicting values in a world increasingly polarized between secular and religious, Western and non-Western values, not only in the West itself, but also within developing countries where discourses derived from Western modernity compete with indigenous discourses and practices and hybrids of the two. The staging of Miss World in Nigeria might be seen as another instance of globalization, yet it is complex precisely because it involves struggles within Nigeria over the nature of the nation itself. It is the increasing globalization of Western cultural forms, practices and values, often imported as elements of lifestyles without the economic base to support them, and frequently experienced as cultural imperialism, that among other things has fuelled hostile reactions in non-Western countries and among minorities in the West. This experience of the West has produced new forms of subjectivity and identity, defined in opposition to hegemonic Western meanings and values. They include identities produced by the intensification of forms of nationalism and fundamentalism, for example, Muslim, Hindu, Orthodox and other Christian fundamentalisms, and the appeal to conservative versions of traditional values and culture. Moreover, the double standards of the Western powers in their foreign policies, especially where the Palestinian question is concerned, have exposed the limitations of repeated Western claims to represent universal standards of freedom and justice.

Such claims are evident in the political rhetoric of Western leaders. For example, in the introduction to the National Security Strategy of the United States of America published in September 2002, one year after '9/11', George W. Bush stated the following:

> The great struggles of the twentieth century between liberty and totalitarianism ended with a decisive victory for the forces of freedom, democracy and free enterprise. In the twenty-first century, only nations that share a commitment to protecting basic human rights and guaranteeing political and economic freedom will be able to unleash the potential of their people and assure their future prosperity. People everywhere want to be able to speak freely; choose who will govern them; worship as they please; educate their children – male and female; own property; and enjoy the benefits of their labor. These values of freedom are right and true for every person, in every society – and the duty of protecting these values against their enemies is the common calling of freedom-loving people across the globe and across the ages.
>
> *(http/usinfo.state.gov/topical/pol/terror/secstrat.htm:1)*

In this statement, Bush characterizes the twentieth century in terms of struggles of between liberty and totalitarianism in which American values proved to be the only sustainable model for success. For Bush and the American administration as a whole, there can only be one morality, just as there is only one way of reading the history of the twentieth century. Thus, for example, in the National Security Strategy, George W. Bush asserts: 'Some worry that it is somehow undiplomatic or impolite to speak the language of right and wrong. I disagree. Different circumstances require different methods, but not different moralities (President Bush, West Point, New York, 1 June 2002 *(http/usinfo.state.gov/topical/pol/terror/secstrat.htm:1)*). Claims that Western values are universal continue to serve as an ideological underpinning for hegemony, imperialism and negative attitudes to non-Western cultures. The National Security Strategy claims that the United States will 'champion aspirations for human dignity', 'strengthen alliances to defeat global terrorism', 'works with others to defuse regional conflicts', 'prevent our enemies from threatening us, our allies and our friend with weapons of mass destruction', 'ignite a new era of global economic growth through free markets and free trade' and 'expand the circle of development by opening societies and building the infrastructure of democracy' (Department of State 2002). Perhaps this last objective is the most transparently imperialist in its explicit aim of 'opening societies and building the infrastructure of democracy'. It assumes that somehow Western powers have the right to intervene in other societies and that democracy can only take one form.

In much Western discourse on Muslim countries and communities, the language used reflects this assumption that only Western values and standards are valid. Such discourse is also marked by a homogenization of the Muslim 'other' and a failure to understand the real relations in play on the ground. At the centre of the boycott by contestants of the 2002 Miss World contest was Sharia Law and specifically the case of Amina Lawal. This was taken up in a Western internet campaign, part of which included the following widely circulated message:

> Dear Friends,
>
> I have just learned that the Nigerian supreme court has upheld the death sentence for Amina Lawal, who was condemned for the crime of adultery. She is to be buried up to her neck and stoned to death. Her death has been postponed for one month so that she can continue to nurse her baby. Amina's case is being handled by the Spanish branch of Amnesty International, which is attempting to put together enough signatures to make the Nigerian government rescind the death sentence. (A similar campaign saved another Nigerian woman, Safiya, condemned in similar circumstances.) The petition has so far (as of April 7th [2003]) amassed over 4,100,000 signatures. It will only take you a few seconds to sign Amnesty's online petition. . . . Please sign the petition now, then forward this message to everyone in your address book.

On 2 May 2003, another email was circulated entitled 'Please Stop the International Amina Lawal Protest Letter Campaigns.' It read as follows:

> Dear friends,
>
> There has been a whole host of petitions and letter writing campaigns about Amina Lawal (sentenced to stoning to death for adultery in August 2002). Many of these are inaccurate and ineffective and may even be damaging to her case and those of others in similar situations. The information currently circulated is inaccurate, and the situation in Nigeria, being volatile, will not be helped by such campaigns. At the end of this letter, we indicate ways in which you can help us and we hope we can count on your continuing support.

The second email had been sent by Ayesha Imam (Board Member) and Sindi Medar-Gould (Executive Director) of the Nigerian organization BAOBAB for Women's Human Rights[1] who sought to clarify at some length the facts of the case, many of which had been badly misrepresented in the internet campaign. Among the worst errors was the misrepresentation of the state of the appeal and of the judicial system. This, they pointed out, undermined the credibility of those people working on the ground on Amina Lawal's behalf in Nigeria. The Western campaign organizers had assumed, without asking relevant groups in Nigeria, that international internet petitions could do more to help Amina Lawal than Nigerian NGOs. Imam and Medar-Gould pointed out that this was very far from the case:

> Not one appeal taken up by BAOBAB and supporting local NGOs in Nigeria had been lost to date. They had been won in local state Sharia courts – none had needed to go up to the Federal Sharia Court of Appeal, from whence appeals would go to the Supreme Court. . . . Contrary to the statements in many of the

internationally originated appeals for petitions and protest letters, none of the victims received a pardon as a result of international pressure.

Moreover, one extremely serious consequence of the internet campaign was the likelihood that it would provoke 'vigilante and political further (over)reaction to international attempts at pressure'. Imam and Medar-Gould pointed out that:

> This has happened already in the case of Bariya Magazu, the unmarried teenager convicted of *zina* (extra-marital sex) and sentenced to flogging in Zamfara in 1999. Ms. Magazu's sentence was quite illegally brought forward with no notice, despite the earlier assurances of the trial judge that the sentence would not be carried out for at least a year. She was told the night before that it would be carried out very early the next morning (and thus had no way of contacting anyone for help even if this unschooled and poor rural teenager had access to a telephone or organizing knowledge and experience), whilst the state bureaucracy had been instructed to obstruct and was physically refusing to take the appeal papers from BAOBAB's lawyers. The extra-legal carrying out of the sentence was not despite national and international pressure; it was deliberately to defy it. The Governor of Zamfara State boasted of his resistance to these letters from infidels even to sniggering over how many letters he had received.

The Lawal internet campaign betrayed many of the features that postcolonial critics have identified as typifying colonialist modes of representation (see Mohanty 1991 and Narayan 1997). It implicitly assumed that Western modes of protest were the most successful and appropriate, irrespective of local circumstances in Nigeria and of the views of those working on the ground whose views were not sought. Moreover, in their lack of attention to the details of the situation and to the relevant struggles going on in Nigeria, campaigners perpetuated negative stereotyping of Islam and of Africa 'as the barbaric and savage Other'. Imam and Medar-Gould ask recipients of the email not to buy into this:

> Accepting stereotypes that present Islam as incompatible with human rights not only perpetuates racism but also confirms the claims of right-wing politico-religious extremists in all of our contexts. . . . when protest letters re-present negative stereotypes of Islam and Muslims, they inflame sentiments rather than encouraging reflection and strengthening local progressive movements.

The othering of Islam by the West creates monolithic images, which suggest that unlike other religions, it is purely oppressive. Imam and Medar-Gould point out that:

> Muslim discourses and the invocation of Islam have been used both to vindicate and protect women's rights in some places and times, and to violate and restrict them in other places and times – as in the present case. The same can be said of many, many other religions and discourses (for example, Christianity, capitalism, socialism, modernization to name but a few).

At stake is 'who is invoking Islam (or whatever belief/discourse) for what purposes, and also to acknowledge and support internal dissent within the community involved, rather than engaging in a wholesale condemnation of people's beliefs and cultures, which is seldom accurate or effective in changing views within the affected community', As Imam and Medar-Gould suggest, its effects are rather to promote fundamentalist forms of identity. They do not rule out international campaigns but insist that they should only be used when really appropriate. More useful is financial support for local initiatives which have greater power to affect social relations and practices on the ground:

> We are asking for international solidarity strategies that respect the analyses and agency of those activists most closely involved and in touch with the issues on the ground and the wishes of the women and men directly suffering rights violations. . . . There is an unbecoming arrogance in assuming that international human rights organisations or others always know better than those directly involved, and therefore can take actions that fly in the face of their express wishes. . . . Please do liaise with those whose rights have been violated and/or local groups directly involved to discuss strategies of solidarity and support before launching campaigns.

Imam and Medar-Gould seek to counteract monolithic views of Islam by informing their readers that:

> Women's rights activists working on these issues very early on received support from progressive lawyers, Islamic scholars and rights activists from throughout Nigeria, the Muslim world and elsewhere, in the form of legal and religious argumentation (fiqh), case law examples and strategies which were generously shared.

Amina Lawal's appeal was successful in September 2003.

The assumptions underpinning the internet campaign attributed to the Spanish Branch of Amnesty International, displayed many of the features that the late Edward Said identified in his book, *Covering Islam*, published in 1981 at the time of the Iran hostage crisis. In this text, Said pointed out that:

> In no really significant way is there a direct correspondence between the 'Islam' in common Western usage and the enormously varied life that goes on within the world of Islam with its 800,000,000 people, its millions of square miles of territory principally in Africa and Asia . . .
>
> (Said 1981: x)

> Yet there is a consensus on 'Islam' as a kind of scapegoat for everything we do not happen to like about the world's new political, economic and social patterns.
>
> (Said 1981: xv)

He continued:

> It is always the West and not Christianity, that seems pitted against Islam. Why? Because the assumption is that whereas 'the West' is greater than and has surpassed the stage of Christianity, its principal religion, the world of Islam – its varied societies, histories and languages not withstanding – is still mired in religion, primitivity, and backwardness. Therefore, the West is modern, greater than the sum of its parts, full of enriching contradictions and yet always 'Western' in its cultural identity; the world of Islam, on the other hand, is no more than 'Islam,' reducible to a small number of unchanging characteristics, despite the appearance of contradictions and experiences of variety that seem on the surface to be as plentiful as those of the West.
>
> (Said 1981: 10)

The modes of representation described here by Said rely on denying complexity, diversity and change to Islamic societies, much as in the case of Amina Lawal. These are moves that postcolonial critics associate with colonial modes of representation. Little appears to have changed in the two decades since Said's book was published. Now as then, the binaries that govern Western discourses about Islam do not allow Muslim people or nations to be diverse or democratic and modern. This form of binarism is supported and reinforced by the limited range of images of Muslim societies that predominate in the West. From representations of Osama Bin Laden and the Taliban to non-Western Islamic societies and fundamentalist movements in the Western world, the images that predominate are of repressive, often violent systems, based on belief rather than reason that constantly violate Western notions of human rights.

In its post-war pronouncements on the future of Iraq, the US administration reiterated its policy of instating what it calls 'freedom' and 'democracy' as part of a wider programme of so-called 'democratizing' the Middle East. Yet for the US, democracy does not necessarily mean what the majority of the people in Iraq might want. The practice of the occupying forces suggests that it signifies a secular state, sympathetic to the US, with a free market economy where it can have military bases, that is a state conforming to US values. In US rhetoric, the Muslim world as a whole is more often than not anti-thetical to freedom and democracy.

Aware of criticisms of this discursive strategy, some American politicians and their British counterparts have made efforts to distinguish between 'fanatical strain[s] of religious extremism' and 'the true and peaceful faith of Islam' (British Prime Minister Tony Blair in his speech to the US Congress on 17 July 2003 (available at *www.washingtonpost.com*)). Yet even allowing for this distinction, Blair continued his speech by asserting the universality of the Western values and juxtaposing them with repressive regimes in an attempt to justify the war against Iraq:

> There is a myth that though we love freedom, others don't; that our attachment to freedom is a product of our culture; that freedom, democracy, human rights, the

rule of law are American values, or Western values; that Afghan women were
content under the lash of the Taliban; that Saddam was somehow beloved by his
people; that Milosevic was Serbia's saviour.

(Blair: Speech to the US Congress, 17 July 2003 available at
www.washingtonpost.com)

Here the only possibilities are Western discourses of freedom or repressive regimes.
Unclear in all of this is what a 'true and peaceful of Islam' might look like and where it
is to be found, since a specific and singular idea of 'freedom' and 'democracy' is taken
to be universal.

Members of Congress, ours are not Western values, they are the universal values of
the human spirit. And anywhere, any time ordinary people are given the chance to
choose, the choice is the same: freedom, not tyranny; democracy, not dictatorship;
the rule of law, not the rule of the secret police.

(Blair: Speech to the US Congress, 17 July 2003 available at
www.washingtonpost.com)

Belief versus reason: Islamophobia in the West

This binary discursive strategy sets the parameters for much discourse on Islam and
Muslims in the West. The competing cultures and values that come to the fore when
secular discourses meet religious ones are not just effects of imperialism and
globalization in the non-Western world, as in the case, for example, of Miss World in
Nigeria. They are also central to Western societies. From the ongoing campaigns of
right-wing Christian fundamentalists in the United States to institute their specific
versions of Christian values, sexuality and family life, to the claims of minorities
within Western societies for respect for their religions and traditional beliefs and
practices, the status of religion in particular – of faith versus reason – in Western
societies creates serious tensions even in those societies where liberal pluralism is the
hegemonic discourse.

In the second half of this chapter, I take up Edward Said's critiques of representations of Islam in the West and look at cultural narratives about Muslims in Britain in
the context of Islamophobia and questions of culture and identity. I ask to what degree
they transcend the limitations that Said has identified in representing Islam. My focus
is on how competing cultures and values are treated in the representation of British
Muslims in the work of British South Asian writer, Hanif Kureishi, who has published
a novel on this issue, *The Black Album* (1995) and one of whose short stories was made
into the film *My Son The Fanatic* (1997).[2]

Among the most pressing current social issues in the West is Islamophobia. In its
1997 report, *Islamophobia: A Challenge for Us All*, the Runnymede Trust offered the
following definition of the practice:

The term Islamophobia refers to unfounded hostility towards Islam. It refers also to the practical consequences of such hostility in unfair discrimination against Muslim individuals and communities, and to the exclusion of Muslims from mainstream political and social affairs.

(Runnymede Trust 1997: 4)

The hostility on which contemporary Islamophobia is founded is not new to the West, but has a long history with roots going back at least as far as the Crusades. Widespread negative media coverage of Islamic revolutions and Islamic states over the past few decades has served to reinforce many long established stereotypes. Fed by this long history of negative images of Muslim societies and by recent political developments, Islamophobia has been taken up over the past few years by government in Britain as a serious social problem in need of attention. This is in part a response to Muslim minorities that have become more organized and vocal, but also to the sort of violent unrest that occurred in northern English cities with large Muslim populations such as Oldham and Bradford in 2001. These communities, often located next to predomin-antly white working-class areas, have high levels of social deprivation and low levels of social interaction between different ethnic groups. Both Islamophobia and Muslim fundamentalism in Western Europe increased markedly throughout the Western world in response to the events of 11 September 2001 and the wars in Afghanistan and Iraq.

In Britain the arrival of substantial numbers of Muslims, after 1945, mainly from Pakistan, Bangladesh and India, but also refugee populations from Muslim countries like Somalia, helped change the face of society in the second half of the twentieth century. Previously, port cities such as Cardiff, Liverpool and South Shields had Mus-lim communities and the first purpose-built British mosque in Cardiff dates from the 1930s. In the new millennium most British cities boast several mosques. With most of its substantial Muslim population now settled for two or three generations, multi-cultural Britain is being faced with demands for parity from its Muslim citizens in the form, for example, of government finance for Muslim schools and the extension of the blasphemy law to cover Islam. At the same time, hostility to Muslims and a lack of understanding of Islamic culture remain a serious problem. Questions of the blas-phemy law and of censorship came to the fore with the publication of Salman Rushdie's *Satanic Verses* in 1988. The ensuing debates, protests and the *fatwa*, call-ing for Rushdie's execution, helped fuel negative perceptions of and hostility to Islam in Britain. One of the effects of this increased hostility has to been to strengthen fundamentalist tendencies among young Muslims, a theme picked up in Kureishi's texts. How, then, do these texts by a prestigious British mixed-race, Muslim South Asian writer address the question of Muslim difference?

A controversial author, Kureishi's work has been read by some as contributing to Islamophobia. In both his short story and film, *My Son the Fanatic* and his novel *The Black Album*, Kureishi addresses the question of Muslim beliefs and values in con-temporary Britain. The Rushdie affair forms the backdrop to *The Black Album*, which

Plate 4. Muslim Procession in 1950s Cardiff.
(Butetown History & Arts Centre archive.)

references the protests over the *Satanic Verses*. One question of interest here is how do they help a non-Muslim readership understand the complex issues involved in Muslim difference? Both texts contrast radically different worlds. *My Son the Fanatic* brings together the world of the local prostitutes, whom the central character, Parvez, chauffeurs in his role of taxi driver, and that of radical Muslims from the local mosque. Parvez's son, Farid, joins the mosque, becomes a devout Muslim and is active in the attempt by a group from the mosque to clear the prostitutes off the streets. In *The Black Album* the beliefs, actions and values of a Muslim student group, dedicated to protecting the interests of the local Pakistani community, is contrasted with the world of sexual and drug-induced pleasure. In both cases the opposition deployed is an extreme one which has implications for how readers are encouraged to interpret Muslim beliefs, values and identities.

My Son the Fanatic focuses on one working-class Muslim family, who having settled in the UK some twenty-five years previously, only to find their hopes of prosperity disappointed after years of hard work. It raises issues of racist induced alienation, identity and belonging, bi-culturalism and Muslim fundamentalism. It suggests that the appeal of extreme forms of religion lies in the positive sense of place and identity that it offers young British Pakistanis, who, despite being born and raised in Britain, still find themselves subject to racism and social exclusion. While first generation immigrant Parvez, with his strong South Asian accent, tries hard to assimilate and become thoroughly bi-cultural, his wife retains much closes ties to traditional culture and supports her son in his turn to religion. Parvez is intimately familiar with the seamy side of city life. He earns his living driving prostitutes and their clients around at night. At the opening of the film, Farid, his son, who speaks like a local Yorkshire man, is engaged to the daughter of a local white police chief inspector, but faced by racism and influenced by friends from the local mosque, he breaks off this relationship and turns to religion. To his father's dismay, he totally rejects his Western education, lifestyle and values, especially those of his father and eventually moves out of the family home. His mother, who has learned of her husband's relationship with a prostitute, returns to Pakistan and by the end of the film the family has disintegrated completely.

The film offers a bleak picture of Parvez's life. Unlike his friend, Fizzi, with whom he emigrated to Britain and who has become a rich and successful restaurant owner, Parvez has remained poor. As he has become increasingly bi-cultural, so he has grown away from his wife and is no longer able to discuss with her the contradictions and problems that he faces on a day-to-day level in his life outside the home in a racist society, nor the changes in his son. He finds a degree of understanding, love and affection from one of the prostitutes whom he drives around in the course of his work and in the course of the narrative this relationship develops into a love affair.

This film depicts a radical shift in Farid's subjectivity and identity. Before his involvement with the mosque, he is a young man who plays the guitar, has a white girlfriend, is studying to be an accountant and is thoroughly westernized. As he turns to a radical form of Islam, he gives away his belongings, including his guitar and breaks off his relationship with his fiancée, Madeleine, calling her chief superintendent father the 'only pig he wants to eat'. The son of a secular Muslim who rejected religion while in Pakistan because of mistreatment in the mosque and an insistence on the part of the Mullah that his Hindu friend would go to hell, Farid learns how to pray from a cassette. In his turn to religion, he claims to be seeking 'belief, purity and belonging to the past'.

Questions of identity and belonging are shown to be key motivations in the turn to fundamentalism. When Farid's father, Parvez, follows him to the mosque, he is told by an older man that the elders do not like the young radicals because they are always arguing with them, but that they are not afraid of the truth and stand for something. This 'something' is shown to be intolerant, dogmatic and even violent. As his identity and beliefs shift, Farid begins to talk like a fundamentalist. Addressing his father, he maintains that women lack belief and reason and he begs Parvez to ask Allah for forgiveness for his wayward lifestyle. His rhetoric becomes increasingly anti-Jewish and anti-capitalist and he joins other Muslim youths in their attacks on the prostitutes on the streets. He says of the white British: 'They say integrate, but they live in pornography and filth.'

Parvez, confides his problems to his prostitute friend, Sandra, who replies: 'You can't blame the young for wanting to believe in something apart from money.' He experiences both Western racism and sexual decadence while working for Shitz, a German entrepreneur, who plans to transform an old factory site into a shopping mall. In the course of his driving, he is taken to a club where he is subjected to serious racist abuse from both stand-up comic and audience. He is called upon to organize alcohol and prostitutes for a party that Shitz is holding. This provokes extreme hostility in his son. Parvez's involvement with the entrepreneur coincides with Farid's invitation to a religious leader from Pakistan to stay in the family home. The Maulvi arrives from Lahore and moves into the house, only to exploit Parvez's hospitality, running up bills that Parvez cannot afford to pay.

When they collect the Maulvi from the airport, Parvez drives through the part of town where the prostitutes loiter. Farid explains: 'In the West there is immorality everywhere.' The Maulvi replies: 'And you take no action,' setting the agenda for the rest of the film as he motivates the young Muslims to drive the prostitutes off the streets, to physically attack them and to fire bomb the building in which they gather. As things deteriorate, Parvez turns increasingly to Sandra and starts a sexual relationship with her. By the end of the film, Parvez's family have left him and he reflects to Sandra: 'I have managed to destroy everything. I've never felt worse or better.'

The Black Album offers a more detailed and differentiated picture of young Muslim fundamentalists in Britain. It is a novel about second generation Pakistanis in London and engages with questions of identity through a radical contrast of life-styles ranging from affluent westernized middle-class living, through Muslim fundamentalism to serious involvement in drug culture. The central character, Shahid, is the younger son of a successful secular, Pakistani travel agent with offices in Kent. To escape the family business, Shahid moves to London to a small college to pursue his interest in literature and writing. At college he becomes involved both with a group of fundamentalist students and with his middle-aged, left-wing, libertarian literature tutor with whom he develops a sexual relationship and who acts as a counterforce to the appeal of the student group.

The Muslim students are depicted as dedicated activists who help their local Pakistani community with advice surgeries and physical protection against racist attacks. Membership, however, is shown to require unquestioning belief, something that Shahid cannot accept, and his involvement with the student group comes to a violent end over the group's burning of an unnamed text, perceived as blasphemous by the students. This clearly references Rushdie's *Satanic Verses*. Shahid's failure to support blind censorship is compounded by his own sensual and even pornographic adaptation of the poems of the group's leader Riaz, which he is delegated to transcribe onto computer.

The appeal of Islam in the novel is shown to be linked directly to questions of identity in a racist society and it is presented as based on faith and solidarity in the face of a rationalist, racist Western decadence. While the leader of the student group, Riaz, is from a small village in Pakistan, his followers are bi-cultural British Muslims. The primary motivation for British-born and educated Muslims turning to fundamentalism is shown to be the need for a positive sense of identity. This is seen most tragically in the case of Chad, the most devoted members of the group. Formerly known as Trevor, he was adopted by a white family as a child, suffered crises of identity and became seriously dependent on drugs. His rehabilitation through Islam is contrasted with Shahid's elder brother Chili, who follows a playboy life-style, becomes addicted to hard drugs and is abandoned by his wife who returns with their child to her upper-class family in Karachi.

The depiction of the Muslim students in the novel is focused on Riaz and Chad. Origins and individual formation are shown to be crucial to the meaning of Islam for individuals. Riaz works with the local Asian community, holding weekly surgeries to discuss problems, and preaches at the local mosque. He takes up immigration cases, writes for newspapers and plans to start his own. His political and religious affiliations are with Iran and he has pan-Islamic politics: 'We're not blasted Christians. . . . We don't turn the other cheek. We will fight for our people who are being tortured in Palestine, Afghanistan, Kashmir!' (Kureshi 1995: 68). He is depicted as regarding westernized Muslims as having lost themselves. Yet even he is not quite a unified, fundamentalist subject. He is still seduced by designer labels and he writes poetry. Chad recounts how:

> Riaz is dangerous, too radical. To us he is a friend but many important people in the community wouldn't like him being creative. It's too frivolous, too merry for them. Some of those guys go into a supermarket and if music playing, they run out again.
>
> (Kureishi 1995: 58)

One of the most popular speakers in the mosque, Riaz's talks cover topical issues such as rave culture, homosexuality and democracy. When Shahid tells Riaz that he has so many questions, the answer is uncompromising: 'Dismiss them! . . . Just believe in the truth.' As the narrative unfolds, Shahid finds himself shocked by some of Riaz's views, for example, his cool and certain hatred of homosexuals (Kureishi 1996: 146).

For the South Asian characters, whether fundamentalist or westernized, religion is related to social class. Thus, both Shahid's family and Riáz, see religion as something belonging to the masses and that raises people above the level of animals. Whereas Riaz wants to import this understanding of religion into Britain, Shahid's sister-in-law Zulma, sees it as a sign of an underdeveloped peasant society.

The figure of Chad contrasts strongly with that of Riaz and is used to explain part of the attraction of fundamentalism to British born Pakistanis. Chad's crisis of identity in white racist Britain is more extreme than Shahid's since he is not only brought up totally westernized but also by white adoptive parents:

> When he got to be a teenager he saw he had no roots, no connections with Pakistan, couldn't even speak the language. So he went to Urdu classes. But when he tried asking for the salt in Southall [West London] everyone fell about at his accent. In England white people looked at him as if he were going to steal their car

or their handbag, particularly if he dressed like a ragamuffin. But in Pakistan they looked at him even more strangely. Why should he be able to fit into a Third World theocracy?

(Kureishi 1995: 89)

Chad is depicted as violent and unquestioning and he ends up fatally burned in a fire bombing of a bookshop, which he has undertaken as part of a campaign against the apparently blasphemous novel.

For Shahid, who has been brought up without religion, the appeal of the Muslim student group is directly rooted in questions of identity, belonging and the racism of white Britain. Shahid has been brought up in Kent, a predominantly white area of Britain. This is shown to cause him serious problems. His first attempt at writing, 'Paki Wog Fuck Off Home' (Kureishi 1995: 60), depicts his experience of racism in secondary school at the hands of his classmates. Like religion, racism is something that his family has chosen to ignore. His mother is horrified when she finds and reads his article:

> More than anything she hated any talk of race or racism. . . . Even when Shahid vomited and defecated with fear before going to school, or when he returned with cuts, bruises and his bag slashed with knives, she behaved as if so appalling an insult couldn't exist, And so she turned away from him. What she knew was too much for her.

(Kureishi 1995: 61)

In London, Shahid tells his new student Muslim friends how growing up in an all white area of Kent made him paranoid and provoked a desire to join the white racists. When confronted with white people:

> I was convinced they were full of sneering and disgust and hatred. And if they were pleasant, I imagined they were hypocrites . . .

(Kureishi 1995: 8)

> My mind was invaded by killing-nigger fantasies. . . . Of going around abusing Pakis, Niggers, Chinks, Irish, any foreign scum . . . The thought of sleeping with Asian girls made me sick. . . . I have wanted to join the British National Party.

(Kureishi 1995: 9)

This desperate need to belong is also shown to motivate his involvement with the fundamentalist student group who try to teach him about the racist oppression of ordinary Pakistani families and the pressure under which they live. One of these pressures is Islamophobia. Tahira, one of the group, recounts:

> But we women go to a lot of trouble to conceal our allures. Surely you've heard how hard it is to wear the hijab? We are constantly mocked and reviled, as if we were the dirty ones. Yesterday a man on the street said, this is England, not Dubai and tried to rip my scarf off.

(Kureishi 1995: 88)

Shahid's previous experience of religion had been on visits to Pakistan with his parents, where he went to the mosque with his cousins. As in London, so too in Karachi, religion is depicted as having strong links to social and political issues: hostility to Hindus and to westernized Muslim Pakistanis. While Hat, one of the members of the student group, explains the Koran to Shahid and shows him how to pray, Shahid remains a hybrid subject, failing to acquire the requisite form of spirituality and he fills the lack with a westernized content.

> While praying, Shahid had little notion of what to think, of what the cerebral concomitant to the actions should be. So, on his knees, he celebrated to himself the substantiality of the world, the fact of existence, the inexplicable phenomenon of life, art, humour and love itself – in murmured language, itself another sacred miracle. He accompanied this awe and wonder with suitable music, the 'Ode to Joy' from Beethoven's Ninth, for instance, which he hummed inaudibly.
>
> (Kureishi 1995: 77)

Shahid is depicted as living a double life. While he is attracted to the student group, he is also strongly drawn to the world of sensual pleasures, which he experiences through his relationship with his college tutor. In addition to their sexual relationship, she feeds him drugs and takes him to raves. Shahid is ultimately unable to reconcile his Western upbringing and desire for experience of a complex world with the requirement just to believe. He comes to realize that what is really in question is belonging:

> All this believing wasn't so much a matter of truth or falsity, of what could be shown and what not, but of joining. He had noticed, during the days that he walked around the area, that the races were divided. The black kids stuck with each other, the Pakistanis went to one another's houses, the Bengalis knew each other from way back, and the whites too. Even if there were no hostility between groups – and there was plenty, if only implicit; his mother, for instance liked to make derogatory remarks about blacks, saying they were lazy, while middle-class whites she revered – there was little mixing.
>
> (Kureishi 1995: 111)

The Black Album, through the figure of Shahid, ultimately rejects the limitations of fundamentalist Islam and espouses a position of multiple identities and openness to all sorts of experience (Kureishi 1995: 122). At the burning of the blasphemous book, Shahid stands in the centre of the crowd unable to join in, feeling ashamed.

> People hooted and clamoured as if they were at a fireworks display. Fists were raised at the flaming bouquet of the book. And the former Trevor Buss and Muhammad Shahabuddin Ali-Shah, alias Brother Chad, who was brandishing it at the sky, laughed triumphantly. . . .
> Looking across the crowd at Chad's expression, he was glad of that. He never

wanted his face to show such ecstatic rigidity! The stupidity of the demonstration appalled him. How narrow they were, how unintelligent, how . . . embarrassing it all was! But was he better because he lacked their fervour, because he was trying to slink away? No; he was worse, being tepid. He was not simple enough!

(Kureishi 1995: 188)

Kureshi's depictions of Muslim difference raise issues that polite white society often chooses to ignore. They show extreme examples of a clash of beliefs and values that are irreconcilable. Yet by choosing aspects of white Britain that the white majority, too, would reject – prostitution and drug culture – they avoid engaging with difference as it affects most people's lives and relieve the white majority of the need to engage with Islamophobia. Like *My Son the Fanatic*, *The Black Album*, too, works with extreme binary oppositions in which the sameness and differences of ordinary everyday Muslims and Muslim life become invisible. In this respect the texts, while much more complex, are not so far removed from those that Said critiques in *Uncovering Islam*.

Conclusion

Muslim minorities in Western societies offer the greatest challenge to liberal pluralism and the acceptance or even the celebration of diversity. Tolerance, with all its limitations as a discourse, becomes a political issue when religious values compete for the secular terrain of politics and civil society. While many religious communities, including Christians, have fundamentalist wings, they are not widely depicted or perceived in these terms. In the case of devout Muslims (like Orthodox Jews), they are marked as different by dress, food and modes of family life. It is the meanings attributed to these visible differences that produce the forms of cultural racism to which Muslims in the West are subjected. Both the Runnymede Report on Islamophobia (Runnymede 1997) and the Parekh Report on the *Future of Multi-ethnic Britain* (2000) argue that there are open and closed views of Islam. Closed views see it as 'monolithic, static and unresponsive, whereas open ones see it as diverse and developing, with internal differences and disagreements' (Parekh 2000: 246). As Said pointed out in 1981, closed views predominant in the media where widespread preconception about Muslims that are integral to Western media and popular culture are recycled and make the cultural political battle to promote open views all the more difficult. Writing of the media the Parekh Report commented that:

Any one news story is interpreted by the reader or viewer within the context of a larger narrative, acting as a kind of filter or template. If the larger narrative is racist – or, more benignly, representative of a 95/5 society – then the story is likely to be interpreted in a racist or majority-biased way, regardless of the conscious intentions of reporters, journalists and headline writers. For example, any reference to Muslims is likely to switch on the notion, implanted by numerous other stories, that most Muslims are terrorists and/or fundamentalists in their interpretation and practice of their faith.

(Parekh 2000: 169)

Yet this is a misrepresentation of the majority of Muslims in Britain today. As the Parekh Report points out:

What Islam means is that 'new ways of living and the process of gradually becoming part of British society have to be ultimately justified in terms compatible with a Muslim faith.' It does not inevitably mean 'a rigid, fundamentalist, anti-Western, anti-modernist religiosity'.

(Parekh 2000: 31)

As various examples in this chapter have suggested, recognition of this and the promotion of open views of Islam are crucial not just to the future of multi-ethnic Britain, but to global politics.

Further reading

Anwar, M. and Bakhsh, Q. (2003) *British Muslims and State Policies*. Warwick: University of Warwick, Centre for Research in Ethnic Relations.

Modood, T. (1992) British Asian Muslims and the Rushdie Affair, in J. Donald and A. Rattansi, *'Race', Culture and Difference*, pp. 260–77. London: Sage in association with the Open University.

Moore-Gilbert, B. (2001) *Hanif Kureishi*. Manchester: Manchester University Press.

Runnymede Trust (1997) *Islamophobia: A Challenge for Us All*. London: The Runnymede Trust.

Yuval-Davies, N. (1992) Fundamentalism, Multiculturalism and Women in Britain, in J. Donald and A. Rattansi, *'Race', Culture and Difference*, pp. 278–291. London: Sage in association with the Open University.

CONCLUDING REFLECTIONS

> Moving from silence into speech is for the oppressed, the colonized, the exploited, and those who stand and struggle side by side a gesture of defiance that heals, that makes new life and new growth possible. It is that act of speech, of 'talking back', that is no mere gesture of empty words, that is the expression of our movement from object to subject – the liberated voice.
>
> (hooks 1989: 211)

The importance of 'talking back' for marginalized and colonized groups has been a central theme of this book. It enables people who find themselves subject to racist, sexist, colonial and homophobic power relations to resist negative definitions of what and who they are, to rewrite their history, to explore existing identities and to create new ones. Identity is important to occupying the position of 'knowing subject' and it is as knowing subjects that we speak and act most effectively in the world. Foremost among the claims of the knowing subject is the belief that we know who we are and are in control of meaning. Of course, this knowledge and control is a partial fiction, but it is a fiction by which we live and which has real effects in the world.

Yet identities are not just enabling, in defining their own sense of identity, individuals and groups tend to fix the identity of others, often working within long-established binary modes of thinking that help sustain inequalities, exclusions and oppression. This is why it is important to see identities as both changing and changeable cultural constructs. Cultural narratives, historical and fictional, such as those discussed in this book, are sites where cultural political struggles over identity take place. They are also sites from which we learn about others.

For those who inhabit privileged, seemingly obvious identities, and witness the role that identities play in oppressive social practices and even wars, the question arises as to whether we can move beyond identities. This question is important, but it is articulated from that privileged space, usually of whiteness, in which people are able to see themselves as simply 'human'. To move beyond identities as divisive, we would need to move beyond material power relations that privilege some groups over others. For those who find themselves excluded from the space of the simply 'human', and are defined as 'other' in discourses of race, gender, sexuality or ethnicity, it is clear that having a voice, representation and respect are crucial. More often than not, this comes from a sense of belonging to a recognized group or community.

In his essay on new Caribbean cinema, Stuart Hall argues that recent diasporic Black cultural production is:

> Putting the issue of cultural identity in question. Who is this emergent, new subject of the cinema? From where does he/she speak? Practices of representation always implicate the position from which we speak or write – the position of *enunciation*. What recent theories of enunciation suggest is that, though we speak, so to say, 'in our own name', of ourselves and from our own experience, nevertheless who speaks, and the subject who is spoken of, are never identical, never exactly in the same place.
>
> (Hall 1990: 51)

As we saw from the quotation at the beginning of Chapter 1, Stuart Hall argues that identity is neither as transparent nor as unproblematic as we tend to think. He argues that rather than assuming that identity is already an accomplished fact, we might usefully see it as a 'production'. Identity from this perspective is never complete, it is always in process, and constituted within representation. From this poststructuralist perspective, identity becomes an effect of culture.

In these final reflections, I want briefly to consider what conclusions might be drawn about the three major concerns of this book. The first of these was how we might usefully theorize the relationship between subjectivity, identity and agency and understand their constitution in and through cultural texts and practices. The idea that cultural practices, such as those discussed in earlier chapters, produce identities through the process of representation, rather than reflect already existing identities is central to the arguments of this book. Because cultural identity is neither one thing nor static, it is a key focus of cultural political struggle: it is constantly produced and reproduced in practices of everyday life, in education, the media, the museum and heritage sectors, the arts, history and literature. It is textually constructed in the narratives of these discourses and institutions and performed by individuals who assume the modes of subjectivity and identity that the discourses offer them. In the process, the individual, interpellated as a particular subject, works by herself or himself as if she or he were a sovereign, knowing subject.

For Stuart Hall cultural identity is:

> A matter of 'becoming' as well as of 'being.' It belongs to the future as much as to the past. It is not something which already exists, transcending place, time,

history and culture. Cultural identities come from somewhere, have histories. But like everything which is historical, they undergo constant transformation. Far from being eternally fixed in some essentialised past, they are subject to the continuous 'play' of history, culture and power. Far from being grounded in a mere 'recovery' of the past, which is waiting to be found, and which, when found, will secure our sense of ourselves into eternity, identities are the names we give to the different ways we are positioned by, and position ourselves within the narratives of the past.

(Hall 1990: 52)

A second concern of this book has been the importance of history to identity. As we saw in Chapters 2, 3 and 4, history matters and it is a site of cultural political struggle for both the hegemonic and the marginalized. In this struggle, issues such as having a voice that is recognized and heard, are clearly crucial to the formation of positive forms of identity. Narratives of the past that depict a collective experience for marginalized groups have important social, ideological and political roles. They can begin to inform and transform the relations of dominant groups to these narratives and to the histories they inscribe. As was suggested in Chapters 2 and 3, having a history within which one can position oneself positively is crucial to identity. This holds true both at the level of personal history and of the larger stories of the communities and nation with which a person identifies. The level of hostility from the conservative press to the suggestion that Britain needs to produce a more inclusive history and more plural conceptions of Britishness, discussed in detail in Chapter 2, illustrates the perceived importance of history to identity. Chapter 4, which focused on Black British writing, suggested ways in which hegemonic constructions of British identity and their grounding in particular narratives of history are being challenged. This writing attempts to reposition Black Britons in relation to hegemonic white-centred narratives of Britishness and provide the basis for positive Black British identities.

Like most societies, Britain has never had a singular and homogenous culture or national identity. It has always had different white ethnic groups with their own senses of history and identity. It has always had strong regionalisms and different forms of class and gender identity. It has had non-white citizens for centuries. Yet the last fifty years have seen a massive expansion in cultural diversity in Britain, as a wide variety of migrants have settled in the UK, diversity that is often strongly grounded in religious differences. The British South Asian writing, films and television discussed in Chapters 6 and 7 point to the ways in which the second and third generation children of migrants to the UK are creating new modes of subjectivity and new hybrid identities. These are emerging both from conflicts and contradictions between 'traditional' cultural values and life-styles and those of mainstream British society, and as a response to forms of racism and ethnocentrism on the part of white Britain. The establishing of minority cultural and religious institutions has lead to an increase in forms of cultural racism, in the face of which it becomes difficult to develop a positive sense of belonging. As we saw in the previous chapter, which looked at conflicting and competing values and that form of cultural racism, known as Islamophobia, cultural racism makes this process of identifying with and belonging to mainstream Western societies very difficult.

In his story 'The Body', Hanif Kureishi's main character tells how he became dissatisfied with his ageing body. At the age of 65, Adam, a well-known writer, is offered the chance to have his brain transplanted into the beautiful body of a much younger man. Intending to return to his old body after six months of hedonistic living, he finds himself trapped as a 'Newbody' for the rest of his now much extended life. In the course of his pleasure filled life as a 'Newbody', detached from family and friends, he discovers the value of the known, familiar and well loved, however old and decaying it may be. Above all he discovers the importance of having a personal history, a past that he can narrate and share with others. In his new incarnation, he has no knowledge of his body's actual past and no one has any knowledge of him, not even his wife recognizes him. He has lost all sources of meaningful identity.

As the various case studies in this book have suggested, meaningful identity is most often linked to a sense of place, personal and social belonging and history, actual or imagined. It is structured by class, gender, ethnicity and sexual orientation but also by racialized forms of subjectification, which seek to limit what any individual can claim to be. A sense of belonging can be variously found in families, communities and groups united by oppression (real or imagined) or marginalization. Sometimes identity combines all these elements as in the case of the Aboriginal people of Australia or, very differently, in the white supremacist groups discussed in Chapter 5. What the case studies in the various chapters demonstrate is that identity both matters to individuals and groups and plays an important role in governing how people treat others.

The final issue that this book has raised is how one might challenge the 'knowing subject' that inheres in various forms of identity, and how one might make hegemonic forms of subjectivity and identity strange, problematizing and relativizing them in the interests of a more tolerant and diverse society. As we saw in Chapter 7, comedy is one mode of doing this, since it ables us to produce moments of undecidability that put the fixity and sovereignty of the knowing subject into question. In multi-ethnic, predominantly white Western societies, where racism and ethnocentrism still hold sway, a key cultural political task for those committed to cultural diversity is the problematization of the often unquestioned issue of whiteness. One of the questions that the book has asked is how cultural texts and practices both construct identities and put fixed notions of identity into question. In the case of whiteness, non-white writers have done this by voicing the experience of non-white 'others' in relation to whites and alerting readers and viewers to the fact that white identities are constructs that often rely on negative assumptions about others. At stake here is the displacing of any assumption about whiteness as either 'natural' or universal. In other texts, it has been done effectively by a total change of perspective, as for example in comedy sketches that work with role reversal, or in fictional rewritings of history. For example, the Australian Aboriginal novel about the colonization of Tasmania by Mudrooroo, *Doctor Wooreddy's Prescription for Enduring the Ending of the World* (1983), vividly depict the devastating effects of initial white colonization by 'nums' (ghosts), that is, white men. Many contemporary writers, both in the West and in the developing world, are mobilizing recent history in support of the postcolonial project of decolonizing Black and indigenous identities, producing new forms of identity and reshaping ideas of culture and nation. They are using fiction to articulate silenced voices, to explore inter-cultural and cross-generational conflicts, and to produce new hybrid identities and cultural forms. They are offering challenges to those forms of white subjectivity and ideas of history and nation that allow racism and ethnocentrism to flourish and refuse to acknowledge white complicity in and responsibility for the position in which non-white people find themselves in today.

It is only very recently that cultural critics have begun to look at the hegemony of whiteness as an apparently unmarked subject position and identity that is thought to be equivalent to being human. This is a crucial move in the struggle to decentre Eurocentrism and residual forms of white supremacism. It can lead to an undermining of fixed white subjectivities and identities that puts the white knowing subject into question. This is an important task, since whiteness and the failure to problematize it remain key obstacles in cultural struggles to challenge the fixed forms of subjectivity and identity that underpin racism and ethnocentrism.

This leaves us with the final question of what is at stake in cultural struggles over identity? The answer, for course, is social power. As we have seen from examples in several chapters of this book, identity is variously regarded as something to be fought over, protected or celebrated, and different forms of cultural narrative and cultural practice: historical, political, fictional and visual play an important role in these processes, helping to constitute subjectivity and identity for the individuals who engage with them. Important here is how cultural practices can offer new forms of identity and agency and serve as ways of subverting and negotiating dominant forms of identity. In analysing how cultural narratives work, the book has been primarily concerned with the social power relations that structure the subject positions and forms of identity in play, realizing that some discourses, and the subject positions and modes of subjectivity and identity that they constitute, have more power than others.

As many marginalized and oppressed people have argued, it is the responsibility of privileged majorities in society to inform themselves about the experience, subjectivities and identities of those who are part of minorities, marginalized or oppressed. Audre Lorde, for example argues that:

> Whenever the need for some pretence of communication arises, those who profit from our oppression call upon us to share our knowledge with them. In other words, it is the responsibility of the oppressed to teach the oppressors their mistakes. I am responsible for educating teachers who dismiss my children's

culture in school. Black and Third World people are expected to educate white people as to our humanity.

(Lorde 1981: 114–15)

Without making the effort, for example, to learn about and understand Islam in the West in the face of Islamophobic caricatures, we will not be in a position to create a vibrant, diverse society in which difference is enriching. As Gloria Yamato has argued in relation to race:

You [as a white person] can educate yourselves via research and observations rather than rigidly, arrogantly relying solely on interrogating people of color. Do not expect that people of color should teach you how to behave non-oppressively. Do not give in to the pull to be lazy. Think hard. Do not blame people of color for your frustration about racism, but do appreciate the fact that people of color will often help you get in touch with that frustration. Assume that your effort to be a good friend is appreciated, but don't expect or accept gratitude from people of color. Work on racism for your sake, not 'their' sake. Assume that you are needed and capable of being a good ally. Know that you'll make mistakes and commit yourself to correcting them and continuing on as an ally, no matter what. Don't give up.

(Yamato 1990: 23–4)

The cultural narratives of minorities – historical and fictional – are one place to begin to acquire the knowledge needed to dislodge both hegemonic narratives and the oppressive binaries that they perpetuate. This is crucial to the development of plural societies that are accepting of difference, and that even celebrate it. As examples in this book have shown, these narratives articulate positions that challenge hegemonic constructions of identities, histories and traditions and enable us to think in new ways about both past and present about who – in our diversity – we are, how we became what we are and what we want to become.

NOTES

Introduction

1 Al Qaeda was formed around 1989 by Osama bin Laden and Muhammad Atef. One of its principal goals is to remove the United States armed forces from Saudi Arabia and other Islamic territories. For more on radical Islamic fundamentalism see Khatib (2003).
2 Sally Morgan (1988) *My Place*. Fremantle: Fremantle Arts Centre Press (1987) (published in the UK by Virago). *Rabbit Proof Fence* (2002) directed by Philip Noyce. Available on DVD from Miramax Home Entertainment.

Chapter 1

1 According to Marx, the history of human kind is the history of a series of modes of production (slave-owning, feudal, capitalist) governed by specific forms of class relations. With the industrial revolutions from the eighteenth century onwards, capitalism changed the face of Western societies. In the twentieth century it moved beyond the borders of individual nation states to encompass imperialism, multi-nationalism and most recently globalization. In its classical form, capitalism is based on the relationship between capital and labour. The capitalist class owns the means of production, i.e. the capital to set up and run factories and to employ labour in order to produce both goods and surplus value. The proletariat has only its labour power, i.e. its ability to work. Class is first and foremost an economic category, determined by whether or not an individual has access to control of the means of production.
2 In linguistic theory, the French linguist Emile Benveniste has been central to theorizations of subjectivity and identity. Benveniste takes as his starting point Descartes' rationalist premise *cogito, ergo sum* ('I think, therefore I am') according to which the act of thinking points to the existence of the knowing subject as the source and guarantee of meaning. Benveniste challenges and complicates this model of subjectivity by distinguishing between the subject of the

enunciation and the subject of the enounced, a distinction that is also important in Lacanian psychoanalysis (see Benveniste 1971).

3 According to Lacan, both meaning and subjectivity are structured in relation to a primary signifier, the Phallus, which governs the symbolic order of society and culture. Control of the Phallus is control of the laws and meanings of society. This position of control is the position of the 'Other'. It is not a position open to either men or women. It could only ever be occupied by figures such as the all-knowing, self-present God of the Judeo-Christian tradition. Subjectivity is founded on the misrecognition by the individual of himself/herself as Other.

4 The project of racial science was to describe and classify the different 'races' of mankind. Opinions varied as to whether these so-called races actually constituted different species or were just variations of a single species. Different theorists came up with different numbers of races, classified by skin colour, phenotype and the practices of phrenology. For more on this see Stanton (1960), Winthrop Jordan (1969) and Young (1994).

Chapter 2

1 'Whose Heritage? The Impact of Cultural Diversity on Britain's Living Heritage.' National Conference, Manchester 1–3 November 1999. The conference was sponsored by the Arts Council of England, the Heritage Lottery Fund, the Museums Association, the Museums and Galleries Commission, the North West Arts Board and the North West Museums Service. Keynote speakers were Chris Smith, then Secretary of State for Culture, Media and Sport, Professor Stuart Hall and Maya Jaggi. For more on cultural diversity in contemporary Britain (and Europe) see Black 1996, Modood and Werbner 1997, Werbner and Modood 1997 and Alibhai-Brown 1999.

2 See www.channel4.com/history.

3 Sir William MacPherson's report on the Stephen Lawrence Case was published in 1999. Stephen Lawrence was a Black schoolboy, brutally murdered by a gang of white youths at a bus stop in London. The police failed to convict anyone with the crime and eventually, after the Labour Government was elected in 1997, a public inquiry was held which concluded that the Metropolitan Police had not followed proper procedures and was institutionally racist. It gave rise to a widespread debate on institutional racism throughout British society.

Chapter 3

1 The Mabo case involved Eddie Mabo's claim that Murray Islanders held 'native title' to three islands on the eastern fringe of Torres Strait. It finally came before the High Court of Australia in 1992. It successfully overturned the doctrine of *terra nullius*, according to which Australia was an empty land when the first European settlers arrived.

2 For more on the history of the indigenous people of Australia see Kevin Gilbert (1978) *Living Black*. Ringwood: Penguin Books Australia; Lorna Lippmann (1981) *Generations of Resistance*. Melbourne: Longman Cheshire; Anna Rutherford (ed.) (1988) *Aboriginal Culture Today*, vol. X, nos 1 and 2 of *Kunapipi*. Sydney, Australia, Coventry, England and Geding Sovej, Denmark: Dangaroo Press).

3 *100 years: The Australia Story*, directed by Deborah Masters and Sue Spencer, Australian Broadcasting Company 2001, 286 minutes. Distributed by Roadshow Home Entertainment.

4 For examples of Aboriginal women's life writing see Moreton-Robinson (2000) 'Telling It Straight: Self-Presentation within Indigenous Women's Life Writing,' pp. 1–31.

5 'Kick the Tin' was a game we played as children at Colebrook Home. The idea of the game was that we all had to stand around the tin. One person, 'It', stood next to the tin. Then someone would run in and give one hell of a kick to the tin and all us *maru* (Black, Aboriginal) kids would run for our lives scattering to hide (Kartinyeri 2000: 2).

6 For more on this see Mohanty (1991, 2003) and Narayan (1997).

Chapter 4

1 *Windrush*, Four Part documentary, BBC 2 1998, produced by Mike Phillips and accompanied by *Windrush: A Guide to the Season*, London, BBC Publications (1998).

2 In the case of football, where in Britain Black players found themselves verbally abused on the football pitch, a counter movement was set up, supported by the Football Association, to, in their words, 'kick racism out of football'.

3 For more on recent Black British culture see Kwesi Owusu (2000) *Black British Culture & Society. A Text Reader*. London and New York: Routledge. For more on Black art see the journal *Third Text*. For photography see various publications by the London-based Association of Black Photographers. For recent work in film and television see Ross (1996).

4 *Does Britain have a Colour Bar?* BBC Television, 1955.

5 For more on race in Britain see John Solomos (2003) *Race and Racism in Britain*, 3rd edn. Basingstoke: Palgrave Macmillan and Andre Pilkington (2003) *Racial Disadvantage and Ethnic Diversity in Britain*. Basingstoke: Palgrave Macmillan.

Chapter 5

1 For examples of websites promoting Confederate memorabilia see www.americastore.com and www.dixieoutfitters.com.

Chapter 6

1 Recent theory raises this issue from a wide range of perspectives, as for example in the very different works of Jacques Derrida and Luce Irigaray. In postcolonial theory Jean-Paul Sartre, Aimé Césaire, Franz Fanon, Edward Said, Gayatri Spivak and Homi Bhabha have been particularly influential.

2 Randhawa had previously published in the anthologies *More to Life than Mr Right* (London: Picadilly Press, 1987), *A Girl's Best Friend* (London: The Women's Press, 1987), *Right of Way* (London: The Women's Press, 1987) and *Flaming Spirit* (London: Virago, 1994). She has also

published a teenage novel, *Harijan* (London: Mantra, 1992). Her novel, *A Wicked Old Woman* was published by the Women's Press in 1987. In addition to writing, Randhawa has worked for a South Asian women's organization which sets up refuges and resource centres for Asian women. She has been involved in the Black and Asian Women's Movement and in anti-racist campaigns.

Chapter 7

1 For a brief histories of Black British and Asian film and television see Ross 1996; John Twitchin (ed.) (1992) *The Black and White Media Show Book*. Stoke-on-Trent: Trentham Books; Therese Daniels and Jane Gerson (eds) (1989) *The Colour Black: Black Images in British Television*. London: BFI; and Jim Pines (ed.) (1992) *Black and White in Colour. Black British People in British Television Since 1936*. London: BFI.
2 *Heat and Dust* (1983) Merchant Ivory Productions; *Gandhi* (1982), directed by Richard Attenborough; *A Passage to India* (1984) directed by David Lean (based on E.M. Foster's novel), *The Jewel In the Crown* based on Paul Scott's *Raj Quartet* (1984) Granada Television and the *Far Pavillions* (1984) Channel 4 Television (based on the novel by M.M. Kaye).
3 *The Bhuddha of Suburbia* is available on video from BBC Worldwide Ltd.
4 *Goodness Gracious Me*, BBC 2, Series One, 12 January 1998 to 16 February 1998. Anil Gupta, Sanjeev Bhaskar, Meera Syal, Nina Wadia, Sanjev Kudi, Sharat Sandana and Richard Pinto. Extracts are available on the BBC video: *Goodness Gracious Me: The Very Best of Series 1, Plus Unseen Out-Takes*, BBC Worldwide Ltd 1998. Complete versions of Series One and Series Two are also available from BBC Worldwide.
5 *The Millionairess* (1960) starred Peter Sellers and Sophia Loren. Loren plays a spoilt wealthy heiress able to buy anything she wants. She meets an Indian Doctor whose sole concern is to help the poor and she sets out to buy him.
6 *Live and Loud Tour* (1994), produced by Brian Klein. On the Box Productions in association with Crucial Films. Video Collection International Ltd, 1994.

Chapter 8

1 BAOBAB for Women's Human Rights has been closely involved with defending the rights of women, men and children in Muslim, customary and secular laws and in particular of those convicted under the Sharia Criminal legislation acts in operation in Nigeria since 2000. BAOBAB was the first (and for several months the only) NGO with members from the Muslim community, who were willing to speak publicly against retrogressive versions of Muslim laws and to work on changing the dominant conservative understanding of the rights of women in enacted Sharia (Muslim religious laws), as well as in customary and secular laws. BAOBAB identifies victims and supports their appeals, raising funds for the costs, putting together a strategy team of women's and human rights activists, lawyers and Islamic scholars who contribute their expertise and time voluntarily.
2 *My Son the Fanatic* (1997) was written by Hanif Kureishi and directed by Udayan Prasad. It is a BBC film available on video from Feature Film Company/VCI.14.

GLOSSARY

Colonialism refers to the occupation, conquest and control of the land, raw materials and products of other peoples. In the case of European colonies this led to complex links between colonizing and colonized countries. As Ania Loomba puts it:

> Modern colonialism did more than extract tribute, goods and wealth from the countries that it conquered – it restructured the economies of the latter, drawing them into a complex relationship with their own, so that there was a flow of human and natural resources between colonised and colonial countries. This flow worked in both directions – slaves and indentured labour, as well as raw materials, were transported to manufacture goods in the metropolis, or in other locations for metropolitan consumption, but the colonies also provided captive markets for European goods.
>
> (Loomba 1998: 3)

The effects of colonialism are still present in postcolonial nations today.

Discourse has different meanings according to theory employed in a particular analysis (for example, linguistic discourse analysis, Foucault or work drawing on Bakhtin). In this book discourse comprises both linguistic meanings and the material social institutions and practices in which meanings inhere and are realized (see Foucault 1981). Thus, for example, the competing discourses that constitute femininity not only define subjects and subjectivities, but shape bodies. Discourses are the site for the articulation of both knowledge and power (see Weedon 1997).

Discursive field. This term comes from Michel Foucault and was developed as part of a theorization of the relationship between discourses, social institutions, subjectivity and power. Discursive fields (for example, sexuality, femininity or medicine) consist of competing discourses that constitute meanings in different and sometimes conflicting ways. The discourses that constitute a discursive field are located in social institutions, or developed in resistance to institutionalized meanings and practices (for example, the women's heath movement). Discursive field are structured by shifting relations of knowledge and power.

Fundamentalism. The term 'fundamentalism' was first used in the nineteenth century by a movement in American Protestantism. In 1919, the World Christian Fundamentalist Association was founded. It insisted on a 'literal' interpretation of the Bible and opposed modernizing or liberal tendencies. It was first applied to Islam in 1957 in the *Middle East Journal*, but widely taken up from the 1980s onwards and applied to many different groups and regimes that were perceived as grounding oppressive practices in particular readings of the Qur'an (see Runnymede 1997: 7).

Globalization is widely applied to many different aspects of contemporary life, ranging from the spread of multi-national corporations and Western capitalist interests, to the international appropriation of popular cultural forms and practices and the worldwide web. Writers on globalization point to the ways in which the structures and integrity of nation states are being challenged by economic and cultural developments, as well as postcolonial diasporas and the migration of peoples, particularly from the 'South' to the 'North'.

Hegemony as used by the Italian Marxist, Antonio Gramsci, refers to how capitalist bourgeois democracies maintain social power relations in the interests of dominant social groups. Hegemony is the outcome of cultural struggle and is never stable, final or guaranteed. It refers to the shifting balance of power in the cultural and social arenas. It relies on consent and is achieved via cultural institutions.

Hegemonic refers to those meanings and forms of social relation that emerge as dominant at any particular moment from the shifting balance of power in the cultural and social arenas.

Hybridity. This term has recently become an important theoretical and political concept, particularly in the areas of postcolonial theory, theories of race, and work on diasporic identities. Here it is often linked with related terms such as *mestiza* (Anzaldúa 1987), creolization, and the 'Third Space' (Bhabha 1990). The origins of the term 'hybrid' can be found in botany and biology where, since the eighteenth century, it has been used to denote a cross between two species. Racial science advanced various theories about the nature of the 'hybrid', most of which suggested that he/she was unviable. The term 'hybridity' was further used in the nineteenth century to denote forms of language such as creole and pidgin. Whereas in the nineteenth century, hybridity was usually used in the context of racial science to refer to people of mixed race, in the later twentieth century it has been reactivated to describe cultural mixing. In this usage, hybridity is most often seen as an effect of the slave trade, colonialism and the ensuing movements of peoples, which have created a range of diasporas throughout the world. In its new formulations, hybridity is used to challenge the very concept of 'racial' categorization. It is used to deconstruct binaries, revealing their constructed nature (see Bhabha 1990 and Anzaldúa 1987).

Interpellation. This Althusserian term refers to the process of direct address or hailing a person by which ideologies (in Althusser) or discourses constitute individuals as subjects (see Chapter 1 for details).

Islamophobia. Unfounded hostility towards Islam together with the practical consequences of such hostility (unfair discrimination against Muslim individuals and communities, and the exclusion of Muslims from mainstream political and social affairs) (see Runnymede Trust 1997).

Orientalism is derived from Said's classic study of the ways in which Western discourses constructed the East. Said argues that the Orient was 'almost a European invention . . . which helped to define Europe (or the West) as its contrasting image'. It is 'one of its deepest and most recurring images of the Other'. Orientalism is 'a mode of discourse with supporting institutions, vocabulary, scholarship, imagery, doctrines, even colonial bureaucracies and colonial styles' (Said 1978: 1–2).

Othering refers to the process of constructing another people or group as radically different to oneself or one's own group, usually on the basis of racist and/or ethnocentric discourses.

Postcolonial. A contested term often used to refer to the period since the end of European colonial dominance in Africa and Asia. It is also used to refer to ideas, scholarship and forms of cultural production that challenge and contest colonial meanings and modes of representation and address the ongoing effects and consequences of imperial domination long after the historical end of colonialism has occurred.

Postmodern. A complex and contested term, originally used in the field of architecture but rapidly taken up throughout the humanities and social sciences. Sometimes it is used to refer to the historical period that started in the 1960s. Often it refers to specific modes and styles of cultural production. It is further applied to poststructuralist cultural theories. Postmodern thought suggests that the criteria that theories use to establish what is true or false, good or bad are not universal and objective but internal to the structure of the discourses themselves.

Primitivism refers to movements in modern art and culture that looked to non-Western cultures for inspiration and for qualities that are thought to be missing in the industrialized West. It is characterized by a search for unspoilt nature and 'primitive' cultures, which are variously said to be more authentic, intuitive, spiritual, sensual, rhythmic, sexual and closer to nature. Working within a set of binaries that associates these qualities with the 'primitive other' against which white Western 'man' is defined, primitivism celebrates the qualities it attributes to the primitive.

Race. The classification of human beings according to categories that are grounded in physical features such as skin colour, type and colour of hair and facial characteristics. Contemporary racial categorizations have their root in eighteenth- and nineteenth-century racial science. Racial categorizations usually claim to be biological and therefore natural. Yet they are never purely descriptive. The physical differences that they identify are almost always linked to other intellectual, emotional and physical categories of difference. Racial categories, like all language, are historically specific cultural constructs. For this reason, some writers on cultural and social issues choose to place them within inverted commas. I do not do this in this book, since although, like all discourse, racial categories are cultural not natural, they have material effects in the world.

Racial science is a now discredited body of writing and research that developed in the eighteenth and nineteenth centuries out of the discourse of natural history. Its project was to identify, describe and classify the different 'races' of mankind. Opinions varied as to whether these so-called races actually constituted different species or were just variations of a single species. Different theorists came up with different numbers of races, classified by skin colour, phenotype and the practices of phrenology. For more on this see Stanton (1960), Winthrop Jordan (1969) and Young (1994). Racial science was invoked in the instigation of both Nazism and Apartheid.

Slave Trade. As European powers colonized the Americas, they required a suitable workforce – both the indigenous peoples and Europeans proved unsuited to conditions on the plantations. From the 1450s to the end of the nineteenth century, enslaved Africans were transported from the coast of West Africa to North and South America and the Caribbean. The slave trade formed a triangle according to which ships carried goods from Europe to Africa with which to purchase slaves, slaves were then transported from Africa to the New World and in the third leg of the triangle, commodities such as sugar and cotton were shipped to Europe. Lovejoy (2000) gives statistics on the transatlantic slave trade between 1650 and 1900, which specify the transportation of 10,240,200 slaves.

Stereotyping. The construction fixed and often negative images of another social group, which is then applies without differentiation to all members of that group. For example, the assumption that all people of African descent are rhythmic and musical, or that all women are less rational or more emotional than men, are based on reductive, stereotypic thinking.

BIBLIOGRAPHY

Adebayo, D. (1996) *Some Kind of Black*. London: Virago.

Ahmad, R. (1988) 'The Nightmare', in *Asian Women Writers' Workshop*, pp. 19–25.

Ahmad, R. and Gupta, R. (eds) (1994) *Flaming Spirit*. Stories from the Asian Women Writers' Collective. London: Virago.

Aho, J. (1995) *The Politics of Righteousness*. Seattle: University of Washington Press.

Ali, A. and Ali, I. (1992) *Ancient African Civilization in Ireland and Britain*. Cardiff: Punite Publications.

Alibhai-Brown, Y. (1999) *True Colours: Public Attitudes to Multiculturalism and the Role of Government*. London: Institute for Public Policy Research.

Althusser, L. (trans B. Brewster) (1971) On Ideology and Ideological State Apparatuses. Notes Towards an Investigation, in *Lenin and Philosophy and Other Essays*, pp. 121–73. London: New Left Books.

Anderson, B. (1991) *Imagined Communities: Reflections on the Origins and Spread of Nationalism*. London: Verso.

Anzaldúa, G. (1987) *Borderlands. La Frontera. The New Mestiza*. San Francisco: Aunt Lute Books.

Anzaldúa, G. (ed.) (1990a) *Making Face, Making Soul. Haciendo Caras. Creative and Critical Perspectives by Feminists of Color*. San Francisco: Aunt Lute Books.

Anzaldúa, G. (1990b) Haciendo caras, una entrada. An introduction by Gloria Anzaldúa, in G. Anzaldúa, *Making Face, Making Soul. Haciendo Caras. Creative and Critical Perspectives by Feminists of Color*, pp. xv–xxviii. San Francisco: Aunt Lute Books.

Araeen, R. (1992) How I Discovered my Oriental Soul in the Wilderness of the West, *Third Text*, 18: 85–102.

Arnold, M. (1869) *Culture and Anarchy*. London: Smith Elder.

Asian Women Writers' Workshop (1988) *Right of Way*. London: The Women's Press.

Associated Press (2001) *Confederate T-shirts Sparks Debate*. www.ap.org, accessed 2 July 2003.

Barkun, M. (1997a) *Religion and the Racist Right*. Chapel Hill: University of North Carolina Press.

Barkun, M. (1997b) Millenarians and Violence: The Case of the Christian Identity Movement, in T. Robbins and S.J. Palmer (eds) *Millennium, Messiahs, and Mayhem: Contemporary Apocalyptic Movements*, pp. 247–60. New York: Routledge.

BBC News World Edition (2002) Miss World Boycott Spreads. www.bbc.co.uk/2/hi/africa/2240970.stm. Accessed 2 December 2002.

Bentham, M. (2000) Critics of a 'racist' Britain are misguided, says report, *Daily Telegraph*, 8 October.

Benveniste, E. (1971) *Problems in General Linguistics*. Miami: Miami University Press.

Berger, S., Feldner, H. and Passmore, K. (eds) (2003) *Writing History: Theory and Practice*. London: Arnold.

Bhabha, H. (1990) Interview with Homi Bhabha, in J. Rutherford (ed.) *Identity, Community, Culture, Difference*, pp. 207–21. London: Lawrence and Wishart.

Bhaskar, S. (1998) Interview, *The Independent*, 4 July.

Black, L. (1996) *New Ethnicities and Urban Culture*. London: UCL Press.

Blair, T. (2003) Speech to US Congress on 17 July. www.washingtonpost.com, accessed 18 July 2003.

Blunkett, D. (2003) Foreword to the Home Office *Connecting Communities* Race Equality Support Programmes. London: HMSO.

Boswell, D. and Evans, J. (eds) (1999) *Representing the Nation: A Reader*. New York and London: Routledge in association with the Open University.

Bourdieu, P. (1993) *The Field of Cultural Production*. New York: Columbia University Press.

Brah, A. (1996) *Cartographies of Diaspora: Contesting Identities*. London and New York: Routledge.

Bush, G. (2002) Introduction to the National Security Strategy of the United States of America. http/usinfo.state.gov/topical/pol/terror/secstrat.htm:1. Accessed 10 January 2003.

Butler, J. (1990) *Gender Trouble*. New York and London: Routledge.

Butler, J. (1993) *Bodies That Matter*. New York and London: Routledge.

Chandran, R. (2000) An insult to all our countrymen, *Daily Mail*, 11 October.

Chiahemen, J. (2002) Nigeria struggles to cope with Miss World pageant, *Reuters* 12 November. www.signonsandiego.com/news/world accessed on 2 December 2002.

Dabydeen, D. (1997) *The Counting House*. London: Vintage (original 1996).

Dabydeen, D. (1999) *A Harlot's Progress*. London: Jonathan Cape.

Dabydeen, D. (2000) *The Intended*. London: Vintage Books (original 1991).

Daily Mail (2000) The flashy vacuity of the Dome, 11 October.

Daily Mail (2000) Comment: What an insult to our history and intelligence, *Daily Mail*, 11 October.

Daily Telegraph (2000) Britishness. People in these Isles are at a crossroads, *Daily Telegraph*, 12 October.

Daily Telegraph (2000) Editorial comment: The British Race, 10 October.

Daily Telegraph (2000) Editorial Comment: Turning point at Runnymede, 13 October.

Daniels, J. (1997) *White Lies: Race, Class, Gender and Sexuality in White Supremacist Discourse*. New York and London: Routledge.

Department of State (2002) *National Security Strategy of the United States of America*, Washington DC, September 2002, p. 4. www.usinfo.state.gov/topical/terror/secstrat.htm accessed on 10 January 2003.

Derrida, J. (trans. G. Spivak) (1976) *Of Grammatology*. Baltimore: The Johns Hopkins University Press.

Djebah, O. (2002) Obaigbena On CNN, *This Day*, Lagos reproduced by BBC World Service 1 December, accessed on www.allAfrica.com, 2 December 2002.

Donald, J. and Rattansi, A. (eds) (1992) *'Race', Culture and Difference*. London: Sage in association with the Open University.

Doughty, S. (2000) Racism slur on the word 'British', *Daily Mail*, 11 October.

Dyer, R. (1997) *White*. London: Routledge.

Foucault, M. (1981) *The History of Sexuality. Volume One. An Introduction*. Harmondsworth: Penguin.

Freud, S. (1975) *The Psychopathology of Everyday Life*. Harmondsworth: Penguin.

Freud, S. (1976) *The Interpretation of Dreams*. Harmondsworth: Penguin.

Fryer, P. (1984) *Staying Power*. London: Pluto.

Fuller, V. (1992) *Going Back Home*. London: The Women's Press.

Gould, S.J. (1981) *The Mismeasure of Man*. New York and London: W.W. Norton.

Gupta, R. (1988) Leaving Home, in *Asian Women Writers' Workshop*, pp. 32–45.

Gupta, T. (1994) Rebecca and the Neighbours, in R. Ahmad and R.Gupta (eds) *Flaming Spirit*, pp. 67–79. Stories from the Asian Women Writers' Collective. London: Virago.

Hague, W. (2000) Why I am sick of the anti-British disease, *Daily Telegraph*, 13 October.

Hall, S. (1990) Cultural Identity and Diaspora, in J. Rutherford (ed.) *Identity, Community, Culture*, Difference, pp. 222–37. London: Lawrence and Wishart.

Hall, S. (1999) Un-settling 'The Heritage': Re-Imagining the Post-Nation, in *Whose Heritage?* Keynote Addresses, pp. 13–22. The Arts Council of England.

Haraway, D. (1991a) *Simians, Cyborgs, and Women. The Reinvention of Nature*. London: Free Association Books Ltd.

Haraway, D. (1991b) Situated Knowledges: The Science Question in Feminism and the Privilege of Partial Perspective (original 1988), in D. Haraway, *Simians, Cyborgs, and Women. The Reinvention of Nature*, pp. 183–202. London: Free Association Books Ltd.

Harris, M.(1968) *The Rise of Anthropological Theory*. New York: Harper Row.

Hegel, G.W.F. (1971) *Philosophy of Mind*. Oxford: Clarendon Press.

Hiller, S. (ed.) (1991) *The Myth of Primitivism: Perspectives on Art*. London and New York: Routledge.

Hobsbawm, E. and Ranger, T. (eds) (1992) *The Invention of Tradition*. Cambridge: Cambridge University Press.

hooks, b. (1989) *Talking Back: Thinking Feminist Thinking Black*. Boston, MA: South End Press.

hooks, b. (1991) *Yearning: Race, Gender and Cultural Politics*. London: Turnaround.

Huggins, J. (1998) *Sister Girl: The Writings of Aboriginal Activist and Historian Jackie Huggins*. St Lucia: University of Queensland Press.

Huggins, R. and Huggins, J. (1994) *Auntie Rita*. Canberra: Aboriginal Studies Press.

Imam, A. and Medar-Gould, S. (2003) Please Stop the International Amina Lawal Protest Letter Campaigns. Lagos: BAOBAB.

Jackson, T. (2003) *What is Racism?* www.stormfront. org/defaultnf.htm. Accessed 18 July 2003.

Jenkins, K. (ed.) (1997) *The Postmodern History Reader*. London and New York: Routledge.

Johnson, B. (2000) The Thursday Column: Why I give way to righteous paranoia about Britain, *Daily Telegraph*, 12 October.

Johnson, P. (2000) *Daily Mail* Essay: In Praise of Being British, *Daily Mail*, 11 October.

Johnson, P. (2000) *Daily Mail* Essay, *Daily Mail*, 11 October.

Johnston, P. (2000) Straw wants to rewrite our history, *Daily Telegraph*, 10 October.

Johnston, P. (2000) Thinkers who want to consign our island story to history, *Daily Telegraph*, 10 October.

Jordan, G. (2004) 'We never really noticed you were coloured': Postcolonial Reflections on Immigrants and Minorities in Wales, in J. Aaron and C. Williams (eds) *Postcolonial Wales*. Cardiff: University of Wales Press.

Jordan, G. and Weedon, C. (1995) *Cultural Politics: Class, Gender, Race and the Postmodern World*. Oxford: Blackwell.

Jordan, W. (1969) *White Over Black: American Attitudes Towards the Negro 1550–1812*. Baltimore, MD: Penguin Books.

Julien, I. and Mercer, K. (1988) De Margin and de Centre, *Screen* 29(4): 2–10.

Khan-Din, A. (1999) *East is East*. London: FilmFour Books.

Khatib, L. (2003) Communicating Islamic Fundamentalism as Global Citizenship, *Journal of Communication Inquiry*, 27(4): 389–409.

Kartinyeri, D. (2000) *Kick the Tin*. Melbourne: Spinifex.

Kavanagh, T. (2000) Curse of the Britain Bashers, *The Sun*, 11 October.

Kureishi, H. (1990) *The Buddha of Suburbia*. London: Faber & Faber.

Kureishi, H. (1995) *The Black Album*. London: Faber & Faber.

Kureishi, H. (2002) *The Body*. London: Faber and Faber.

Lacan, J. (trans. A. Sheridan) (1977) The Mirror Phase as Formative of the Function of the Eye, in J. Lacan, *Écrits*, pp. 1–7. London: Tavistock (original 1949).

Laville, S. (2000) I feel so proud when I see our Union flag, *Daily Telegraph*, 12 October.

Loomba, A. (1998) *Colonialism/Postcolonialism*. London and New York: Routledge.

Lorde, A. (1981) *Sister Outsider*. Freedom, CA: The Crossing Press.

Lovejoy, P.E. (2000) *Transformations in Slavery*. Cambridge: Cambridge University Press.

Lugones, M. (1990) Hablando cara a cara/Speaking Face to Face: An Exploration of Ethnocentric Racism, in G. Anzaldúa (ed.) *Making Face, Making Soul. Haciendo Caras. Creative and Critical Perspectives by Feminists of Color*, pp. 46–54. San Francisco: Aunt Lute Books.

Lyotard, J.F. (1984) *The Postmodern Condition: A Report on Knowledge*. Manchester: Manchester University Press.

MacPherson, Sir William of Cluny (1999) *The Stephen Lawrence Inquiry*. London: The Stationery Office.

Makinde, O. (2002) Interview, *ThisDay*, Lagos, 1 December accessed via www.allAfrica.com on 21 December 2002.

Marx, K. and Engels, F. (1970) *The German Ideology*. London: Lawrence and Wishart (original 1845).

Meehan, D. (2000) *It is no Secret: the Story of a Stolen Child*. Milsons Point, NSW: Random House.

Mercer, K. (1990) Welcome to the Jungle: Identity and Diversity in Postmodern Politics, in J. Rutherford (ed.) *Identity, Community, Culture, Difference*, pp. 43–71. London: Lawrence and Wishart.

Mirza, H.S. (ed.) (1997) *Black British Feminism: A Reader*. London and New York: Routledge.

Modood, T. (1992) British Asian Muslims and the Rushdie Affair, in J. Donald and A. Rattansi (eds) *'Race', Culture and Difference*, pp. 260–77. London: Sage in association with the Open University.

Modood, T. (1997) 'Difference', Cultural Racism and Anti-Racism, in P. Werbner and T. Modood (eds) *Debating Cultural Hybridity*, pp. 154–72. London and New Jersey: Zed Books.

Modood, T. and Werbner, P. (1997) *The Politics of Multiculturalism in the New Europe*. London and New York: Zed Books.

Mohanty, C.T. (1991) Under Western Eyes, in *Third World Women and the Politics of Feminism*, pp. 51–80. Bloomington and Indianapolis: Indiana University Press (a revised version is published in Mohanty 2003: 17–42).

Mohanty, C.T. (2003) *Feminism Without Borders: Decolonizing Theory, Practicing Solidarity*. Durham and London: Duke University Press.

Moore-Gilbert, B. (2001) *Hanif Kureishi*. Manchester: Manchester University Press.

Moreton-Robinson, A. (2000) *Talkin'up to the White Woman: Indigenous Women and Feminism*. St Lucia: University of Queensland Press.

Moreton-Robinson, A. (2000) Telling It Straight: Self-Presentation within Indigenous Women's Life Writing, in A. Moreton-Robinson, *Talkin'up to the White Woman: Indigenous Women and Feminism*, pp. 1–31. St Lucia: University of Queensland Press.

Morgan, P. (1992) From a Death to a View: the Hunt for the Welsh Past in the Romantic Period, in E. Hobsbawm and T. Ranger (eds) *The Invention of Tradition*, pp. 43–100. Cambridge: Cambridge University Press.

Morgan, R. (1993) *The Word of a Woman: Selected Prose 1968–1992*. London: Virago.

Morgan, S. (1988) *My Place*. London: Virago.

Morris, M. (1984) Introduction, in S. Selvon, *Moses Ascending*, pp. vii–xviii. Oxford: Heinemann.

Morrison, T. (1981) *The Bluest Eye*. London: Picador.

Morrison, T. (1988) *Beloved*. London: Picador.

Mudrooroo (1983) *Doctor Wooreddy's Prescription for Enduring the Ending of the World*. South Yarra, Victoria: Hyland House.

Narayan, U. (1997) *Dislocating Cultures. Identities, Traditions and Third World Feminism*. New York and London: Routledge.

National Library of Australia, *Bringing Them Home Project*, leaflet published by the National Library of Australia: Canberra.

Newswatch online (2002). Accessed 2 December 2002.

Oladunjoye, P. (2002) Let's Never Have Miss World Here Again, *Newswatch* 1 December. www.allAfrica.com. Accessed on 2 December 2002.

Parekh, B. (2000) *Report of the Commission on the Future of Multi-Ethnic Britain*. London: Profile Books.

Phillips, C. (1989) *Higher Ground*. London: Faber & Faber.

Phillips, C. (1991) *Cambridge*. London: Faber & Faber.

Phillips, C. (1999) *The Final Passage*. London: Faber & Faber (original 1985).

Phillips, C. (2000) *Crossing the River*. London: Faber & Faber (original 1993).

Phillips, M. (1998) *Windrush: A Guide to the Season*. London: BBC Publications.

Phillips, M. (1998) *Windrush*, four-part documentary, BBC TV.

Pilkington, A. (2003) *Racial Disadvantage and Ethnic Diversity in Britain*. Basingstoke: Palgrave Macmillan.

Procter, J. (2003) *Dwelling Places: Postwar Black British Writing*. Manchester: Manchester University Press.

Randhawa, R. (1987) *A Wicked Old Woman*. London: The Women's Press.

Raychaudhuri, S. (1994) Sisters, in R. Ahmad and R.Gupta (eds) *Flaming Spirit*, pp. 16–28. Stories from the Asian Women Writers' Collective. London: Virago.

Riley, J. (1985) *The Unbelonging*. London: The Women's Press.

Riley, J. (1987) *Waiting in the Twilight*. London: The Women's Press.

Riley, J. (1988) *Romance*. London: The Women's Press.

Ritzer, G. (2000) *The Macdonaldization of Society*. Thousand Oaks, CA: Pine Forge Press.

Ross, K. (1996) *Black and White Media*. Cambridge: Polity.

Roy, L. (1998) *Lady Moses*. London: Virago.

Runnymede Trust (1997) *Islamophobia: A Challenge for Us All*. London: The Runnymede Trust.

Rutherford, J. (ed.) (1990) *Identity, Community, Culture, Difference*. London: Lawrence and Wishart.

Said, E. (1978) *Orientalism*. Harmondsworth: Penguin.

Said, E. (1981) *Covering Islam*. London: Routledge and Kegan Paul.

Scarman, The Rt. Hon. Lord (1981) *The Brixton Disorders, 10–12 April 1981*. London: HMSO.

Selvon, S. (1984) *Moses Ascending*. Oxford: Heinemann (original 1975).

Selvon, S. (1998) *The Lonely Londoners*. Harlow: Longman (original 1956).

Shimizu, A. (2003) Lying Bodies: Survival and Subversion in the Field of Vision. Unpublished PhD thesis, Cardiff University.

Solomos, J. (2003) *Race and Racism in Britain*, 3rd edn. Basingstoke: Palgrave Macmillan.

Soyinka, W. (2002) Soyinka wants Federal Government to take blame for death toll, *ThisDay*, Lagos, 2 December, accessed via allAfrica.com on 2 February 2002.

Stanton, W. (1960) *The Leopard's Spots. Scientific Attitudes Towards Race in America 1815–59*. Chicago: University of Chicago Press.

Syal, M. (1999) *Life isn't all ha ha hee hee*. London: Doubleday.

The Sun (2000) Editorial comment: The Sun Says, 11 October.

Thompson, D. (2000) It's ridiculous, *The Sun*, 11 October.

Utley, T. (2000) The Wednesday Column: They met at Runnymede – to boss us around, *Daily Telegraph*, 11 October.

Wagg, S. (ed.) (1998) *Because I Tell a Joke or Two: Comedy, Politics and Social Difference*. London: Routledge.

Weedon, C. (1997) *Feminist Practice & Poststructuralist Theory*, 2nd edn. Oxford: Blackwell.

Weeks, J. (1990) The Value of Difference, in J. Rutherford (ed.) *Identity, Community, Culture, Difference*, pp. 88–100. London: Lawrence and Wishart.

West, C. (1982) *Prophesy Deliverance: An Afro-American Revolutionary Christianity*. Westminster: John Knox Press.

Werbner, P. and Modood, T. (1997) *Debating Cultural Hybridity*. London and New Jersey: Zed Books.

Williams, C. (2002) *Sugar and Slate*. Aberystwyth: Planet.

Woodward, K. (ed.) (1997) *Identity & Difference*. London: Sage in association with the Open University.

www.africanamericanjourneys.com, accessed 10 January 2003.

www.infoplease.com/spot/confederate1.html, accessed 18 July 2003.

www.pbs.org/newshour/extra/features/jan–june00/flag.html, accessed 2 July 2003.

www.religioustolerance.org, accessed 18 July 2003.

www.youdebate.com/DEBATES/confederate, *Confederate Flag Debate and Poll*, accessed 2 July 2003.

Yamato, G. (1990) Something About the Subject Makes It Hard to Name, in G. Anzaldúa (ed.) *Making Face, Making Soul. Haciendo Caras. Creative and Critical Perspectives by Feminists of Color*, pp. 20–4. San Francisco: Aunt Lute Books.

Yggdrasil (2003) *White Nationalism FAQ*. www.stormfront.org. Accessed 18 July 2003.

Young, R. (1990) *White Mythologies: Writing, History and the West*. London and New York: Routledge.

Young, R. (1994) *Colonial Desire: Hybridity in Theory, Culture and Race*. London and New York: Routledge.

Younge, G. (2000) Celebrate, don't tolerate minorities, *The Guardian*, 11 October.

Yuval-Davies, N. (1992) Fundamentalism, Multiculturalism and Women in Britain, in J. Donald and A. Rattansi (eds) *'Race', Culture and Difference*, pp. 278–91. London: Sage in association with the Open University.

INDEX

Related books from Open University Press
Purchase from www.openup.co.uk or order through your local bookseller

---

RETHINKING CULTURAL POLICY

Jim McGuigan

- What are the possibilities and limitations of public policy in the cultural field under late-modern conditions?

Issues of cultural policy are of central importance now because forms of media are growing at an astonishing rate – new media like video games and chat rooms as well as modified older forms such as virtual access to museums, libraries and art galleries on the Internet. The digital revolution gives rise potentially to a culture of 'real virtuality' in which all the cultural artefacts of the world, past and present, may become instantly available at any time.

This innovative book charts the decline and renewal of public cultural policy. It examines a wide range of contemporary issues and blends a close reading of key theoretical points with examples to illustrate their practical import.

This is the perfect introduction to the area for undergraduate students in culture and media studies, sociology of culture, arts administration and cultural management courses, as well as postgraduates and researchers.

Contents
Introduction – Cultural Analysis, Technology and Power – Discourses of Cultural Policy – Cultural Policy 'Proper' and as Display – Rhetorics of Development, Diversity and Tourism – Culture, Capitalism and Critique – Glossary – References – Index.

192pp   0335 20701 4 (Paperback)   0 335 20702 2 (Hardback)

MEDIA, POLITICS AND THE NETWORK SOCIETY

Robert Hassan

- What is the network society?
- What effects does it have upon media, culture and politics?
- What are the competing forces in the network society, and how are they reshaping the world?

The rise of the network society – the suffusion of much of the economy, culture and society with digital interconnectivity – is a development of immense significance. In this innovative book, Robert Hassan unpacks the dynamics of this new information order and shows how they have affected both the way media and politics are 'played', and how these are set to reshape and reorder our world. Using many of the current ideas in media theory, cultural studies and the politics of the newly evolving 'networked civil society', Hassan argues that the network society is steeped with contradictions and in a state of deep flux.

This is a key text for undergraduate students in media studies, politics, cultural studies and sociology, and will be of interest to anyone who wishes to understand the network society and play a part in shaping it.

Contents

Series editor's foreword – Acknowledgements – Introduction – What is the network society? – The informationisation of media and culture – Addicted to digital: the wired world – Life.com – Civil society and the network society – Tactical media – A networked civil society? – Glossary – Bibliography – Index

176pp   0 335 21315 4 (Paperback)   0 335 21316 2 (Hardback)

Related books from Open University Press
Purchase from www.openup.co.uk or order through your local bookseller

---

RETHINKING CULTURAL POLICY
Jim McGuigan

- What are the possibilities and limitations of public policy in the cultural field under late-modern conditions?

Issues of cultural policy are of central importance now because forms of media are growing at an astonishing rate – new media like video games and chat rooms as well as modified older forms such as virtual access to museums, libraries and art galleries on the Internet. The digital revolution gives rise potentially to a culture of 'real virtuality' in which all the cultural artefacts of the world, past and present, may become instantly available at any time.

This innovative book charts the decline and renewal of public cultural policy. It examines a wide range of contemporary issues and blends a close reading of key theoretical points with examples to illustrate their practical import.

This is the perfect introduction to the area for undergraduate students in culture and media studies, sociology of culture, arts administration and cultural management courses, as well as postgraduates and researchers.

Contents
Introduction – Cultural Analysis, Technology and Power – Discourses of Cultural Policy – Cultural Policy 'Proper' and as Display – Rhetorics of Development, Diversity and Tourism – Culture, Capitalism and Critique – Glossary – References – Index.

192pp   0335 20701 4 (Paperback)   0 335 20702 2 (Hardback)